PR   TY

Other books by the author

No Pope of Rome: Militant Protestantism in Modern Scotland
(Mainstream 1985)

God Save Ulster! The Religion and Politics of Paisleyism (Clarendon
Press 1986)

*The Rise and Fall of the New Christian Right: Conservative Protestant
Politics in America, 1978-1988* (Clarendon Press 1988)

A House Divided: Protestantism, Schism, and Secularization (Routledge
1990)

PRAY TV

TELEVANGELISM IN AMERICA

STEVE BRUCE

London and New York

First published 1990
by Routledge
11 New Fetter Lane, London EC4P 4EE

Simultaneously published in the USA and Canada
by Routledge
a division of Routledge, Chapman and Hall, Inc.
29 West 35th Street, New York, NY 10001

© 1990 Steve Bruce

Typeset by LaserScript Limited, Mitcham, Surrey
Printed and bound in Great Britain by
Mackays of Chatham PLC, Chatham, Kent

British Library Cataloguing in Publication Data

Bruce, Steve
Pray TV: televangelism in America.
1. United States. Christian church.
Evangelism. Christian evangelism. Role in television
I. Title
306'.6

Library of Congress Cataloging in Publication Data

also available

ISBN 0-415-03097-8
0-415-03098-6 (pbk)

For David Martin on his retirement

CONTENTS

TABLES

PREFACE

This book was suggested to me by Chris Rojek of Routledge who felt that there was a need for a serious study of American religious broadcasting, especially one written with a European readership in mind. I was happy to accept the challenge because I had just finished *The Rise and Fall of the New Christian Right*, a study which concentrated on the recent political mobilizations of American conservative Protestants. In order to keep that study narrowly focused on the new Christian right as a socio-political movement, I had either to pass over or deal very briefly with a number of intriguing questions about American religious broadcasting and its audience. A chance to address those questions directly was welcome. I was also pleased to once again challenge what I regard as the hysterical exaggerations of the power of the new Christian right, this time armed with the evidence provided by Pat Robertson's failed campaign for the Republican party's presidential nomination.

It is worth saying a brief word about methodology. Most of my claim to understand the things I write about rests, not so much on the cited sources of quantitative research data (although such material has been influential), but on my direct involvement with the producers and consumers of televangelism. To be technical about it, I am an 'interpretative' social scientist. While I do not entirely reject surveys and statistics, I do believe that the claim to be 'scientific' must rest, not on apeing the quantitative methods of the natural sciences (although such methods have their place), but on being able to support one's arguments with sound reasoning from good evidence. That we are concerned with the beliefs and actions of people rather than with the regularities of chemical reactions means that our evidence consists largely of the accounts which are given by the people we strive to understand. I have not quoted from my original interview material or from the many notes on my observations because such material would not be available for critical examination by people who doubted my conclusions. That any reasonable person looking at and hearing the same things would have come to the same conclusion is something which the reader has to take on trust; the occasional illustrative quotation from any interview would not change that fact. But by way of presenting my credentials, I would like to stress the extent to which my work has been informed by considerable first-hand experience of American conservative Protestantism. Many hours have been passed in church services and crusade rallies in Fort Worth, Charlottesville, Washington, Greenville, Lynchburg, and Cincinnati. More time has been spent on a motel room bed staring at Oral, Pat, Jerry, and their many less well-known minor league colleagues on a television screen. Casual conversations with strangers in the cafes and bars of small southern towns always produced interesting glimpses of what members of the public thought of televangelists, and the dreariness of weeks away from home was lifted on a number of occasions by the generous hospitality of fundamentalist and pentecostal families who invited me to abandon Ramada, Econo-Travel, and Howard Johnson for their spare rooms. Although there is little direct reference in the text to the mass of 'data' one inadvertently acquires just by being there, that experience laid the foundation on which the study is built.

Wherever possible I have avoided the technical language of sociology, not because I am ashamed of my discipline (far from it, I once tried to have 'sociologist' listed on my passport as my occupation; the clerk said 'Yes, but what do you do for a living?'), but because I find such technical language unnecessary. With little or no loss of sense, most sociological notions can be expressed in ordinary English. A more difficult matter is to estimate accurately the theological knowledge of the typical reader. Some of you may wonder why I am telling you what you already know and others may wish for more clarification. I can only ask that members of each group remember the existence of the others and bear with me.

ACKNOWLEDGEMENTS

As always a number of debts were incurred in the course of the research that informs this book. The Nuffield Foundation has been a generous supporter of my work. It allowed me to spend six weeks in America in 1983 and two months in 1986. On the second visit, I was also assisted by an invitation to be a visiting scholar in residence at the University of Virginia. Donald Black, chairman of the Department of Sociology, provided me with office facilities and he and his colleagues made my stay pleasant and stimulating.

My own university has been generous with study leave and with travel funds which allowed me to make a third visit to America in the spring of 1987. I arrived the day before the Bakker scandal broke in the news! As always Professor Roy Wallis and Dr Steven Yearley of the Queen's University have acted as sounding boards and copy editors.

Professor Colin Bell kindly invited me to spend some time in the Department of Sociology in Edinburgh, away from the clamour of the telephone and the small but persistent voice of everyday university business. I am grateful to him and his colleagues for the chance to put my thoughts together in tranquillity.

Finally, my greatest debt is to the many American Christians – supporters and detractors of televangelism – who willingly gave their time and effort to guide a stranger in a foreign land. In particular, I would like to thank Gil Brightsen, associate pastor of Thomas Road Baptist Church, and his family; Steve Hankin, Alan Cairns, and the staff of Bob Jones University of Greenville, South Carolina; Tim and Beverley La Haye; Carl McIntire and Edgar C. Bundy; Moral Majority/Liberty Federation; Gary Jarmin of Christian Voice; Pro-Family Forum, Fort Worth; Heritage

Foundation; People for the American Way; Chuck Bergstrom of the Lutheran Office of Government Affairs; James Dunn of the Baptist Joint Committee on Public Affairs; and above all, the many ordinary Americans who talked to me about their religious beliefs.

Chapter One

A BRIEF HISTORY OF AMERICAN PROTESTANTISM

INTRODUCTION

It is one of the many paradoxes of America that a large part of the population of one of the most advanced and productive industrial economies in the world claim to follow a deviant schism of the ancient religion of a small, pastoralist people and believe that God created the world in six days, that all our animals are descended from the pairs saved by Noah from the Flood, and that the world will end shortly in a plan announced in the Bible books of Daniel and Revelations. Western Europeans find much American religion incomprehensible. Even if the beliefs themselves can be accepted, the styles in which they are presented and the enthusiasm with which they are embraced are thought to be strange. Few aspects of American religious life cause more interest, confusion, and derision than television evangelism. Although Europeans have become accustomed to the brashness, commercialism, and *ersatz* spontaneity of the television game show, they have yet to view American religious television with anything other than horror or morbid curiosity. This book is a description of the phenomenon of 'televangelism' (to use the abbreviation coined by Hadden and Swann 1981) and an explanation of its appeal.

Before we can make sense of American religious television, we must consider some of the forces that have shaped the history of religion in the United States. Any brief account is bound to be selective; this selection will describe the rise and distribution of conservative Protestantism, introduce some of the religious ideas and arguments which are important to televangelists and their supporters, locate 'fundamentalism' and 'evangelicalism', and describe the cultural institution of 'revival' religion.[1]

1

THE EARLY COLONIES

The key to following the complexities of American religious history is its basis in migration. Unlike many of the old world countries which exported population, the new world never had one dominant legally established 'state' church. Although many historians treat the puritanism of the New England colonies as if it were an early informal establishment, setting the tone for future developments, the colonies of North and South Carolina, Maryland, Virginia, and later Georgia were founded by Episcopalians and had established Episcopalian churches until the 19th century.[2] And then there was the Roman Catholicism of the French settlers, initially numerous in the north-eastern part of America, and later a small but important component in the culture of the deep south. The annexation of Mexican territory meant acquiring a large Spanish Catholic presence in the south west and west (Gaustad 1962). Even in New England, not all settlers were puritans; some were indeed convinced believers, seeking to establish the kingdom of God on earth outside the reach of the persecuting Church of England, but many were freebooters and adventurers, interested in the colonies for the economic rather than the spiritual opportunities the new world had to offer.

Although it was given considerable legitimacy by being the religion of the gentry, the Episcopalianism of the colonies on the south-eastern seaboard was prevented from growing with the population by its inappropriate parish structure and by its politics. Controlled by an out-of-touch bishop in London, resources stretched over vast areas, and staffed by low calibre clergy, the Episcopal churches already had difficulty gaining and retaining the support of their supposed parishioners before being divided by the rebellion against Britain (Bolton 1982).

Congregationalism, as New England puritanism became, was for a time the strongest bloc in American Christianity and its 749 congregations at the time of the Declaration of Independence gave it a considerable lead over its rivals. It is a common pattern that increased wealth and status bring with them a decline in religious rigour, commitment and personal piety. As the puritans prospered in commerce and manufacture, their religion became institutionalized and conventional:

The successful business or professional man acquired an increasingly positive self-image. Eventually, he was no longer willing to hear his pastor call him names in church he would resent if called in the street. He began to disregard exhortations to humility and to ape aristocratic tastes and values.

(Howe 1972: 321)

In theological terms what gradually occurred was a shift from the hard creed of Calvinism to the more individualistic and democratic optimism of Arminianism. The strand of the Protestant Reformation influenced by John Calvin and his followers stressed that God was all-powerful, God was all-knowing, and man was entirely sinful. A God who would be swayed by the actions of humankind was, for Calvin, no God at all. If we could not influence God and there was a heaven and a hell, it followed that whatever destination was ours must have been decided at the start of time, before our births, let alone before we had a chance to displease God by sinning. Man's very existence (since the Fall) was displeasing to God. Calvinists believed that some people have been 'elected' by God, or 'predestined' to salvation. Although God had sent his only son into the world so that his death would be a sacrifice to redeem us, this atonement was directed only to the sins of the elect.

Although the puritans were by no means as joyless as they are commonly portrayed (after all, confidence that one is part of the small band of elect saints is a reason to be cheerful), theirs was a hard elitist religion which made their God an unapproachable, firm but fair, and distant father (McLoughlin 1978: 56-62). By making salvation entirely a product of God's inscrutable will, it removed all room for human striving or improvement, while at the same time demanding the fiercest discipline from the saints and from the unregenerate (who were to be ruled by God's laws whether they liked it or not). While Calvinists believed in conversion, this was a process which was only effective for the saints although it might appear to be experienced by many. The simplest analogy is of those 'two tube' adhesives where the substance in the second tube only becomes a glue when added to the contents of the first tube; being elected is the first tube and being converted is the second. For those who are not among the saints, apparent conversions, while good in the sense of showing that the

3

unregenerate can become concerned about their sinfulness, will not save them.

In contrast, the 'free will' or Arminian version of Protestantism favoured by the Methodists allowed that Christ died for us all and that we could *choose* to be saved; although we could not buy God's favour with our works (the Roman Catholic heresy) we had a part to play in accepting God's freely given gift of his only son. By having faith in God's grace, we would be saved from hell.

Although apparently different theological grounds have been used as the occasion for the argument and different labels have been used to identify the contending parties, the basic divisions between Calvinist and Arminian – what part could man play in his own salvation and what proportion of mankind would be saved – have been at the heart of many disputes within Protestantism and the Arminians have won. Only in small pockets (usually in contexts such as South Africa and Ulster where the notion of a small elect band of saints resonates with the position of a minority settler population) does one now find popular Calvinism (Wallis and Bruce 1986: Ch. 10).

THE FIRST GREAT AWAKENING

The history of American religion is often written in terms of waves of revival. Recently detailed local area studies remind us that terms such as the 'first great awakening' impose a degree of artificial tidiness upon what is always a messy history. There was no clear start or finish, just a period when large parts of the population were struck by a new enthusiasm for conversion. Why these times rather than some others should have seen sermons, preached often before but with no noticeable effect, bringing audiences to their knees in fear and trembling as they come 'under conviction of sin', is not easily explained, although McLoughlin (1978) offers one of the best brief accounts. There is no doubt that social and economic changes in the colonies were disrupting the previous social order and creating considerable uncertainty in relationships. The puritan family was changing, as was the church. The stable pastoral village which the puritans had hoped to create could not be sustained when sons were forced to break away from their fathers to acquire land outside the original township. It

4

seems general strains and tensions rather than spectacular disasters produced the New Englanders' new readiness to contemplate the state of their souls.

Many of the ministers involved in preaching to the enthusiastic crowds of the 1740s – Jonathan Edwards certainly – described themselves as Calvinists and did their best to present the observably great work within the framework of Calvinist theology. They hoped to confine the impact of the upheaval to introducing 'into an essentially Calvinist context a new style of emotional intensity, personal commitment to Christ, and holy living' (Marsden 1980: 44). Yet perhaps the greatest of all the preachers – the Methodist George Whitefield – despite his protestations of Calvinism, believed that all sinners could repent and urged them to do so.

The predictable consequence of revival was the erosion of distinctive Calvinist doctrines and this was seen in changes within Presbyterianism and Congregationalism, in the spread of Methodism, and – important in the history of fundamentalism – in the rise of the Baptist movement. Although small numbers of European Baptists settled in America in the eighteenth century, the core of what is now the largest group of American Protestants came from the revival congregations. Not surprisingly, they felt the Congregationalist notion of infant baptism incompatible with the revival's emphasis on conversion and personal commitment; they began to argue that adults should be immersed in water as a signal of their new found faith.

Emerging in New England during the campaigns for religious freedom (despite their experience of persecution in England, the puritans were not advocates of toleration), these revival Baptists joined the earlier Baptists under Roger Williams, who had moved his people to Rhode Island to avoid the puritan hegemony, and then spread into the south. There they took advantage of the Episcopalian Church's lack of a popular base, and in those areas where there was interest, the revival took on elements of a movement of the oppressed, a means by which the poor and dispossessed could make sense of their own condition while launching a spiritual critique of their social superiors. It was not radical or revolutionary but the Baptist movement was a 'rejection of the style of life for which the gentry set the pattern and . . . a search for more powerful popular models for proper conduct. . . . The Baptists' salvationism and sabbatarianism effectively redefined morality and human relationships.' (Isaac in McLoughlin 1978: 94).

THE SECOND GREAT AWAKENING: CONVERTING THE FRONTIER

The occasion for the second awakening (dated from around 1800 to 1830) was the expansion of population into the hinterlands and the creation of a constantly expanding frontier. On the frontier people would have to negotiate new social relations with each other and would have to face new hardships and privations. Although thinly spread, the pioneers were a new market for religious offices. Many Presbyterian ministers were active and Presbyterianism consequently enjoyed growth, but the revivals of the second awakening were led by Baptists and Methodists who, because they placed personal piety and preaching skills above theological education in the recruitment of clergy, had the resources to take advantage of the new markets. Itinerancy had already proved its value in the first great awakening; instead of pastoring a stable congregation or looking after a parish, the revival preachers worked an area, or in the Methodist case, a circuit. Moving from one meeting to another, speaking perhaps twice a day, gave a preacher the opportunity to deliver the same address over and over until the dramatic delivery had been fine-tuned.

Itinerancy also allowed the most efficient direction of resources. A Baptist clergyman offered the following judgement of the Methodist system:

> their complete system of mission circuits is by far the ablest for domestic missionary effort ever yet adopted. They send their labourers into every corner of the country; if they hear of any particular attention to religion in a place they double the number of labourers in those circuits, and place their best men there, and endeavour generally to adapt the charac-ter of their preachers to the character of the people among whom they are to labour.
>
> (Quoted in Johnson 1955: 19)

The important innovation of the second revival was the extended 'camp meeting'. The meeting usually taken as the first of

6

the new genre occurred in a clearing by the Gasper River in Kentucky in July 1800. Already the practice of large numbers of serious Christians from the sparsely populated countryside gathering at some central creek or ferry crossing to hear a number of different preachers, as well as to take communion, had become established. Here the numbers of people who gathered for the series of services far exceeded the capacity of the tiny wooden church and so an area of bush was cleared.

> On the first night, after formal indoor services were over, discussion groups of 'seriously exercised Christians' spontaneously staged a revival of their own. The net result was that most of the ministers and several hundred worshippers remained at the meeting house all night. Some pioneers, more materially minded, who had carried along 'victuals mostly prepared' also set up makeshift tents of bushes or branches, sheets or quilts, or rested in open or covered wagons. Thus the camp meeting came into being, a convenience if not a necessity in the American backwoods.
>
> (Johnson 1955: 35)

A characteristic of these meetings, as it had been of many in the first awakening, was bodily manifestation of the emotional intensity of being under conviction of sin. Many hearers cried out, screamed, wept, shook and rolled themselves on the ground before achieving the joyful release. Some would, in the words of Methodist leader John McGee, 'with a piercing scream, fall like a log on the floor, earth or mud, and appear as dead'. Those who succumbed were variously affected.

> Some, when unable to stand or sit, they have the use of their hands, and can converse with perfect composure. In other cases, they are unable to speak, the pulse becomes weak, and they draw a difficult breath about once a minute; in some instances their extremities become cold, and pulsation, breathing and all the signs of life leave them for nearly an hour. Persons who have been in this situation have uniformly avowed, that they felt no bodily pain; that they had the entire use of their reasons and reflection, and when recovered, they could relate everything that had been said or done near them.
>
> (Quoted in Johnson 1955: 58)

7

While some preachers saw these exercises as signs of the power of the Holy Spirit, many were concerned about excess and about the opportunities for licentiousness caused by so many men and women spending the night together after occasions of great emotional intensity. Leading churchmen spoke in favour of control. The meetings themselves became routine. Camp sites were planned with the sexes segregated and the edges better lit. Instead of being spontaneous expressions of the Holy Spirit, the camps became arranged events. By 1806, it was routine for the last quarterly Methodist 'conference' in any circuit to take the form of a camp. Some Baptist associations also held camps as annual affairs. The bodily expressions also became routinized, part of an expected role performance, until they passed away altogether.

This question of spontaneity and order is important background for the later discussion of urban revivalism and broadcast religion. There are obviously many exceptions but as a general principle we can suggest that spontaneity, while lauded in the rhetoric of miracles, is seen as a threat. It is chaotic, it is disruptive, and it endangers interaction by making it impossible for any one person to predict how any other will behave. The instinct, the drive, is always to harness the driven and the instinctive, to make them ordered, routine, and predictable. In the history of American Protestantism there is a dual process of increasing control. At the first level one has a repeated pattern of a period of dullness and lifelessness in the churches being disrupted by an outburst of spontaneous religious enthusiasm, usually from some marginal social group. While endorsing it and trying to spread this new manifestation of God's work, ministers and others representing the mainstream of ordered civilized life seek to control it. And even those who are not consciously trying to control the enthusiasm inadvertently contribute to its routinization by scheduling meetings where the Spirit will be expected to move. Rather than demonstrate their lack of true religion, those in the locale of the planned meeting will feel obliged to produce their own revival. Once the time, place, layout, and timetabling of the camp meeting are arranged, it is not long before the enthusiasm becomes equally contrived.

Out of fellowships and camps come congregations and annual meetings and the religious life develops its orders and routines – until the next outburst. Yet each wheel turns within a process of ever-increasing *civilization*. The frontier was thinly populated and there was very little company or society. The work was long, very hard and monotonous. There was little or no law or custom. Where there was little need for co-operative social interaction (and indeed very little interaction beyond the immediate family) there was little need for co-ordination. Hence there was no premium on controlling one's physical urges. As settlements developed into towns and cities it became increasingly important to exercise self and social control. The self-disciplining diligent tradesman relegated the frontiersman to the place of archaic hero in children's books.

The spontaneity of the early days of the revivals was the last flourish, in a sanctioned context, of the primitive and uncivilized character of the frontier, which it both expressed and tamed. Those brought into the churches were socialized into teetotal self-control and personal discipline.[3]

In terms of religious geography, the result of the second great awakening was to leave the south predominantly Baptist and Methodist.

The story so far puts the first 'British' settlers in place. At the first census in 1790, 83.5 per cent of Americans were found to be English in origin, 6.7 per cent Scots, 5.6 per cent German, 2 per cent Dutch and 1.6 per cent were Irish. But this was the end of British predominance; sixty years later it was found that the largest groups of newcomers were the Irish (43 per cent) and Germans at 26 per cent, with only 14 per cent coming from England and Wales (Gaustad 1962: 43-5). The Germans and Dutch (and later Swedes) brought Lutheranism to the upper states. The main contribution of the Irish to the history of American Protestantism was to inadvertently stimulate local revivals as the arrival of poor Roman Catholics gave the longer established Protestants two reasons to recommit themselves to their religion: gratitude that they were not poor Catholics and fear that poor Catholics would undermine the world of good honest Protestants (Billington 1964).

PERFECTIONISM, REFORM, AND CIVIL WAR

One way of thinking of the shift from Calvinist election to Arminian free will is to see it as an increasingly positive view of man. From being so much in sin as to be helpless before God, man

9

had come to be viewed as having at least the sense to choose to respond to God's offer of salvation. While still stressing faith over works, the religion of the Baptists and Methodists saw man as largely competent. Charles Finney, the leading figure in the second wave of revivals, entirely repudiated Calvinism. In one of his phrases borrowed by many a preacher: the sinner's 'cannot is his will not. The will is free and . . . sin and holiness are voluntary acts of mind' (quoted in McLoughlin 1978: 125). Finney held that God was benevolent and that he had gifted man with reason. The logical extension of the new confidence which could be derived from these beliefs was to appear in the second quarter of the nineteenth century as 'perfectionism' or 'holiness'. Its advocates believed that the first blessing of the conversion experience could be followed by a further blessing which gave the believer the confidence to live a saintly life of what was called 'entire sanctification'. One element of the movement expected only that the second blessing would bring peace and deep piety. Another strand expected it to endow the believer with such gifts of the Holy Spirit as the ability to prophesy and to speak in 'the tongues of men and angels'. This second position is the forbear of modern *pentecostalism*.

Initially perfectionism or holiness was an interest movement which drew most support from Methodism and which was organized around camp meetings, conferences, and a number of regular publications. It was only towards the end of the century and largely as a result of criticism from non-pentecostal Methodists, that holiness and pentecostal groups began to see themselves as a distinct denomination. The Assemblies of God, the largest white pentecostal denomination – in which televangelists Jim Bakker and Jimmy Swaggart were ministers – grew out of a meeting in 1914 of representatives of 300 isolated pentecostal congregations. By 1980 it had grown to having some 9,000 congregations, concentrated in Texas, California, Oklahoma, and Arkansas (Gaustad 1962: 125).

The cultural change of which Arminianism and perfectionism were part also brought a great movement for social reform. Although we now see concern with the social and material environment as a distinctly liberal preoccupation, many of the nineteenth-century reformers were convinced evangelicals for whom the improvement of this world and the winning of souls were part of the same project. Most surprising, given the later association between conservative Protestantism and racism, evangelicals were at the forefront of the anti-slavery campaigns; the Evangelical Alliance excluded slave-owners and the students of Charles Finney's Oberlin College were committed to both revival preaching and emancipation. Phoebe Palmer, one of the leaders of Methodist perfectionism, was active in social work. William G. Boardman, whose *The Higher Christian Life* was a best seller, was executive secretary of the Christian Commission's social work department (Smith 1965: 175).

Such Protestants did not deny original sin but believed that the Holy Spirit was working to help us overcome it.

> Who does not see that, with the termination of injustice and oppression, of cruelty and deceit; with the establishment of righteousness in every statute book, and in every provision of human legislation and human jurisprudence; with art and science sanctified by the truth of God, and Holiness to the Lord graven upon the walls of our high places, and the whole earth dwelling in the rain of righteousness, this world would be renovated by the power of holiness. Oh, this is the reign of Jesus!
>
> (quoted in Smith 1965: 221)

Although this preacher speaks of the whole world dwelling in the rain of righteousness, he meant by that something importantly different from what a puritan in the early days of the New England colonies would have meant by it. The puritans were not individualists; they believed in a justly ordered society and were willing to debate at length the just price for goods, for example (Berthoff 1971: 68-72). In 1639 Robert Keayne, the wealthiest man in the Massachusetts Bay Company, was fined $200 for amassing unfairly large profits and was made to confess his sin in church (Carroll and Noble 1982: 73). The shift from Calvinism to Arminianism was also the shift from the ideal of a righteous community to the idea of the saved individual. For some time the enthusiasm, almost hyper-activity, of the pious reformers disguised the fact but 'community' now meant either the self-selecting society of saints (who shared a common religious culture) or the rest of the population who were the usually unwilling objects of evangelical compassion and impulse to regulation. This change made it

11

possible for a further turning inwards. Once the community, in the broader sense, failed to show the appropriate gratitude for the compassion of the evangelicals and resisted their desire to legislate social goodness, it could be abandoned to its fate.

THE FRACTURE OF AMERICAN PROTESTANTISM

The victory of the North in the Civil War, although it could be read by evangelicals as a proof of God's blessing, also marked the end of an era in American Protestantism. Although there were many for whom the horizon of religious life never extended beyond their own particular congregation or denomination (especially if it was an ethnic church), tacit support for the dual strategy of conversion and reform was so widely spread that one could almost talk of it as being the orthodox core of nineteenth-century Protestantism. But between the end of the Civil War in 1865 and the start of the First World War, major social, economic, and cultural changes saw the centre of gravity of American Protestantism shift so that what had for a century been taken-for-granted became marginalized.

The re-shaping of Protestantism can be considered in two parts: the social and the theological. This period saw a major revision of the attitudes of conservative Protestants to social reform. Southern evangelicals drew inwards, responding to their defeat and the emancipation of slaves by thinking of improvement in individual terms and leaving society to its own devices. Reforming evangelicals themselves seemed short of energy and their purposes seemed narrower and meaner. Marsden notes that while Jonathan Blanchard had before the Civil War been enthusiastic in the promotion of emancipation, the rights of Indians, peace, and popular democracy, his son Charles, in reviewing his own labours for improving society mentioned:

> in addition to education and Anti-Masonry, only his reform efforts against Sabbath-breaking, strong drink, and 'narcotic poisons' (mainly tobacco). Apparently he perceived these causes as the essentials of the 'Puritan' heritage.
>
> (Marsden 1980: 31)

Such a change has to be seen against the background of a sustained challenge to evangelical good works from two sources: a growing secular labour movement and liberal churchmen. Leading clergymen such as Washington Gladden and Walter Rauschenbusch (later identified as 'social gospellers') were also promoting secular notions of reform and progress. For them, the alteration of individuals was not enough and not even the main task. The Christian's responsibility was to improve the world, irrespective of the conversion potential of such social amelioration.

Many of the clergymen who were active in taking social reform to the left were also spokesmen for what acquired the unfortunately arrogant sobriquet of the 'higher criticism'. Pioneered by German rationalists, the higher critical approach to the Bible attempted to bring the bright (and sometimes harsh) light of modern scholarship to bear on the texts. Good historians and anthropologists, its proponents treated their own faith and its sources in the same way as they examined other religions. For them, the Bible was a document compiled by many different hands and shaped by many different cultural antecedents. Historical scholarship would strip away the accretions and sedimentations of other more primitive cultures and reveal the 'real' Bible and the 'real' Christianity. In practice, of course, the real Bible was the old one rewritten to suit the philosophical views of a modern industrial intelligentsia; the supernatural was reduced to the bare minimum and Christian revelation was changed from an historical event to an existential moment.

Until the challenges of the higher criticism, conservative Protestants had not thought much about the authority of the Bible. It was simply taken for granted by most Christians as the word of God and little thought was given to what that might mean. The threat to the assumption that, give or take the odd short passage, the Bible meant what it appeared to mean, produced an equal and opposite reaction. If the higher critics were going to reduce the word of God to the writings of man, conservatives felt obliged to argue that the Bible was inerrant, faultless, the dictated and revealed word of God, true in absolutely every detail. One conservative spoke of 'the Holy Spirit in the last letter He dictated to the apostle Paul'; another described the prophesies of the Bible as a 'photographically exact forecasting of the future' (Marsden 1980: 56).

In addition to the findings of geology which threatened

previous assumptions about the age of the earth, an important part of the new scholarship which liberals and higher critics felt should be brought to bear on Protestant theology was Darwinian evolution. For conservatives it was a major challenge, not just because it offered an explanation of the origins of species at odds with that in Genesis 1-12, but because it was part of a cultural current which saw the possibility of human improvement without the aid of God. It is important to note that the conservatives did not generally see themselves as in any sense anti-scientific. Far from it; they were firmly committed to an old-fashioned Baconian notion of scientific reasoning in which one collected all the 'facts' and then induced natural laws. For them God's statements in the Bible were facts and, provided one read them with an open mind, one could not fail to come to the conclusions to which the conservatives had come. Only later, in the 1920s, would one find conservatives arguing that the Bible and science were indeed in conflict and science was wrong. And even that was a minority position. By the 1960s, one would again find conservatives arguing that Darwinism failed to qualify as scientific, that evolution had not been established as a 'natural law', and that the Genesis account of creation was entirely compatible with 'real' as opposed to 'pseudo' science; creationism was re-launched as creation science.

Millennialism

The composite picture of American conservative Protestantism at the end of the nineteenth century is now almost complete. It only remains to introduce what later became a constituent element of fundamentalism.

In 1818, William Miller developed an interest in the problem of the timing of Christ's return. His examination of the Book of Daniel convinced him that there were only some twenty years before the end of the world. His lectures on the 'second coming of the Lord' were published in 1835 but attracted little attention until his cause was taken up by a Boston minister who was a gifted publicist.

> Between 1840 and 1843 meetings were organized all across the country, with Miller himself lecturing over three hund-red times during one half-year period. Despite warnings and

condemnation from many quarters, thousands, no doubt
hundreds of thousands, began to prepare for the Lord's
coming. As in Reformation times, there was even a comet to
heighten popular apprehension.

(Ahlstrom 1972: 480)

But the appointed dates came and went and nothing happened.
The movement collapsed but, inspired by the prophetic leadership
of Ellen G. Harmon, a remnant grew and developed into the
Seventh Day Adventists. Although never as specific about the date
of the end of the world, many conservative evangelicals in the
second half of the nineteenth century became concerned with 'the
end times'.

The early Calvinists were post-millennial. That is, they believed
that the millennium – the thousand years of God's righteousness
on earth – would be followed by Christ's second coming, the day
of judgement and so on. Pre-millennialists expect the sequence to
be reversed. Although details differed from one school to another,
the basic order is the continued decline of this world, second
coming, day of judgement, and then millennium, enjoyed only by
those who have been saved.

There is no necessity for pre-millennialists to be disdainful of
social reform but there is an obvious affinity between the expectation that the world will end soon (and get worse before it does)
and the idea that there is little point improving the world. One
does not redecorate when the wrecking crew are at the door.
Instead of social improvement what is required in the end times is
the conversion of as many people as possible and the preservation
of one's own purity. Note, however, that anxiously awaiting the
end does not necessarily lead to introversion. In some schools, the
conversion of large numbers is seen as a precursor and even as a
pre-condition of Christ's return. Hence the stress on missionary
activity to be found in pre-millennial circles and the continuing
popularity of plans to evangelize the whole world by the year 2000
(see below, pp. 229–32).

Conservative Protestant reform was some time dying and it had
one last campaign: temperance. Organizations such as the
Women's Christian Temperance Union (Gusfield 1963) had built
up enough public support for a number of states to vote
themselves dry in the 1890s. Full national prohibition was not won

until 1919 when the Volstead Act and the 18th amendment to the Constitution made the production, distribution, and retail of beverage alcohol illegal. The unwillingness of a large segment of the population to abide by the law created the climate in which organized crime could develop and in 1933 the 21st amendment to the Constitution repealed the 18th (Martin and Gelber 1981: 665). Many counties which were dominated by conservative Protestants continued to vote themselves dry but the debacle of the unintended consequences of prohibition seriously embarrassed the legal enforcement of righteousness and it was not tried again.

THE ENCLAVE

By the last quarter of the nineteenth century the broad centre of Protestantism was breaking up and the forces we now know as 'fundamentalism' were coalescing. In part fundamentalism was a response to the rise of secular labour politics, higher criticism, and Darwinism but more generally it was a response to the modern world. Just as liberalism was one possible reaction to the development of mass industrial urban societies interrelated in ways which seemed difficult to understand let alone control, so fundamentalism was a response to what many conservative Protestants saw as the terminal decline of civilization (by which they meant Christian and Protestant and Bible-believing civilization).

At first fundamentalism developed an organizational structure similar to the early days of the holiness movement. People remained in their denominations but read fundamentalist periodicals and books, held bible-study groups with like-minded believers, established educational institutions, and attended great summer rallies which were refined versions of the 'camp meetings' of the second awakening. But as it became clear that fundamentalists were not going to be able to distract their denominations from the apostate direction in which they were headed, pressure built for secession. Most denominations experienced schism and by the 1920s, fundamentalists were more likely to be in fundamentalist denominations than to form awkward pressure groups in mainstream churches.

Marsden describes the institutional structure of fundamentalism very well by using the analogy of an ethnic enclave.

Raised with middle-class Victorian ideals they might find themselves in new and unsettled situations; 'in-migrants' within a pluralistic and not always friendly society, or simply outside centers of cultural influence. Faced by a culture with a myriad of competing ideals, and having little power to influence that culture, they reacted by creating their own equivalent of the urban ghetto. An over view of fundamentalism reveals them building a subculture with institutions, mores and social connections that would eventually provide acceptable alternatives to the dominant cultural ethos.

(Marsden 1980: 204)

The conflict between fundamentalism and the modern world came to a head in the 1925 dual between William Jennings Bryan, the ageing Populist Democrat politician, and Clarence Darrow in a courtroom in Little Rock, Arkansas, when John Scopes, a biology teacher, was prosecuted for teaching Darwinian evolution. For the fundamentalists, Bryan argued that it was better to know the Rock of Ages than to know the age of rocks. Nowadays most people suppose that the creationists lost the Scopes case. In fact they won, a decision that was no surprise when three members of the jury said they read nothing but the Bible. The verdict was later overturned on a legal technicality. However, the public perception reflects the general response. To many Americans, Bryan was a ridiculous old man defending a lost cause with bad arguments and fundamentalism was a religion of small town and small mind hicks and hayseeds.

Although they had lost the argument in the major denominations and been humiliated in the Scopes trial, fundamentalists did not abandon their faith. Rather they drew strength and comfort from their public rejections and devoted their energies to creating a network of fundamentalist institutions which would sustain them and their faith. Bible Institutes flourished. In 1937, the Moody Bible Institute in Chicago had some 15,000 attenders at its courses and about the same number in correspondence classes. Between 1930 and 1940, the circulation of *Moody Monthly* rose by over 13,000 to some 40,000 readers (Carpenter 1980: 65-70). Bob Jones founded his fundamentalist liberal arts university. In the cities and in the north east, the fundamentalist strategy of the inter-war years was the creation of alternative social institutions; in the south and parts of the mid-west and west, it was continuing to exert the influence it already had on local state institutions. And, as we will see shortly, first radio and then television stations were an important part of the alternative world of fundamentalism.

THE INSTITUTIONALIZATION OF REVIVALS

Europeans who watch Jimmy Swaggart or James Robison strutting and sweating his message on to the television screen are often over-awed by the theatricality of the performance but these men are but thin impressions of some of their forbears and, as we have seen, the emotionalism of their meetings is nothing compared to that of the Kentucky camp meetings of the 1820s where there were actual 'holy rollers'.

I have already suggested that the evolution of revivalism can be seen as a process of increasing routinization and control. Charles Finney in the 1820s was keen to make a powerful impression on his listeners and to stir strong emotions. Although his preaching style was pedestrian, graphic language was used to stimulate fear. Here is a typical Finney description of the fate awaiting the unconverted:

> Look! Look! See the millions of wretches, biting and gnawing their tongues as they raise their scalding heads from the burning lake. See! See! How they are tossed and how they howl. Hear them groan, amidst the fiery billows, as they lash and lash and lash their burning skins.
>
> (Quoted in Weisberger 1958: 115)

He also prayed for sinners in the audience by name and used an 'anxious seat' for inquirers at the front of the hall to supplement personal fear with social pressure as incentive to experience conversion. But he expected the listeners to repress their emotions and channel them into the decision to convert. Vocal expressions of enthusiasm – the amens and hallelujahs – were not encouraged nor were the groans of a soul brought under conviction of sin. The various fainting, rolling, dancing, and laughing 'exercises' of the frontier were also discouraged. Fifty years later, Dwight L. Moody's style was so bland as to attract almost no criticism except for the rather folksy way in which he talked about God and the mawkish-

18

ness of the ballads sung by his partner Ira D. Sankey. Moody saw himself as the businessman's evangelist. He frequently used metaphors from commerce to describe and justify his evangelistic work and 'business-like' was one of his favourite forms of praise.

Billy Sunday (which actually was his name!) was a professional baseball player who went from working for the YMCA, to being the advance organizer for evangelist J. Wilbur Chapman, to holding his own crusade meetings. He borrowed from Chapman the idea of a decision card which converts could sign. It read: 'I have an honest desire henceforth to live a Christian life. I am willing to follow any light God may give me. I ask the people of God to pray for me.' There were spaces for the convert's name, his address, and his preferred church or pastor (a little touch which suggested that most converts would have some contact with the churches). The climax of a Sunday service was the call for members of the audience to show they were 'with him' (what they were assenting to was kept deliberately vague to ensure large numbers) by leaving their seats, coming to the front, and shaking Billy's hand. As the wooden floor of the tabernacles which Sunday had specially constructed for his meetings were covered in sawdust, the exercise quickly got the name of 'hitting the sawdust trail' and during his career, millions did it for him. The question of numbers will be raised again but it was characteristic of Sunday's operation that he directed every effort to persuading as many as possible to hit the sawdust trail and gave great publicity to the numbers who did so. The much smaller number of people who signed decision cards and the even smaller proportion who became involved in local churches after the Sunday circus had left town were not widely advertised either by the Sunday machine (as one would expect) or by local newspapers, for whom it was not an exciting story.

In terms of spontaneity and enthusiasm, Sunday combined some of the wild anarchy of the old Kentucky frontier camp meetings with the dull business-like delivery of Moody or Reuben A. Torrey (Moody's successor as head of the Chicago, later Moody, Bible Institute). He offered in his own rough and tumble performance a sanitized and scaled-down version of the old camp fire meeting. Instead of four days of anarchy, there was a neat two hour service and such shouting and rolling around as there was came, not from the audience as an expression of coming under conviction of sin or being filled with the Holy Spirit, but from

19

Sunday himself, as an entertainment. Members of the audience who ventured to participate by shouting 'Amen' or 'Hallelujah' were chastised by Sunday in humour: 'Never mind, my friend, I can do all the hollering.' The very rare individual who essayed the bodily exercises of the first camp meetings was forcibly removed before any damage was done to Sunday's reputation for respectability.

In that sense his meetings provide a convenient bridge from early revivalism to mass media evangelism where the audience are passive, distant recipients of radio and television signals, and the evangelist is the one who by his mannerisms shows the work of the Holy Ghost.

CONSERVATIVE PROTESTANTISM 1919-1970

Billy Sunday died before the final defining fracture of American Protestantism. The difference between liberal or 'mainstream' Protestantism and the conservative variety was clear. But there was an important difference within the conservative camp, reflected in the more careful uses of the terms 'fundamentalist' and 'evangelical'.[4]

Both sides agree that (a) the Bible is infallible because it is the word of God; (b) Christ was God's only son sent into the world to die for our sins; (c) salvation (eternal heaven instead of eternal hell) is attained by undergoing a conversion experience, by being 'born again' in Christ. To some extent, fundamentalists can be distinguished from evangelicals by the rigour with which the first of these beliefs is worked out. For all their protestations, no-one takes every part of the Bible literally. Even the most conservative interpreter recognizes that Lamb of God is metaphor and not mutton. But fundamentalists take more of the Bible at face-value than do evangelicals. Fundamentalists tend also to be more sure than evangelicals of the imminence of the end of the world. Although most fundamentalist pastors would not insist on subscription to a particular scenario for the apocalypse (beyond being sure that the day of judgement would come pre- rather than post-millennium), they could probably do so without alienating much of their congregation.

A third difference concerns American nationalism. Since the first settlement some Protestants have identified the white anglo-saxon settlers of America with God's chosen people. The Republic, the shining city on the hill, the new Israel; all are common themes. Evangelists such as Moody and Sunday were convinced of the superiority of the social and political structures of America over all else and this has continued to be a strong theme in conservative Protestantism. In the period since the end of the Second World War, the identification of America and God's chosen land has become even stronger as the threat from the Soviet Union has been theologized into a threat from *atheistic* communism and the anti-Christ of the future apocalypse. Leading fundamentalists such as Carl McIntire, Billy James Hargis, Fred C. Schwartz, and Major Edgar Bundy combined attacks on communism with criticism of liberal Protestantism and the ecumenical movement by accusing liberal and mainstream churchmen of being closet communists and fellow travellers.[5] In the heyday of McCarthyism, these men were to be found supplying names and information to the House Committee on Un-American activities. Although evangelicals tend to be anti-communist and pro-American, they are much less likely to link the fortunes of the gospel and the foreign policy of their country.

But what most readily distinguishes the two parts of the conservative Protestant tradition is attitude to liberals and other non-believers; as James Davison Hunter has neatly put it, the principle point of disagreement is *politeness* (1983: 84-91). Since they lost their fight to take over the major denominations and walked out, separation from apostasy has been an article of faith with fundamentalists. Paul's 'Be ye not yoked with unbelievers' is extended from advice about marriage to a philosophy of life. Although it is intended pejoratively, the common fundamentalist description of evangelicals as people with the right beliefs but the wrong friends is pretty close to the mark. While fundamentalists could not fault most evangelicals on their own personal beliefs they do fault them for not 'separating' from others who do not have the right beliefs. Fundamentalists wish to make ideological soundness a test for association; evangelicals tend to be more flexible about their relationships. Thus Bob Jones denounces Billy Graham for allowing Roman Catholics and liberal Protestants to be associated with his crusades and, worse, passing on 'converts' to such apostate bodies. While the American Council of Christian Churches (formed by Carl McIntire as a fundamentalist alternative to the ecumenical Federal Council of Churches) demands total separation, the National Association of Evangelicals permits its denominations to be associated with the Council.

RELATIVE STRENGTHS

This brief history of Protestantism in America has introduced most of the principal denominations and theological positions. Finally I will present a brief summary of the relative strengths of the main groups in the mid-1950s, a convenient point to turn to religious broadcasting.

Table 1 Religious identification in 1957 (in percentages)

Roman Catholic	25
Baptist	21
Methodist	14
Lutheran	7
Presbyterian	6
Episcopalian	3
Jewish	3
Other and none	21

Source: Greeley 1972: 89

Given that televangelism is largely evangelical, fundamentalist or pentecostal, we can eliminate first the Catholics and Jews, and second, the Methodists, Presbyterians, and Episcopalians, who tend to be moderate in theology. Having said that, the broad confessional categories disguise important distinctions. Among the Lutherans, for example, there were 2.5 million members of the theologically moderate Lutheran Church in America and 2 million members of the conservative Lutheran Church-Missouri Synod. Among the Baptists are liberal northern Baptists (about 1.5 million in the American Baptist Church) and 8 million conservative Southern Baptists. Included in the 'others' would be a number of important theologically conservative groups: independent Baptist fundamentalists, pentecostalists, and adventists. Very roughly speaking, of the about 33 million members of the twelve largest Protestant denominations, one-third were in evangelical, fundamentalist, or pentecostal denominations and two thirds were in mainstream or moderate denominations.[6]

22

The main trend from the 1950s to the present has been the relative decline of the moderate denominations and the growth of the theologically conservative ones (Hoge and Roozen 1979; Bruce 1989). Particularly dramatic has been the growth of the pentecostal Assemblies of God which in 1953 reported 370,000 members and now about one million. We need not bother with the detail of individual denominational careers. A good rough guide to theology is interdenominational affiliation. In the 1950s, the churches affiliated to the ecumenical Council (which changed from Federal to National Council of Churches of Christ in America in 1950) accounted for two-thirds of Protestants. In 1987, the NCC had 22.8 per cent of American Christians in membership but a larger number – 33.6 per cent of American Christians – were in conservative denominations not affiliated with the Council. It is against that background that we need to consider the rise of televangelism.

Chapter Two

RELIGIOUS BROADCASTING IN AMERICA

RADIO DAYS

In the radio boom which followed the end of the First World War, the strident voices of the hucksters, if not the most common, were the most interesting and memorable. Initially there was no federal regulation of radio and anyone who could afford the equipment could broadcast. The result was a chaos of thousands of transmitters, varying in power from those which could barely be heard across town to those which carried clear across the country, shifting frequency and changing their broadcast schedules as new businesses came and went. According to Robert Landry:

> There were hysterical clergymen, enemies of Wall Street, enemies of chain stores, enemies of Catholics, Jews and Negroes, promoters of patented heavens. . . . The meaning of the stars, the stock market, the future life could all be learned by enclosing cash. Falling hair or teeth could be arrested – just write. Fortunes in real estate could be made over-night – just write. Home cures for this, or the other thing were available.
>
> (Quoted in Emery 1969: 7)

Public pressure eventually led Herbert Hoover, then Secretary for Commerce and Labor, to push Congress into passing the 1927 Radio Act which established the Federal Radio Commission (FRC).

One radio operator with strong feelings about chain stores was W. K. Henderson, a prominent businessman in Shreveport, Louisiana. In addition to defying the FRC's authorized power limits and shifting frequency, Henderson also stretched its patience with his language. Retail chain stores were described as 'dirty low down

24

burglars' and 'damnable low down thieves from Wall Street' (Pusateri 1977: 86). In one of the rare uses of its power to protect the public interest, the FRC made it clear that it would close Henderson down and he sold his station. Another minor star of the free-for-all days was Dr John Brinkley, a physician in Milford, Kansas, who operated station KFKB. He used his airtime to advertise his hospital and his own surgical expertise. He also diagnosed conditions of people he had never seen and prescribed medicines from a mailed out sheet. Emery gives the following example of his on-air doctoring method:

> Probably he has gall stones. No, I don't mean that. I mean kidney stones. My advice to you is to get prescription No. 80 and 50 for men, also 64. I think he will be a whole lot better. Also drink a lot of water.
>
> (Quoted in Emery 1969: 10)

Brinkley's licence was not renewed.

Such government interference in broadcasting was rare. Despite high sounding statements about public interest, the FRC did little more than regulate the mechanics of radio broadcasting; frequency allocation and transmitter power fixing were its main concerns. Beyond removing those whose broadcasting consisted of nothing but quackery or whose language was so intemperate as to offend local dignitaries (and that had to be pretty intemperate), little was done to regulate content. The restructuring of the FRC as the Federal Communications Commission, with added responsibility for first telephone and telegraphic communication and later television, made little difference.

From the very first, religion was an important part of the material which was pumped into the ether. The first professional radio voice broadcast took place in December 1920 in Pittsburgh. Only a month later Calvary Episcopal Church of the same city broadcast its regular worship service. Perhaps more surprising, many of the early stations – sixty-three of the 600 stations operating in 1925 – were church owned (Ellens 1974: 16). Although many broadcast only on Sundays, this was a considerable church involvement in the new medium and it might have increased had the new Commission not required higher standards (and hence more costly equipment) and the depression not hit churches as hard as secular institutions.[1]

From the first, secular stations gave air time free ('sustaining time') to religious broadcasting so that they could claim that at least part of their output was in the public interest when it came to licence renewals. This then created the problem that the demand from religious groups for such time far outstripped what the stations were prepared to allocate and they needed some manner of regulating the demands. The Federal Council of Churches of Christ in America (later the National Council of Churches) represented twenty-five mainstream denominations. It encouraged local churches to co-operate in ecumenical broadcasting. The fledgling NBC radio network saw the value in using the Council to distance itself from squabbling denominations and asked it to organize all NBC's Protestant religious broadcasting. The arrangement had the desired effect of leaving it to the major churches to sort out their competing demands and was pursued with the other main traditions through the Jewish Seminary of America and the National Council of Catholic Men (Horsfield 1984: 3).

The Columbia Broadcasting Service (CBS) began by offering some commercial time for religious broadcasting but then switched to providing only sustaining time in 1931 as a subtle way of ridding itself of Father Charles E. Coughlin, whose notoriety was becoming an embarrassment (see pp. 163–4). CBS shifted to an NBC-like arrangement with the Federal Council selecting people to preach on the *Church of the Air* programme. By 1934 the Council had control of six hours of regularly broadcast programmes (Hadden and Shupe 1988: 47). At this time, the Mutual Broadcasting System – which transmitted Charles E. Fuller's *Old Fashioned Revival Hour* and Walter A. Maier's *The Lutheran Hour* – was the only network offering unrestricted commercial time. And in 1944, it responded to criticism of its programmes by the mainstream denominations and placed conditions on its sold time. Religious broadcasters would no longer be able to solicit funds on the air or air programmes longer than thirty minutes and outside Sunday morning.

For a short period, religious broadcasting was almost monopolized by the denominations of the FCCC and by one or two of the largest evangelical denominations which managed to secure their own sustaining time. Not only did they have all the free time but there were very few opportunities for others to buy onto the air.

Leading liberal broadcaster Harry Emerson Fosdick rejoiced in this predominance: 'it is sure that we have opportunity in religion-on-the-air to make an incalculable contribution that will outflank, overpass and undercut sectarians in religion' (quoted in Saunders 1968: 101). The recently formed National Association of Evangelicals campaigned against this virtual lock-out and had some initial success: Mutual and what later became the ABC network both allocated free time to the NAE. Another response to the Mutual policy changes was the formation of the pressure group National Religious Broadcasters.[2]

Although those who were excluded clearly saw the allocation of sustaining time to the Federal Council and its affiliated denominations as a considerable boon which they were being denied, it is not clear that free time was an unalloyed blessing. It certainly benefited the networks in allowing them to claim public service credit without having to bother with the rival suits of competing religious groups but because it was freely given, the churches could not be too insistent about the quality of the time, which could always be in the unpopular margins of Sunday morning and 'deep sleep'. Furthermore, as I will later suggest, the cosy cartel, as most such arrangements do, acted as a damper on initiative and innovation and resulted in a long term fall in the quality and popularity of the programmes made and aired in this manner.

Although there were some institutional changes and there was a gradual increase in the extent to which individual denominations produced their own material, the basic arrangement of religion on network radio remained the same to the present although there was a steady rise in the number of *local* stations which offered commercial time.

The early radio giants: Maier and Fuller

Although the mainstream denominations dominated sustaining time, it was the few conservative programmes on paid time which had the largest audiences. Just before CBS abandoned its policy of selling time, a contract was signed with the Lutheran Church-Missouri Synod (a conservative schism from the main Lutheran tradition) to air a weekly show at a price of $200,000 for a season. Walter Maier, who in addition to teaching Old Testament at the Missouri Synod Seminary had been running its radio station

KFUO ('Keep Forward Upward Onward!') for four years, believed it was worth it and began *The Lutheran Hour* in October 1930. The format was typical – sacred singing from a large choir followed by a short sermon – but it soon built a large and loyal audience whose contributions paid more than half the costs. When the Mutual Broadcasting System started its network, Maier paid to have it air his shows and as MBS expanded, he increased his payments to reach the expanding potential audience.

Contemporaneous with Maier was Charles E. Fuller. Unlike Maier who began broadcasting from the institutionally strong position of being on the staff of a denomination's seminary, editor of one of its magazines, and speaker on its station, Fuller was an independent. He was pastoring a small congregation (which had grown from a bible-study group he led) when he first became involved in radio. In February 1930 a Santa Ana educational station began to broadcast the Sunday worship services from his church. In May additional time was purchased for a programme of religious music 'and a phone-in time with Fuller answering questions directed to him from the radio audience' (Armstrong 1979: 41). In an interesting example of positive feedback, the programmes attracted more people to the church which forced the programme to go off the air while the building was modified. The larger congregation made Fuller more ambitious and he re-started the programme on a more powerful station in Long Beach.

Fuller's ambitions clashed with those of his congregation. The church officers preferred a traditional view of the church's role and were not happy about broadcasting beyond the immediate local area to people who would not attend the services. Fuller resigned and devoted himself full-time to a series of radio shows supported solely by listeners' contributions. The series got off to an unfortunate start, opening in the week of March 1933 in which Roosevelt closed the banks and an earthquake killed 115 in Long Beach, but the shows built an audience, expanded to an hour as *The Radio Revival Hour* and in 1937 became a national programme on Mutual with the title *The Old Fashioned Revival Hour*. The expansion of the Mutual network – more stations meant a higher price – both forced Fuller's hand (as it had done with Maier) and gave him an excellent opportunity to appeal to his listeners for more money to reach the larger possible audience. By the end of

1939 Fuller was heard on all 152 of the Mutual stations. By 1943 he was the network's largest customer and was buying 50 per cent more time than the secular company in second place.

When Mutual dithered over its policy towards religion on commercial time, Fuller bought time on hundreds of small independent stations. The changeover was so smoothly effected as to hardly diminish his audience. The fall in advertising revenue after the war caused the networks to change their minds about excluding paid religious broadcasting and by 1949 *The Old Fashioned Revival Hour* was back on network, this time ABC. Further changes of network policy forced the programme to be cut to half an hour and then Fuller to change back to independent stations but until he retired in 1967 and against the competition of television, *The Old Fashioned Revival Hour* regularly drew audiences in the twenty millions.

TELEVISION

The first regular television broadcasts were made in 1939 and 1940 by the NBC network. Early output included Protestant, Catholic, and Jewish religious programmes but it was not until 1947 that any religious organization really grasped the potential of television and, importantly for a later argument, it was the Southern Baptist Convention, which was outside the ecumenical cartel of the Federal Council of Christian Churches, which first seized the chance.

As with radio, the networks came to an agreement to work with the three major faiths through central organizations rather than themselves arbitrate the competing demands of various denominations. The networks provided the resources to make the programmes and sent the product to their affiliated stations for broadcast on sustaining-time. In addition to the centrally produced network product, a number of local ecumenical groups developed the same sort of arrangement with local stations.

A problem was that this arrangement, as critics to both right and left agreed, led to bland inoffensive programmes. Even the large conservative denominations which were powerful enough to lever their own free time out of local stations – the Southern Baptists and the Missouri Synod Lutherans – managed to produce dull and lifeless programmes. The National Religious Broadcasters campaigned against a system which appeared to benefit the FCCC-affiliated denominations but what finally destroyed the near-monopoly of the mainstream churches was not a change of heart by the networks (to this day most broadcasters must contract on a syndicated basis with the plethora of individual stations) but a ruling by the Federal Communications Commission.

In 1960, the FCC declared that no public interest was served by it discriminating between commercial and sustaining-time. That is, whether or not a station was broadcasting in the public interest would depend on the nature of its output and not the contractual basis on which the decision to air that output was made. Although it seemed innocuous, the FCC decision radically changed the nature of religious broadcasting in America. If a radio or television station needed to fill some of its time with religious material in order to claim to be broadcasting in the public interest and sold time was as good for that purpose as freely given time, then it would sell time rather than give it free to the local council of churches.

Station managers dropped those programmes (both network and local church council-produced shows) they had been airing free and sold their time to the clamouring evangelicals. By 1970 there were thirty-eight independent syndicated evangelical programmes buying time from local stations; by 1978 this had risen to seventy-two. The fierce competition among potential paying customers allowed the stations to increase their charges for time slots. It also made the previously difficult-to-fill Sunday time more valuable. Eventually, even those stations which had been at first reluctant to join in this rash of commercial activity were tempted by the easy money.

The consequence of that minor policy ruling from the Federal Communications Commission was a major change in the nature of American religious broadcasting. In 1959 58 per cent of religious programming was on commercial time; by 1977 the proportion had increased to 92 per cent. Not all of this, but most, is the evangelical, fundamentalist, or pentecostal material we think of as 'holy roller' or 'televangelist'. The impact is slightly less than one might at first imagine because a lot of this programming is in the smaller markets and in marginal times. But it is amplified by a knock-on effect on the networks. As local network-affiliated stations opted out of the network product to sell their own religion time, the networks reduced their commitment to sustaining-time religious programming. CBS in 1980 cancelled two long-running religion series because 'all but a dozen' of their affiliates preferred to use the time slots for paid, syndicated evangelical programmes (Buddenbaum 1981: 267) and in 1988 it closed its religion unit and ended *For Our Times*, the last sustaining-time programme on any of the major networks.

In addition to dominating the religion output of secular radio and television, conservative Protestants have also been establishing their own television stations, something made possible by the opening up of the cheaper UHF frequency bands in the 1970s. It is a little difficult to quantify the phenomenon because identity as a 'religious' station is not always apparent but by 1978 there were about thirty such stations and a decade later the figure had doubled. However, this may have little overall effect. Horsfield (1984: 98) believes that Christian stations act as a magnet for religious programmes, which shift from buying time on the local secular channels to buying time on the local religious channel with little or no net increase in the total amount of religious programming.

The National Religious Broadcasters Association was founded to create space for its conservative Protestant members by campaigning against the near-monopoly of broadcasting enjoyed by the liberal churches. In fairy-tale fashion, evangelical and funda- mentalist broadcasting has gone from Cinderella to princess. Some of the major denominations are still involved in religious broadcasting but the bulk, perhaps 75 per cent of all religion on radio and television is now evangelical or fundamentalist. Were one looking for near-monopolies, one would simply note that more than half the airings of religion programmes are accounted for by just *ten* programmes and they are all evangelical or fundamentalist.

TELEVISION STARS

Bishop Fulton J. Sheen

The modern televangelism organization and product will be described in great detail in the next chapter; here I want to introduce some of the key figures in the evolution of that product.

Although the programmes which came to dominate television religion were paid commercial time airings, the first television star did not buy his own time but was sponsored by the Admiral company which made televisions. For fifteen years before 1953, Bishop Fulton J. Sheen had been the principal speaker on *The Catholic Hour* which, as is inexplicably often the case, was a half-hour radio show, an NBC sustaining-time programme. In 1952 he moved, with no alteration in style, to a television studio.

> His program consisted solely of a speech or classroom lecture on a religious or moral subject, presented in a study-type set, with the aid of a blackboard on which he occasionally illustrated the point being made. The only assistance he received throughout the programme was from a stagehand who cleaned the board while it was off-camera.
>
> (Horsfield 1984: 7)

Sheen often remarked the cleanness of the board when he next came to use it and attributed it to an 'angel', who became nationally famous. Although his status as a Catholic bishop was made clear by his robes and cape, Sheen drew the huge audience for *Life is Worth Living* from across the religious spectrum. Uniquely for religious broadcasting, his show was a conventionally sponsored commercial programme which held its own against prime-time viewing:

> Many bars tuned their television sets to his program; taxi drivers would stop work for a half-hour in order to watch. A blind couple in Minneapolis bought an Admiral television set to express gratitude to the sponsor of his program.
>
> (Horsfield 1984: 8)

Billy Graham

The best known of modern American preachers, Billy Graham, has made extensive use of mass media but done little to innovate. Graham's preaching career began with an evangelistic organization called Youth for Christ (YFC) and his first contact with radio came in 1944 even before he was widely known as a preacher. In his first year out of college, Graham was asked by YFC leader Torrey Johnson if he wanted to take over Johnson's *Songs in the*

Night show which went out over one of Chicago's most powerful radio stations. Having presented a number of editions, Graham joined Johnson on a YFC tour of Europe. In 1950 he was approached by Theodore Elsner, president of the National Religious Broadcasters, who felt there was a need for someone to fill the gap left by the recent death of Walter A. Maier. Elsner's contacts were able to offer Graham a peak Sunday afternoon slot on ABC that was about to become vacant. At $7,000 a week, assuming that after three weeks the audience would be funding the show, and with arithmetic somewhat awry, Graham decided that he needed $25,000. The rest of the tale is told in classic evangelical style. Unable to make up his own mind, he decided to leave the decision to the Lord:

> I feel the burden for it, but it's up to You, and if You want this, I want You to send me a sign. And I'm going to put out the fleece. And the fleece is for the $25,000 by midnight'.
>
> (Quoted in Pollock 1966)[3]

At the end of that night's crusade, he spoke of the radio opportunity and waited for the money to come in. When the team added up what they had collected, they had only $23,000. One team member, a little short of the evangelical right stuff, suggested that they were near enough the target which would have been a sign from the Lord.

> Billy, almost in tears at the generosity and trust of the people, firmly said, No: the fleece was for $25,000 before midnight, $25,000 it must be. The devil might have sent the lesser sum to tempt him. A subdued team returned to the Multnomah Hotel shortly before midnight. Billy went to his room, Grady to the mail desk, where he was given three envelopes delivered by hand. In each was a pledge from somebody unable to wait in the queue: one for $1,000, two for $250. Together they made up the $25,000.
>
> (Pollock 1966: 118)

With what was again somewhat curious arithmetic, the name chosen for the half-hour slot was *Hour of Decision* and it was filled quite economically by broadcasting a part of a live crusade meeting. With the advent of good taping technology, it became even easier to record crusade meetings and edit them down.

Like his radio show, Graham's television work was primarily an extension of the crusade. Previously land lines had been used to carry the sound signal to halls in neighbouring towns but these meetings were always rather awkward events: with only a disembodied voice, the audience had nowhere to look! Television was at first, and still is, used in much the same way as the land lines: as a device for taking the crusade meeting to those who cannot come to it. Crusade meetings are filmed and time is bought to air them; television is a way of servicing the overspill. Indeed, Graham has never had a regular programme but has bought time to air 'specials' which mirror the rallies; a well rehearsed mass amateur choir sings rousing crusade hymns, local ministers or dignitaries read passages of scripture and pray, Graham preaches a long sermon, and those who respond to his call are filmed coming forward for counselling.

Oral Roberts

A similar naïveté towards the technical visual possibilities of the medium was shown by Oral Roberts in his early years in television. Granville Oral Roberts was the son of a preacher in the Pilgrim Holiness Church in a small town in rural Oklahoma. His father had broken with the Methodists 'because of their lack-of appreciation for his experience and proclamation of the charismatic gift of speaking in tongues' (Ellens 1974: 80). Oral was licensed as a Holiness preacher in 1935 and pastored various small Pilgrim Holiness churches before ending up in Enid, Oklahoma, where in 1947 he rented a local auditorium and conducted a crusade (Hadden and Swann 1981: 23). In 1948 he held his first healing meeting in a tent and launched his career as a faith healer, working the sawdust trail of tent meetings in small country towns and then bigger cities.

He was already well known, or notorious, for his healing crusades and his radio show *Healing Waters* when, in January 1954, he broadcast his first programme on sixteen television stations. This one was filmed entirely in a studio but he felt it to be stilted and, with encouragement from Rex Humbard, whose son he had healed (Humbard 1971), he raised money to film scenes of healing in the tent.

The first program filmed direct during the crusade was aired in February, 1955. It created a national controversy. At our office in Tulsa we were flooded with calls and television stations through North America were totally unprepared for the response they received. Their switchboards were jammed; their mail was unprecedented.

It shook some station managers so much that our program was cancelled. Then they really began to get mail. Millions were excited by our program and wanted it shown on their favourite stations.

(Roberts 1972: 180)

Probably thousands rather than millions but the new format – where he preached a sermon in the studio, direct to camera but filmed himself healing lines of the sick and needy in his tent meetings – was a success. There was some initial difficulty with his core pentecostal support who wondered if his films would have the same healing power as his bodily presence but criticism was silenced by the many testimonies of those healed through the new medium (Harrell 1985: 127-9).

Until the mid-1960s, the television programmes were little more than advertisements for the rallies. Then, appreciating that the increasing sophistication of the medium was making his format look dated, and with public interest in faith healing apparently waning, Roberts folded up his tent and dropped the television show to concentrate on the founding of Oral Roberts University. When he returned to television in 1969, it was with an entirely new kind of show designed to make the most of the medium. It was taped in the NBC studios at Burbank, California, with a technical crew from Rowan and Martin's *Laugh-in*. The announcer was from the cast of *Bonanza*!

The sparkling new TV presentation had everything that would guarantee success for any series – bright contemporary music, attractive young people, a fast pace, superb technical quality, and a well-known presenter at its center.

(Armstrong 1979: 86)

The variety show format with such 'special guests' as Dale Evans, Pat Boone, Anita Bryant, Jerry Lewis and Jimmy Durante caused something of a sensation among conservative Protestants, who had trouble with the claim that the appearance of being nothing more than the best in secular entertainment was a good way of hooking the uncommitted before slipping them the message in the second half, but the audiences were enormous. As will be clear later, specific figures for audience size are difficult to find and even more difficult to interpret but Ellens claims an audience for a Roberts's Thanksgiving Day special of over 27 million viewers (Ellens 1974: 87) and this is not implausible.

Details of the ideological content of the programmes, the 'product', will be discussed in the next chapter. Here it is enough to note that as Roberts has aged, and as he has moved from sawdust-floored tent to university, so he has almost entirely dropped the practice of faith healing on screen. Recently, in an attempt to fight off the challenge from Jimmy Swaggart, he hired a secular production company to devise a new format which, among other things, tried to appeal to a younger audience by having Oral talking to large puppets! It failed but Roberts remains near the top of the first division (Frankl 1987: 123).

Rex Humbard

The position as progenitor of religious television, the first person to appreciate that the new medium offered the opportunity for new formats, almost certainly belongs to Rex Humbard. Humbard was born into an itinerant preaching family and was doing little more than following the family trade when he decided that he was called to build a new congregation in Akron, Ohio, but he had the vision to see the symbiotic relationship between that congregation and a television audience. His life on the road with his parents – he was one of the Humbard Family Singers who warmed up the audience for his tent preaching father – had taught him the importance of entertainment (as well as adding a vast repertoire and enormous experience to an excellent voice). For the first few years Calvary Temple met in a movie theatre but the Cathedral of Tomorrow – specifically designed for television with a stage which revolved – was being built and in 1958 it opened.

Hadden and Shupe (1988: 51) make the simple but important point that the invention of videotape gave an enormous boost to the fortunes of the independent television evangelists. Until then pictures not on motion picture film or transmitted down fixed lines could not be distributed and shown on a number of television stations and film was very expensive. Although pioneering in designing his church for television, Humbard was unwilling to use film and was thus seen on only a limited number of stations in Ohio and West Virginia. With the arrival of video in the early 1960s, he broadcast further afield. By 1968 he could claim to be seen on sixty-eight stations and by 1980 he was on 207.

The Humbard show was a musical entertainment built around the extended Humbard family; in 1980 fourteen of them appeared. The format was glossy Nashville country and western. Contemporary gospel music, sung by the family or guest stars, was interrupted for brief sermonettes from Rex or spots in which he prayed over prayer requests viewers had sent in. In the mid-1970s, the music content increased further when *You Are Loved* was moved out of the Cathedral of Tomorrow and filmed on location in Florida (Hoover 1988: 57).

In the discussion of fund-raising in Chapter Seven, the importance of grandiose building programmes in attracting donations will be discussed. After getting his fingers burnt on the fires of local opposition and the Internal Revenue Service in the early 1970s, Humbard never engaged in such projects and this may explain his being the first of the major televangelists to go out of business. His demise was sudden. For some time he had been losing audience share and in 1985, the cost of airtime was greater than the amount coming in to pay for it. When word of his troubles got around, television stations cancelled his programme. With fewer showings, there was a smaller audience and less revenue and so on. Abruptly, Humbard retired (Hadden and Shupe 1988: 123).

Robert Schuller

The only major television evangelist who is a minister of a mainstream denomination, Robert Schuller began his ministry in a drive-in in Garden Grove, California in the 1950s. Asked by the Reformed Church in America to start a congregation in California, he had commenced preaching to about seventy-five people; them sitting in their cars and him standing on the roof of the snack bar. Even when the congregation had grown enough to fill a normal church building, Schuller continued to preach at the drive-in.

In September 1980, he preached his last sermon in the old

building of the Garden Grove Community Church and led the congregation in a procession to the spectacular Crystal Cathedral which he had built at a reported cost of $16 million. Designed specifically for his television shows by leading modernist Phillip Johnson, the Cathedral is, as its name suggests, walled and roofed entirely in glass and embodies Schuller's beliefs that the faith should have few mysteries and the faithful should not be cut off from the world. Schuller has not forgotten his drive-in days; one end of the Cathedral opens up so that the thousands who drive in to the car park and plug their headphones into the stands can also see Schuller.

Schuller's *Hour of Power* begins with the choir singing a moving anthem while the camera pans over the delightful gardens of the Church, the open blue skies, and the smiling faces of the congregation. Finally it comes up and closes on Schuller standing, arms raised in his bright robes, smiling and announcing: 'This is the day the Lord has made! Let us rejoice and be glad in it.' Although Schuller may sometimes interview a celebrity about his or her faith, the centre of the show is a Schuller sermon which is a well organized and fluent presentation of an emotional therapy he calls 'Possibility Thinking'.

There are two important features of Robert Schuller's success in televangelism and the implications of both will be developed later. The first is that like Humbard, Schuller designed a church and congregation for television, but like Roberts, he made it a major fund-raising building scheme. The second point is that Schuller is not an evangelical or a fundamentalist and yet has succeeded in a medium and a format apparently dominated by conservative Protestant theology.

Pat Robertson and the Christian Broadcasting Network

The most original of contemporary television evangelists is Marion G. 'Pat' Robertson, a man whose programming formats have been so innovative that, even before his campaign for the presidential nomination of the Republican party in 1988 called for a more secular image, he could reasonably disclaim the description 'television evangelist'; organizer, programmer, and presenter might be more accurate descriptions.

In 1961 Robertson bought a defunct UHF television station in

Virginia Beach, Virginia at a 'miraculous' fraction of the asking price (Hadden and Swann 1981: 37). With money raised from preaching in Virginia churches, he put the station back on the air for its first short broadcast, which at two and a half hours was just long enough to ask for further donations.

Robertson experimented with different show formats. Jim Bakker, later to become his own master, worked for Robertson presenting a puppet show! During a 1963 fund-raising 'telethon', Robertson asked for 700 people to pledge ten dollars to meet the monthly operating budget. They did and they were collectively honoured when Bakker started a talk show called the *700 Club*. The format was copied directly from such secular talk shows as *The Johnny Carson Show*. Evangelical 'stars' were interviewed about the miracles in their lives and they even plugged their new books and records. The *700 Club* was a great success. The surplus funds that it brought in were used to expand the organization.

In 1980 the flagship programme was transformed from talk show into 'magazine' show which combined entertainment with in-depth investigative reporting, and a news summary. In 1986, Robertson's commentaries on the news were formally packaged in a section called, appropriately enough, 'Pat Robertson's Perspective on the News' (Hadden and Shupe 1988: 139).

The borrowing of secular programme formats for Christian programming was not new – Oral Roberts had already borrowed the light entertainment variety show – but Robertson has been a pioneer in the technology and organization of communications. While other televangelists produce and distribute showcases for themselves and their product, CBN offers a network structure which services programmes other than Robertson's own vehicles. Feeding 5,500 cable systems, it is now the third largest cable television network. It provides an all-day channel of paid religious programmes from other televangelists, CBN's own religious products (which in addition to the *700 Club* for a short time included a Christian soap opera, killed off because of poor ratings), and repeats of such wholesome family shows as *Gunsmoke*, *Wagon Train*, *Skippy the Kangaroo*, *The Flying Nun*, and *The Man From Uncle*.

Robertson has used the money raised by CBN to diversify: he now offers training in television and radio production techniques to Christian communicators at 'CBN University'. His interest in political issues (which will be discussed at length in Chapter Eight) has led him to support litigation on behalf of fundamentalist groups and he has founded his own law school to train Christian attorneys for the fray.

This very brief survey of some of the stars and pioneers of televangelism suggests one very obvious general point. Since the 1920s when a series of important battles within the churches and in the wider society made it clear that conservative Protestants had lost their grip on mainstream America, they have worked to maintain their distinctive sub-culture (where regional isolation meant that they were still dominant) or to create the social institutions necessary to sustain a deviant world-view in more threatening circumstances. It is easy to suppose that such isolation, and deliberate insulation, means that conservative Protestantism in America has remained untouched by modern culture. Certainly, the name 'fundamentalist' was chosen to assert an unchanging orthodoxy in a shifting world. Yet any brief survey of the use of radio and television by fundamentalists shows very clearly how willing they have been to adopt, not just the technology of the secular modern world, but also its programme formats. Although the church service remains a popular shape (used by Schuller and Falwell, for example) the variety show, the talk show, and the magazine programme have all been adopted once their secular popularity was clear.

Marshall McLuhan's 'the medium is the message' was an inspired and inspiring statement of the proposition that format determines content. Televangelists have always defended their borrowing of secular forms with the two-fold claim that the ends justify the means and that McLuhan was wrong: the devil's frame need not always contain the devil's picture. Whether borrowing secular models has been accompanied by major changes in the fundamentalist product will be considered in the next chapter.

EXPLAINING CONSERVATIVE DOMINANCE

American religious television is so obviously dominated by fundamentalists, evangelicals, and pentecostals that it requires conscious mental effort not to treat televangelism and religious television as synonyms. Yet as the above history of religious broadcasting in America shows there was a time when, far from being dominant, conservatives were all but excluded from the airwaves. The change in fortunes requires explaining and I will argue that, in addition to specific difficulties which resulted from organizational obstacles, liberal Protestantism was hampered by elements in its own character which made it unsuited to mass media.

First though we might note the obvious affinity between reformed Christianity and mass media of all sorts. In contrast to faiths which stress liturgy and participation in ritual, Protestantism largely reduces religion to a matter of right belief which comes from 'hearing the Word'. From the 'Gutenberg Galaxy' to the global village, Protestantism has made use of media which allow 'disembodied access' to the saving faith.

Strong control and stable presentation

There were a number of obvious weaknesses with the sort of programme produced by ecumenical bodies. The first was the constant change of voice or face as the preacher or presenter was rotated. It is very clear from the detailed study of the audience for religious broadcasting in New Haven in the 1950s (Parker *et al.* 1955) that the most popular programmes were those which were structured around a single strong personality – a Charles Fuller or a Father Coughlin. Rotating the preacher prevented the development of audience familiarity and loyalty.

Furthermore, there was a general lack of competence in the early efforts. Parker *et al.* note: 'The ministers' general lack of training in the use of mass media, their ignorance of the audience potential and their failure to plan continuously ... are major blocks to effective local religious broadcasting (1955: 103). The local Council of Churches had recently started two weekly television programmes. One, aimed at children had a full-time producer and featured a single personality. The series for adults 'has been conducted by a committee of ministers working in their spare time, has not had an integrated theme and has not had continuity of format or presenters' (Parker *et al.* 1955: 103). The former was a success; the latter was not.

The independent evangelicals not only provided continuity of presenter but the presenter was the sole begetter of the enterprise and exercised total control. He also had a pressing need to succeed.[4] Evangelical entrepreneurs depended on their winning an audience for at least the continued funding of the programme, and often for their livelihoods. They were not subtly deflected from the need to be popular by the thought that the programme was being funded out of the large coffers of a major organization or that they had another job anyway. And it was not only the finances of broadcasting which gave evangelicals and fundamentalists the entrepreneurial drive; many of them had already acquired and cultivated it in building their own independent ministries. Even those evangelical, fundamentalist or pentecostal denominations which are quite large still set great store by their ministers building a church from scratch. Those who took to the air-waves were the most ambitious and self-motivated products of a tradition which cultivated and lauded entrepreneurial skills.

Clarity of purpose and product

One of the main differences between liberal and conservative broadcasting was clearly identified in the New Haven study in the early days of television. After trying to describe the avowed intent of each of the large number of programmes being surveyed, the researchers note:

> Two comments can fairly be made on this extended list of purposes. The first is that it is noteworthy that frank intent to recruit converts characterized all three Roman Catholic programs and half of those produced by 'other Protestant' groups, but only one of the programs of the National Council of Churches, *This is Life*, a series distributed by the National Council but produced by and representing the view of the Lutheran Missouri Synod which is not a member of the Council.
>
> (Parker *et al.* 1955: 111)

The second comment is that the rest of the programmes show a wide range of diffuse aims:

> when the aims are viewed together with the sweeping designations of target audiences, one suspects that the religious broadcasters are expecting to accomplish too much with too large and heterogeneous an audience. The loose-

ness of the purposes of many of the programs betray lack of thoughtful program policy formulation.

(Parker *et al.* 1955: 112)

But the problem went deeper than policy formulation. In a number of other contexts, I have argued that the failure of liberal Protestantism relative to its conservative rival can be traced to the 'precariousness' at the centre of its belief system (Bruce 1984a; 1989).

Conservatives and liberals do not differ just about specific propositions, about particular truths; they also differ on the basic *epistemological* question of how it is one knows the truth and what sort of status such truth might have. To put it bluntly, conservative Protestantism is dogmatic and authoritarian; it believes that there is just one truth that can be specified in a series of rules, adherence to which separates believers from unbelievers, saved from damned. In contrast liberal Protestantism, although monotheistic, tends to relativism. It no longer claims the certainty of the one truth but rather holds that there are a variety of expressions of the truth, that there is more than one way to God, and so on. It denies the possibility of a 'check list' of dogmas separating the faithful from the unfaithful.

The consequences of this basic difference are considerable and have been explored at length elsewhere (Bruce 1989). Here I will just touch on those with implications for the two traditions' use of television.

One of the features of liberal Protestantism is its sensitivity to alternative perceptions of the world and God's word. Willingness to see other points of view may have appeal in face-to-face interaction but the strident simplicity of the conservative Protestant message makes it better suited for communication by mass media. Radio and television generally have to compete with stimuli from people and other sources which are 'live' in our presence. In such circumstances, the narrow, well-defined product of the conservatives – 'Ye must be born again' - carries better than the hesitations of liberalism.

Conservative certainty also allows them to be free of doubts about the use of mass communication technology. Liberals view with suspicion the 'dummying-down' which seems endemic to television. Further, they tend to see God's revelation as something which is always changing and which is best found in interaction, between people, and between people and their world. The liberal does not believe that God's revelation can be taken in the words of a particular translation of scripture and sent out into the ether, there to be picked up by passers-by, with the expectation that the Word will have the intended effect. Unlike the conservative, the liberal believes that we can never just read and understand, we always interpret. We creatively infer the meaning of things in the light of our experiences and our own culture. Consider the liberal view of miracles. It is not that the miracles of the Bible are not 'true'; rather it is that, for the culture in which the Old Testament was developed, miracles were commonly believed in and hence God's revelation is presented in that way during that period. But we do not believe in miracles so we interpret those stories in a different way. This hermeneutic principle, if accepted, prevents one from believing that messages carry their own interpretation about with them.

Conservatives have an almost magical view of the ability of scripture to *act*, to work independent of the interests of the reader. At a crusade meeting in Oxford in 1979, Billy Graham challenged doubting members of the audience to just sit down with the Gospel of John, read it through five times, and ask to be saved. Understanding is no problem; just read and the text will save you! Some evangelicals have so little time for questions of inter- pretation that one almost expects them to suggest that the Word can save even those who cannot read it. And sure enough, Anita Bryant (1978: 92) suggested exactly that: 'I've heard weird stories from all over the world about where missionaries have gone to odd places and where people have been saved just by seeing a torn page of the Bible on the floor.' The assumption that the Word has exactly the same meaning to all people gives the conservatives a confidence in the use of impersonal and mass means of communication which liberals cannot share. If fragments of scripture can save, then there is nothing at all wrong with having computers writing apparently personal letters to viewers and listeners who write in asking for prayer.

It is worth considering the utility of a powerful belief in the supernatural. Liberal Protestants do not much believe in miracles. If there ever were any, they were confined to an earlier age. Many conservative Protestants still believe in the possibility of God's miraculous intervention in the mundane world of here and now. In the early days of holy roller radio and television, God's divine healing, brought to the sick and needy by his faithful servant Brother Jim or the Reverend Ike, provided many miracles and although faith healing is no longer as popular as it was, there are still plenty of miracles for the fundamentalist to expect and experience. If you send Oral Roberts a seed faith offering to God, then God will reward you ten-fold. Miracles are exciting. They are sensational and sensation is what mass media need.

Although I will later suggest that most conservative Protestants are on rather comfortable terms with the material world, in one sense they are clearly divided from it. Where liberals insist that we can only understand God's word in relation to our position in our societies and cultures, the conservatives wish, in rhetoric at least, to distance themselves from the surrounding culture. They talk of being 'in the world but not of it'. The logical extension of the liberal Protestant position is to reduce the things that separate him from the rest of his culture. Indeed, one often finds liberals arguing that the truly Christian thing to do is to embrace the secular world and secular struggles. In terms of acting out one's Christian commitment this leads to a pattern of actions quite different to those of the conservative. If the evangelical Protestant wishes to do something evangelical, he tries to convert people to his values and beliefs; the liberal activist can only be active in secular causes.

The liberal view is demonstrated clearly by the career of Everett Parker who, through the New Haven research on the audience for religious television, his own production work, and various positions in church bureaucracies, was once the leading spokesman for, and producer of, imaginative and professionally produced broadcasting in the mainstream churches. He has not produced a programme since 1968. He has taken the purpose of church involvement with broadcasting to be sustained criticism of the values portrayed on television. Rather than producing Christian programmes, he produces Christian criticisms of secular programmes which are rarely different to the criticisms of non-Christian liberals. In particular he has been active in trying to establish the rights of blacks to the services of the media (Ellens 1974: 142).

Cohesion and commitment

In contrast to liberal Protestants, with their diffuse notions of the role of the Christian in the modern world, conservatives have considerable cohesion around a single purpose. The conservative preacher reduces everything to the need to preach the gospel and save souls. Members of his audience entirely agree with the primacy of these goals and, because they believe that dire consequences attend the failure to be saved, are willing to give time and money to enterprises that promise to preach the gospel and save souls.

Fortuitously, the organization of the television economy is perfect for conservative evangelicals because every airing of the programme which asks for money to reach a wider audience can be used as a measure of the success of that method of preaching the gospel. The maximum possible audience, whether or not anyone is watching or is at all moved by the show, can be used as an index of souls saved. The continuation of the programme can be mistaken by evangelicals for the very thing which the programme is supposed to achieve. The more money being raised, the more air-time being bought, the more 'souls being saved'; in a nice sleight of hand what is actually an input measure is presented as a measure of output, of success. Liberal Protestants are as likely as anyone else to mistake their efforts to change the world for actual changes in the world but they cannot make that mistake about religious programmes on television because they do not see pumping the gospel into the ether as a plausible interpretation of the Christian mission in the modern world. Fundamentalists, evangelicals, and pentecostalists can displace their goals onto the support of a television programme; liberal Protestants cannot.

The awful consequences which they suppose to attend a failure to get saved explains the greater commitment of conservatives. They are more willing to act than are liberals. But more important than this psychological account of why conservatives and liberals are differently motivated to act on behalf of their beliefs is the social point of cohesion. The singularity of conservative purpose produces a much more unified support than that attracted by the diffuseness of liberal Protestantism. Conservative evangelicals agree more about what they value and they are more likely than

46

liberals to act *in concert*. This cohesion amplifies the power of conservative evangelicalism.

A couple of examples will illustrate the ability of conservatives to mobilize their people. In 1974 two radio owners who had failed to get a licence for a station in Spokane, petitioned the Federal Communications Commission to object to the output of the Moody Bible Institute station and to ask for the access of religious broadcasters to the FM educational channel to be restricted. Letters from fundamentalists opposing the petition broke all previous records for letters to the FCC; about 700,000 were received by August 1975.

> Letters continued to pour in even after the favorable ruling. The NRB, religious radio stations, and the secular press launched an intensive effort to tell the public that religious broadcasting was no longer threatened by petition RM 2493. Eventually the volume of letters against the Lansman-Milan petition dwindled to seven thousand a day. By the end of 1978 almost nine million pieces of mail had come to the FCC about the petition.
>
> (Armstrong 1979: 28)

Or a second example; in February 1979, Texas televangelist James Robison made one of his periodic attacks on homosexuals,

> pointing to the murders of San Francisco mayor George Moscone and city supervisor Harvey Milk as part of God's judgement on homosexuals, citing an assertion in the *National Enquirer* that homosexuals prey on each other, and quoting a police chief as saying that homosexuals recruit and murder little boys.
>
> (Martin 1981: 223)

Having two years earlier given a right to reply to a homosexual rights group after a similar attack, WFAA-TV decided to cancel Robison's programme altogether. Robison hired flamboyant attorney Richard 'Racehorse' Haynes to prepare a request to the Federal Communications Commission to consider whether the decisions restricted his freedom of speech rights. But, more importantly he organized a Freedom of Speech rally in Dallas which drew 11,000 supporters. It is worth quoting part of

Robison's speech to that rally, if only for the flavour of a Bible thumper on form, using the rapid shouted delivery and alliteration more common in the black Baptist tradition:

> It is a shame that America knows more about Mickey Mouse than about Moses, more about *Charlie's Angels* than about God's angels, more about Shell than hell, more about Phillips 66 than about the holy 66 books of the Word of God, more about Hugh Heffner than about the heavenly heralds.
>
> (Quoted in Martin 1981: 224)

WFAA-TV relented under the pressure and started airing Robison's shows again. It is hard to imagine a section of the audience for mainstream Protestant religious television protesting in such a way as to press a television station into changing a decision.

The theme of commitment is a good place to end this discussion. As the brief history of religious broadcasting in America made clear, the lever which turned conservative Protestantism's greater suitability for mass media into actual predominance over mainstream Protestantism was *money*. The evangelicals and fundamentalists took over the air-waves because the stations wanted to sell time and their audience was willing to supply the money to pay for it. Because conservative Protestants were willing to donate towards the cost of broadcasting, televangelists were able to buy the time and the technology to spread the gospel to millions.

WHY AMERICA?

Finally in this chapter I would like to consider the question of why televangelism is common on American television but virtually unknown anywhere else. The first part of the answer has already been given: the history of religious culture in America has been such as to leave a very large evangelical, fundamentalist, and pentecostal sub-culture. In most Protestant European countries, church-going of any sort is rare and conservatives form only a small part of the Christian remnant. The second part of the answer concerns how such people have come to dominate religious broadcasting. We can clarify the question by suggesting that, even if Britain had a large conservative Protestant sub-culture, it would

48

not have televangelism. Some of the particular points have already been made; they will now be placed within the context of a general comparison of the structure of British and American broadcasting.

It would be no exaggeration to describe the United Kingdom system of broadcasting which obtained until 1988 as closed in access and centralized in control in comparison to the American system which is open in access and diffuse in control.[5] The first and most obvious difference is in the proliferation of radio and television stations. It is very, very difficult to gain a licence to broadcast in Britain. There only are four television channels. The publicly-financed British Broadcasting Corporation (BBC) operates two of them. Another channel is used by a number of independent regional commercial companies who co-operate to service one channel (ITV) while periodically 'opting out' for their own regional programmes. Channel 4 is also commercial and airs programmes commissioned by its directorate from independent producers, some of which are the ITV regional companies, others of which are specialized firms created to make one or two series. While in contrast with American broadcasting, four channels seems mean, it should be noted that this figure is the result of recent *expansion.* Channel 4 is a 1980s innovation and the second BBC channel was only added in 1964.

Neither the BBC nor the Independent Broadcasting Authority (which supervises the ITV companies and commercial radio) allow air-time to be sold. Neither permits ideological advertising; indeed the BBC takes no advertising at all. Apart from the occasional 'telethon' fund-raiser for an impeccably non-controversial charity, neither allows programmes to solicit donations.

Broadcasting, like many other things in Britain, is organized in a paternalistic manner. For example, whereas American television companies sell advertising space to political parties and candidates, the British networks give time to the central offices of the parties in proportion to their performance at previous elections and exclude individual candidates from making their own arrangements with the regional independent companies.

Both the BBC and ITV, although not legally obliged to do so, have seen it as part of their public-interest role to provide religious broadcasting and the BBC and the independent companies have religion departments. The early objections to religious radio came, not from broadcasters, but from churchmen who were concerned

49

that services might be 'received by a considerable number of persons in an irreverent manner and might even be heard by persons in public houses with their hats on' (quoted in Dinwiddie 1968: 20).

It is the general practice for the staff to be recruited from the ranks of the ordained clergymen of the main denominations and then trained in broadcasting techniques. Thus a department of three producers would normally have a Catholic priest, an Anglican cleric, and a minister from the Methodists or one of the other dissenting denominations. A large part of the religious output (for television almost as much as radio) is the broadcasting of church services and, with a slight weighting being given to the state 'established' Church of England, the opportunity to broadcast is rotated around the various denominations and some sects in rough proportion to their size.

Both the BBC and the IBA have local religious advisory committees and they share a Central Religious Advisory Committee in which leading churchmen and women can comment on the output of the networks. Allcock (1968) correctly notes that although such committees appear at first sight to do little more than endorse the practices of the television companies, they do actually have some authority in so far as the companies would incur considerable public disfavour if their actions were not rubber-stamped. To give an example, in the autumn of 1988 the ITV companies failed to convince the Central Committee that, in order to compete better with the BBC for the evening audience, they should be allowed to move their prime Sunday evening sacred music programme *Highway* out of what is traditionally the 'God slot'. Unable to carry the committee, they gave up the scheme.

Although the British model differs from the early days of the American networks, in that the television companies do not formally work through ecumenical organizations, the end product is generally ecumenical and middle-of-the-road with not so much a leaning towards liberal Protestantism as a careful avoidance of anything which would seem like proselytization or criticism of competing perspectives. Even when small, aggressively evangelistic sects are given their occasional turn to broadcast a service, it is always made clear to them (informally of course) that any attempt to use the air-waves to criticize their rivals will mark the end of their opportunity to broadcast. For example, when the Religion Depart-

ment of BBC Northern Ireland decided that Ian Paisley's Free
Presbyterian Church of Ulster was due a Sunday service broadcast,
some thought was given to which of the forty or so ministers would
be most broadly 'acceptable'. When Paisley threatened the success
of this filtering process by volunteering to take part in the service
from the chosen congregation, it was subtly but surely made clear
to him that controversy was to be avoided and it was. The service
which was broadcast would have been acceptable to all Presbyterians and most Protestants.

Perhaps the most telling point about British mass media
religion was made by Ronald Falconer at the end of a long career
in the BBC religion department when he said: 'Religious
broadcasting . . . is organized and produced in precisely the same
way as the output of any of the other departments' (1977: 115). He
might have gone on to draw the conclusion: the attitude of the
BBC and ITV to religion is much the same as their attitude to any
other topic about which they make programmes.

Although some churchmen take exception to the failure of the
media to offer them opportunities to proselytize, most recognize
that bland product and more programmes 'about religion' than
'of religion' is the price they have to pay for having so much time
devoted to religion in a country with such low church membership
and attendance.

Although most of the above concerns British television, it
applies equally well to radio. Until the late 1960s there was only
one radio company – the BBC – which had three channels. There
has been a recent opening up of the air-waves with large numbers
of 'local' radio stations being licensed. Most of these spend most
of their time on recorded pop music and carry little or no religious
broadcasting.

The Thatcher government, since it came to power in 1979, has
devoted considerable effort to emasculating the BBC by filling the
board of governors with its placemen and threatening legal action
over controversial programmes. As part of that project, it has
forced the Corporation to take an increasing amount of its programming from independent production companies. Although
these changes, and the proliferation of local radio stations, have
slightly opened up the British broadcasting media, the main
obstacles to a system like that of the USA – the impossibility of
starting one's own television or radio station and the inability to

buy air-time – remain and the government shows little enthusiasm for altering them.

Americans like to depict their broadcasting as the operation of 'the free market' (restrained only by concern for common decency, fairness and the public interest), but in respect of religion, it is organized in such a way as to give a considerably advantaged market situation to paid-time religious broadcasters. The Federal Communications Commission has strict regulations governing fund-raising by stations which hold non-commercial licences (educational stations, for example) but it has failed to enforce these for religious groups holding such licences

> thus making it easier and more profitable for religious organizations to hold noncommercial licenses by lowering the normal restrictions on the raising of money through on-air solicitations, the sale of religious items and so on.
>
> (Horsfield 1984: 14)

Furthermore, the FCC has declared that the restrictions on the amount of commercial time permitted for each hour of programming does not apply to religious programmes.

> This means that television stations may sell unlimited time to religious broadcasters without worrying about usual restrictions on commercial time. This uneven enforcement of FCC policy has made it more than normally profitable for stations to sell time to religious broadcasters who are prepared to buy it. Whereas before the low-audience period of Sunday morning was a difficult one in which to sell commercial time, stations have been able to compensate by selling whole blocks of time to religious broadcasters.
>
> (Horsfield 1984: 14)

Finally, the FCC has made it clear that its regulations requiring fairness and balance do not apply to religious programmes. The fairness doctrine is intended to ensure that various community perspectives on controversial subjects are all aired. The FCC has decided that religion is not a controversial issue and hence there is no need for organized 'balance' and rights to reply.

The consequence is to give religious broadcasters (programme makers and station managers), a favoured position in the market place. Furthermore, as we have already seen the FCC ruling that paid-time programmes could as readily count as 'public service' as sustaining-time ones gives an advantage to religious broadcasters who are prepared to buy time. The mainstream churches, partly because they were used to sustaining time, partly because ideological and organizational obstacles make them less willing and able to compete in paid prime time, are not the ones prepared to buy time. Hence the FCC's position of giving a wide berth to religious broadcasters (and to the thorny thickets of church-state relations that any FCC action would have to confront) is an encouragement to the independent evangelical broadcasters.

Chapter Three

TELEVANGELISM ORGANIZATIONS

Although it is the point of contact between preacher and audience, what visitors to America see when they turn on the television in the motel room on a Sunday morning is only the end product of a vast and complex operation. This chapter describes the organizations which produce televangelism by considering examples of two types of religious television operation: the 'super church' and the network.

THE FALWELL OPERATION

Jerry Falwell's Thomas Road Baptist Church operation is ambitious and shows one genre at its most developed, a position to date shared only with the Oral Roberts Evangelistic Association. Like Graham, Falwell does little or nothing with television other than use it as a way of allowing people who cannot attend his church to spectate on the worship services of Thomas Road Baptist Church. Initially his use of mass media was directed solely towards building a congregation for his church, which began with thirty-five adults and their children meeting in what previously had been a bottling factory for Donald Duck soft drinks. In the best tradition of rags-to-riches stories, Falwell is fond of recalling that, despite days of washing the floors, the feet of that first congregation still adhered to the syrup residues. He keeps a few bottles of Donald Duck on his office shelves.

Falwell graduated from the Baptist Bible College in Springfield, Missouri, and returned to his home town of Lynchburg, Virginia, to lead the first service of the Thomas Road Baptist Church in June 1956. The next month he began recording a short 'service' – *Deep*

54

Things of God – for daily broadcast on a local radio station. The following year he started presenting a weekly service live on a local television station.

Like many founders of small fundamentalist churches, Falwell was attracted to broadcasting not only because it allowed him to take the Word to a larger audience than came to hear him in person but also because it acted as advertising for the church and it worked: the congregation grew. From the first, Falwell had ambitions to diversify and in 1959 a 165 acre farm in Appomattox County was bought to become the Elim Home for Alcoholics.

In 1966 there was a major expansion of the number of radio outlets. Two years later, the church bought its own black and white cameras and replaced the rather stilted 'service in a studio' format with taping of the Sunday morning service at Thomas Road. This was syndicated on an increasing number of television stations and there was a corresponding increase in income and in Thomas Road church members. In the following decade, membership went from around 2,000 to 15,000. Television outlets increased from one to 250 and the number of radio stations which aired the daily programme rose from about ten to 180.

The mid-1960s were the period when the increasing assertiveness of blacks and the civil rights legislation of the Johnson administration challenged the traditional structures of race relations in small towns and cities all over the south. Lynchburg was no exception and in 1967 Falwell launched Lynchburg Christian Schools, which for the first year of their existence were consistently referred to by the local papers as having a 'whites only' admission policy (Goodman and Price 1981: 116). Segregation was popular with Falwell's parishioners and the school grew steadily until it had 1,200 pupils in 1980.[1]

The next stage was the foundation in 1971 of Liberty Baptist College. Two years later Liberty Baptist Seminary was added to the expanding milieu and in 1976 the Liberty Home Institute for bible study was established. It now serves some 10,000 mail students.

The provision of a variety of quasi-social services is a good way of bringing outsiders into the Church's sphere of influence. Some ground and a number of wooden huts in a fork in the James River were bought quite cheaply and turned into 'Treasure Island', a summer camp. Liberty Baptist students and teenage members of the core congregation are encouraged to staff the camp for the summer months. Fees are kept low and efforts are made to enrol children whose parents are not connected with Thomas Road. On average 3,000 children either stay in, or attend daily events at, the summer camp.

The advantage of this peripheral expansion is that one 'limb' can be used to reduce the costs of another. Thus Treasure Island was also useful as dormitory accommodation for the college students when enrolment was pushed faster than the expansion of facilities on the intended campus on 'Liberty Mountain', a green field site on the edge of the city. Students were useful in a number of outreach schemes. In addition to using the radio and television programmes to advertise Thomas Road, Falwell put a lot of money into a bussing programme which had a very practical appeal to parents. Young congregation members and students 'worked' the suburbs of Lynchburg looking for parents who did not take their children to church. They offered to collect the children and return them after the service. If this had no other attraction, its function as a child-minding service would have been appealing.

There is also integration at the other end of the age scale. The church organizes an extensive 'Senior Saints' programme for retired people. Some of the activities of the 'Jolly Sixties' clubs are purely social but the active aged are also encouraged to do voluntary clerical work such as opening envelopes and sorting mail. In the early days and still in periodic slumps when full-time staff are paid off, they form a useful portion of the sixty or so people who work in the mail room. There are plans to build retirement accommodation on Liberty Mountain so that aged church supporters can end their days in Christian company.[2]

Falwell not only condemns abortion but he does something to provide an alternative. Thomas Road Baptist Church runs a nursing and adoption home for unmarried mothers.

Of all the activities of the Falwell operation, the educating of students is the most important. Ten years after the college was started, building began on Liberty mountain. Liberty University – as the Baptist College became – now has about 6,500 students in thirty-three buildings valued at about $30 million. Although at present the courses are those of a liberal arts university, it is Falwell's aim to add a law school and a medical school. Unlike Bob Jones University which, on separatist principle, has deliberately avoided applying for registration by secular authorities, Liberty

University is accredited and is proud enough of its membership of the Southern Association of Colleges and Schools to say in its publicity that 'it is the only independent, fundamentalist, separatist, local-affiliated liberal arts college in the United States to be accredited' (Falwell Ministeries 1981: 52).

The educational expansion has three purposes. One is to supply a cadre of well-educated and qualified conservative Christians to staff the fundamentalist milieu. A second is to provide safe and sanitized high quality education to the children of fundamentalist families; as Falwell put it: 'It is our goal to be the Harvard of academics, the Notre Dame of athletics and the Brigham Young of religious schools to evangelical and fundamentalist boys and girls' (quoted in Hadden and Shupe 1988: 136). The third and unstated purpose is to produce the basis for a new denomination. A small but significant minority of Liberty students intend to start autonomous fundamentalist baptist churches. Although Falwell does not want to make the lives of such pioneers so secure as to blunt their entrepreneurial edge, he does want them to succeed. To that end, he uses his television programme to raise money to offer initial and partial support for fundamentalist church planters. He also gives them good initial publicity by preaching at their inaugural services. The consequence is a slowly increasing number of fundamentalist churches which owe a considerable debt to Falwell and whose ministers have been trained together: a *de facto* Falwellite Baptist denomination.[3]

As such peripherals as the school and college have grown and a twenty-four hour radio station has been established, so the television audience and the home base congregation have expanded. Thomas Road is now in its third auditorium having outgrown the previous two. The home base has two values. First, it functions as a normal albeit very large congregation; there are regular services, prayer groups, and bible studies. A host of associate pastors visit the sick, teach Sunday school, lead old folks outings, evangelize in prisons, and service the round of activities that fills the week of a fundamentalist congregation.

But it has the second value of servicing the television programme. It does so in the obvious sense that the auditorium is the setting for the show and the services provide the bulk of the programme material; but there is a less obvious value of the home base: it provides viewers with something to visit. Viewers are encouraged to visit Lynchburg and many drop in if they are in the area. Special events such as the annual 'bible study' in the local sports auditorium are scheduled to draw in thousands of viewers and, for a few hours at least, to turn a mass of unattached individuals into a 'community', but the regular routine of the congregation offers a tourist attraction which is complemented by a visit to the hill-top Liberty University.

The purchase in 1986 of a small television network adds the final tie. Falwell intends to use it to carry a two-hour daily programme with a phone-in talk segment. The rest of the time will be filled with 'chapel services, convocations and sporting events from Liberty University' as well as regular Sunday services from Thomas Road (Hadden 1986a: 13). Television, university, and church become fully integrated and mutually supporting.

THE SOLICITATION TECHNOLOGY

While developing the university is at the heart of Falwell's ambitions and the medical school at Oral Roberts University has been the founder's main interest for some time, such institutions only exist because of the money raised from the audience for the television shows. The creation and maintenance of the audience requires two sorts of technology: that which makes the programmes and that which raises the funds. The filming, editing, and copying technology is the same for evangelists as it is for secular studios. What is different is the existence of a complex technology for making possible contact between individual members of the audience and the televangelism organization. I will describe in some detail the workings of the system that turns viewers into patrons.

Much British media sociology believes that the consequence (if not the intention) of mass media is the exclusion of ordinary people (McQuail 1983: 60). Because mass media are immensely expensive, access to them can only be bought by those with a lot of money (i.e. capitalists such as Rupert Murdoch and Robert Maxwell) or those whose political power allows them to comman- deer air-time. This observation is offered as an explanation for the class bias in the images (for example, of what counts as normal) which are presented on television. It sounds intuitively plausible but the case of televangelism is quite different. Here the most conservative form of religion offered on television pushed the more liberal version (which had the greatest support from the upper classes) off the air-waves and screens by being able to spend more money. And note how that money was raised. Dwight L. Moody and Billy Sunday had considerable backing from 'fat cat' robber barons; John Wannamaker and the Rockerfellers were among those who gave large sums to Billy Sunday. But the money for Falwell's programme costs (and for his expansive building projects) is raised in very small sums from a very large number of people. In 1976-7, nearly 80 per cent of his $22.2 million income came from 762,000 individual contributions (Horsfield 1984: 28), an average gift of only twenty-three dollars. It was precisely ordinary people who funded the rise of televangelism. If this television is some sort of opiate of the masses, then it is being supplied by a drug empire which the addicts themselves created.

Contact with the ordinary viewer – the 'couch potato' of the stereotypes – comes firstly and obviously through the screen: the evangelist appeals to the viewers. Then the viewers must contact the evangelist and the evangelist must be able to respond personally to the contacting viewer. The second leg has been vastly improved by the spread of the telephone. While many programmes still encourage viewers to 'keep those letters and cards pouring in', shows such as the *700 Club* invite viewers to phone on toll-free numbers for prayer or counselling. Mrs Norman Vincent Peale used to read out some listeners' letters and then reply to them, but such personal contact on an impersonal medium could only touch three or four people each week. The third leg – the televangelist replying to the viewer – has really only been possible since the development of large and fast computers.

A large part of any radio and television religious programme is concerned with getting members of the audience to contact the show. Televangelists have a number of ways of encouraging people to contact them. One is to offer a free gift – a copy of part of the scriptures, a pamphlet, or a small piece of jewellery such as Falwell's 'Jesus First' tie pin. The evangelist may, as Oral Roberts and Pat Robertson do, promise to pray for you if you tell him your troubles.

Obviously the televangelist does not personally answer his toll-free telephones. In the case of Robertson's CBN counselling service, the toll-free number flashed at the bottom of the screen is usually not CBN centre in Virginia Beach but a local office staffed by locally recruited CBN personnel. Despite promising to do so, televangelists do not personally read the letters they are sent; even were they so inclined it would be physically impossible when, for example, Roberts gets over 6 million items of mail a year.

Incoming letters are first sorted into those with a donation and those without. Clerical staff read the letters and code the contents: small donation, regular viewer, wants prayer for alcoholic son. A powerful computer is already programmed to produce stock responses to such stimuli. A letter of thanks from Brother Jim or Oral for the gift, saying that he needs all the regular viewers he can get and promising prayer for the alcolohic son, embellished with appropriate passages of scripture, is then printed out and mailed.

Once the organization has the name and address of a supporter or an interested enquirer, he or she can become a target for direct mail fund-raising. The key to mailed appeals is the ability of a computer to cheaply vary parts of a prepared text. The machine can be loaded with a basic promise to pray for the writer, the usual bromides about the Lord, and an appeal for funds to keep the work going. The secretaries who read the incoming mail log not only the name and address of the writer but their sex and age if they are discernible, and the nature of the problem for which they have asked for prayer. In future direct mail 'shots', the computer can put the recipient's name into its basic text and add other psuedo-personal touches. Such embellishment is normally confined to the first page; it saves money to have all the idiosyncratic elements on the first page and the rest of the letter standard (for examples, see pp. 140–6).

The spurious suggestion of personal interest in the recipient of direct mail is complemented by an equally spurious suggestion of personal interest in the televangelist's reply. The letter appears to come, not from the staff of *The Old Time Gospel Hour* but from Jerry. The computer printer can underline salient bits with a wavy 'pen' line to give the appearance that Jerry had second thoughts on reading through before signing and did a bit of highlighting. The signature will be a perfect facsimile of the preacher's own hand. For added authenticity there may even be what has every appearance of being a hand-written 'PS'. New printers can produce whole letters in what looks like hand-writing on rough-edged vellum letter paper.

If the creation of the appearance of a personal interest in the writer is one major advantage of the computer, increased efficiency in soliciting is another. Lists of names can be sub-divided and additional information constantly added to the records so that the organization can stop sending material to people who do not make donations, differentiate big donors from small donors, and direct energies to the most lucrative section of the audience. Those people who are persistently big donors can then be given genuinely personal treatment; they might be invited to week-end seminars, a conference retreat, or even a dinner with the evangelist.

There is, of course, nothing new about such selective attention. Nineteenth century evangelical organizations were similarly disdainful towards the small giver and attentive to the major bene-factor. The great Victorian philanthropic societies made a point of being especially flattering to those who parted with big sums of money by, for example, listing them on the letterhead and inviting them to grace the platform for the annual meeting. While such attention makes great economic sense, until the age of the computer it could only be pursued with a small number of major donors. Even where there was no strong ideological reason for treating all supporters alike, there was a serious obstacle to doing otherwise: in the absence of electronics, it was too time-consuming.

The new technology not only makes the present generation of preachers more efficient than their forbears by making it relatively cheap to solicit from a very large audience but it further enhances their operations by allowing appeals to be directed and stream-lined. The rather impersonal contact of broadcast media can be followed up by apparently more private and personal contact with potential supporters.

The actual performance of some evangelistic organization mail operations falls some way short of this potential. Horsfield (1985) reports an experiment in which he wrote to five leading paid-time broadcasters with a specific request for advice on how to live a Christian life. One organization sent only one letter, signed by the director of the Counselling Department and answering the question. The other four between them sent forty-four items of mail, most of which were quite unconnected with Horsfield's request. He did not reply to any of the communications yet it was five months before one evangelist gave up and the remaining three organizations were still mailing out ever more urgent requests for money after nine months, at which point Horsfield wrote to them to ask them to stop.

A second qualification should be entered. Direct-mail solicitation is not an Aladin's lamp. Studies of the use of direct mail in commercial and political campaigns suggests that it often costs more than it raises (Rosenberg 1983). Mailing lists are only valuable if they are frequently pruned of people who do not give and up-dated to take care of changes of name and address. The advantage which the televangelists have over commercial companies (such as that of one of the pioneers of direct mail, Richard Viguerie) is that the addressees initiate contact. Viguerie collects the names and addresses of people who, for example, give money to a gun lobby organization. He may later use that list to raise money for the Nicaraguan *Contras*. We can suppose some ideological consonance between being in favour of guns and wanting the Contras to have some, and hence that the people on the first list are more likely than names chosen at random from the phone book to be sympathetic to the second cause. The mailing is not exactly a shot in the dark but it is only loosely targeted and is thus expensive. The names and addresses which televangelists have are those of people who watch their programme and who have taken the initative to contact them.

Falwell has the added advantage over commercial mailers that not every one of his mailings needs to be lucrative for the operation as a whole to be worthwhile. While he often works on the same broad base, Viguerie usually contacts people only once on each contract and although he may wear the odd poor return as being useful in consciousness raising, he really needs to raise money from each job for it to count as a win. Falwell may not get any money back in response to any particular sad story of imminent bankruptcy and yet still see the mailing as worthwhile because it maintains contact with supporters and may increase recipient loyalty to Falwell and to his show. Televangelists work on maintaining long-term contact with those of their viewers who contact them just as they hope to develop audience loyalty and direct-mail technology is an invaluable addition to the mechanisms for developing and maintaining a following.

We should not forget that in developing a committed audience, each televangelist is in competition with all the other mass media evangelists (and with other sorts of Christian work). Christian Broadcasting Network's own research of its 'Partners' showed that the volume of Christian mail coming into their homes was at times overwhelming but concluded, not that there should be less but that CBN had to find new ways of designing its direct mail so that it stood out and was read! (Horsfield 1984: 33).

THE NETWORKS

The same computer technology is used by the organizations in the second major genre of televangelistic enterprise: the network, as represented (in chronological order) by Robertson's CBN, the Crouch's Trinity,[4] the Bakkers' PTL, and Eternal Word Network,[5] which is run by Mother Angelica, a nun of pensionable age (Elvy 1986). Like the churches or evangelistic associations, the networks produce their own material and, in the case of CBN, have been particularly willing to pioneer new programme formats.[6] But the real innovation of the networks has been their demonstration that Christians can construct and manage a communications infra-structure every bit as sophisticated as the secular ones. To the extent that they are used by other televangelists, they have also liberated their brethren from being in bondage to secular gatekeepers.

The networks rent space on satellites to feed their product to cable systems which pass it into individual homes. Using two satellites, CBN, for example, feeds 24 hours a day into 5,300 cable systems. The great advantage of this system is that it replaces the slower and more organizationally complex method of spreading programmes by sending (in the jargon 'bicycling') videos from one station or cable system to the next. But it is costly. Satellite feed has to be paid for and the network has to pay cable systems to accept it. The network covers costs by soliciting from the audience for its own home-produced programmes and by selling air-time to other producers.

Pat Robertson's pioneering move created a major incentive to innovate. It is not just that there is the time to be filled and hence an opportunity for a wide variety of different programme formats, but there is also the confidence which comes from seeing oneself as a rival to CBS or NBC. The ambition of the networks is to provide the mass media counterpart to the fundamentalist world of Thomas Road Baptist Church. The fundamentalist Baptist 'super churches' aim to provide a complete round of activities for all age groups. The networks aim to offer a similar breadth of product for those who prefer to sit at home. By setting the television so that the channel cannot be changed (fundamentalist magazines advertise devices which do exactly that), parents can ensure that nothing will appear on the television which will offend their fundamentalist world-view and principles.

Although one might suppose that the networks have a fairly narrowly circumscribed role, as we have already seen with the case of CBN, the networks are capable of expanding into projects of varying degrees of relevance to the core business. The grand plans of the Bakkers for PTL will be discussed later (Chapter Ten).

CHARISMA AND BUREAUCRACY

A final and vital element of any description of a televangelism operation concerns *power and authority*. Most social scientists will be familiar with Max Weber's famous typology of forms of authority (or non-coercive compliance). Traditional authority is that which depends on the leader holding some traditionally sanctioned office or delivering some traditional message. He is obeyed because that office or that message has always been obeyed; that is how we have always done things. Charismatic authority is that which disrupts tradition and rests on no support other than the person of the putative leader, for whom supernatural gifts are normally claimed. The archtypical charismatic leader is the Christ figure who challenges tradition by saying 'It was written but I say unto you...'. In Weber's view, most previous societies were dominated by patterns of traditional authority periodically disrupted by outbursts of charisma (Weber 1964; Wallis 1982).

In contrast, modern societies are dominated by rational-legal authority. Instead of the weight of tradition or the efflorescence of charisma, there is the rational order of the bureaucracy with its rules and regulations. Things are done one way rather than another because the rules require it or because it is the most efficient procedure. Indeed, the very word 'procedure' suggests the spirit of bureaucracy.

Many new religious movements and political parties are

founded by charismatic leaders. The problem with charisma, of course, is that it is unstable. It is both unstable and unpredictable in the single person of the leader (who may freely change his mind as the Spirit moves him) and unstable in the long-term sense that the leader will die. It is a common pattern in the evolution of new religious and political movements that the charisma of the leader, often during his lifetime, is gradually routinized and finally replaced by the bureaucracy of rational-legal authority. In her otherwise useful examination of televangelism, Frankl attempts to depict the evolution of television evangelism as one of *increasing* routinization and rationalization.

> The traditional authority of the revivalist and his personal calling are no longer the basis for winning souls. Instead, modern, technologically sophisticated organizations have replaced the traditional authority of the revivalist. This represents a clear shift from charismatic authority to rational-legal authority.
>
> (Frankl 1987: 100)

Apart from the confusing sliding between 'traditional' and 'charismatic' to describe the authority of the pre-electronic revivalist preacher, Frankl wishes to attribute to the imperatives of television changes which may well have other sources. The basic 'medium is the message' approach glosses over the vast differences in format, style, and content between equally successful televangelists. It also misses the point, ably exposed in the PTL scandal (of which more later), that the televangelists exercise almost absolute discretion in the construction of their organizations and their product. They can and do do what they like. They are autarchs. Fashions in television production and certain economic imperatives (such as 'be popular enough to pay for all this') may have some part in shaping the product on the screen, but the operation as a whole resembles far more a large feudal estate than a modern bureaucratic corporation. If Falwell wants a university, then a university is what he founds. If Jim Bakker decides to fund emergency social-service centres and then close them three years later when he loses interest, then that is what he does (Hadden and Shupe 1988: 127). If James Robison wants to change from being apolitical to being politically active in Religious Roundtable and then go back to being apolitical (this time because he has moved from orthodox fundamentalist to a more charismatic 'healing' ministry) then he does it.

The feudal analogy is additionally appropriate in drawing our attention to the number of cases where sons have either succeeded their fathers or stand ready to so do. Richard Roberts often appears with his father Oral and now has his own show. Garner Ted Armstrong was as popular a broadcaster for the Worldwide Church of God as his father Herbert W. Armstrong. Bob Jones III, as the name foretold, has followed his grandfather and father in broadcasting and running the university which bears the family name. Robert Schuller's son pastors a part of his father's church and makes ever more frequent appearances on the *Hour of Power.*

In summary, the modern broadcasting evangelistic association is likely to be a vast bureacratic operation which has diversified into a range of supporting enterprises. In most cases, the expansion has been towards creating an alternative community, a subculture of evangelical and fundamentalist piety or, in the case of networks, toward developing a technology which can support such a community. But despite such expansion, the television programme remains at the heart of the matter for it is through it that an audience is created from which, via the modern electronic communications of telephone banks and letter-writing computers, funds are solicited. Although a programme can develop a clear enough identity to continue for periods without the founder (as the *700 Club* did when Robertson was pursuing the presidency), it remains a vehicle for his personality. For all its apparent resemblance to a modern business corporation, the televangelistic association differs in the crucial respect that it exists to market and sustain the ego of the evangelist, who remains free to pursue his angels and demons wheresoever he will.

Chapter Four

THE RELIGION OF RELIGIOUS
TELEVISION

Most discussions of televangelism begin by regarding it as a manifestation of fundamentalism. Although sometimes intended as an
insult, it is more usually just taken at face-value, as the appropriate
description of the major religious broadcasters. With the exception of Robert Schuller, all the leading televangelists have at some
time or other in their careers described themselves as fundamentalists. Although the package of ideas, beliefs, and values signalled
by the term 'fundamentalism' is a good place to start an analysis of
just what it is that is preached on religious television, I will suggest
that the term now functions more as a totem than as accurate
description. Like such ethnic labels as 'Italian' or 'Swede', it tells
us a lot about how the prime-time preachers see their origins and
little about the present except that the claimants have a sentimental loyalty to that 'old time religion'. In his pioneering
examination of the importance of ethnic identity, Herberg (1960)
suggested a generational pattern. The first migrants of, say, Polish
Americans were Poles who happened to settle in America. Their
children usually had little time for the old country, language, or
customs and devoted their energies to passing as real Americans.
But in the third generation, one has people who feel comfortable
enough about their place in America to be able to go back and take
up again some of the more attractive elements of the culture of the
grandparents. They are the Americans who are proud to be Irish,
Greek, Polish, or whatever.

We might usefully add another layer. The present generation of
ethnic Americans are so removed from their ancestral culture that
their attempts to claim it appear cynical or hysterical. In dyeing the
beer green on St Patrick's Day, the descendants of the Irish

demonstrate, not the strength of their identity but its weakness. The frequency with which some modern day televangelists claim to be Bible-believing fundamentalists suggests something similar. I will argue that the theology of the prime-time preachers (in so far as any can be discerned; an important point) differs markedly from that of fundamentalists of Sunday and Bryan's generation.

It might also be supposed that the conservative Protestantism which televangelism offers is 'world-rejecting'. Nothing could be further from the case. As I will argue, televangelists represent a form of conservative Protestantism which has *accommodated* to the modern world almost every bit as much as the liberal Protestantism which they so often disdain for its compromises with the secular world.

Not all televangelists believe the same things and even within a single evangelist's theology there may appear ideas which are either contradictory or at least in tension. I will describe the common core of concerns and, except where they are important for understanding the appeal of a particular preacher, I will pass over idiosyncracies and differences of emphasis. For the sake of brevity I will use 'fundamentalist' loosely to include evangelicals and pentecostalists, except where I wish to make specific points about differences within the conservative camp.

Before the examination of content begins however it is worth saying a word about the relationship between the nature of the medium and the nature of the religious programming it carries. Frankl uses a contrast between urban revivalism and televangelism to draw attention to features of the latter but she makes far too much of the impact of what she calls 'television imperatives' on the product. To give two examples, in listing the artificialities which the medium imposes on the images of the world it presents, she stresses the 'episodic' nature of television programmes: they have a start and an end while real life is continuous (1987: 86). But then church services and crusade revival meetings are similarly episodic. She tells us that television is highly selective in the situations and characters it presents. But then church preaching and revival sermonizing are equally highly selective. Although she does not make as much of this point as others,[1] she supposes that television is *subtly* ideological in that its selective presentations should direct our perceptions of the world. But conservative Protestantism is already ideological and already was when it was presented in print and in the tents of itinerant evangelists. Any subtle ideological overtones it has acquired through being produced for television will be considerably less significant than the gross ideological overtones it has always had irrespective of medium.

References to the consequences for the belief system of this being *mass media* religion will be made as appropriate. Some features of television – close-ups allowing a more subtle and confidential style of presentation or frequent changes of camera angle and subject allowing more variety of image – while they affect the way it looks and sounds, appear to have little impact on the religious content of religious television and it is that to which I now turn.

BIBLE BELIEVING

A very obvious feature of televangelism is the frequent, almost incessant, use of the Bible as a source of authoritative knowledge. The classic pose of the television preacher is with an open Bible in one hand. In the historical introduction I made the point that no-one takes all of the Bible literally but conservative Protestants see themselves as discerning God's will through the study of his Word and most televangelists (Schuller less so than others) construct their addresses around exposition of the Word and constantly turn to it for support for their positions.

EASY BELIEVISM

Surprisingly, televangelists do not talk a lot about what they believe beyond asserting the authority of the Bible and the need to be 'born again'. Especially in the chat show and variety show formats, but even in the more traditional church service format of Falwell's *The Old Time Gospel Hour* there is very little explicit theology and doctrinal teaching. But then pre-mass media urban revivalism was similarly short on theological instruction. Moody and Sunday believed that the Bible was God's word and that one needed to be saved and to live right, but neither gave much time or effort to the details of the faith they promoted. Both protested that they were not learned enough to get involved in the fine print. They also offered a pragmatic justification for avoiding fine detail. Any departure from one or two key principles would bring disagree-

69

ment from the supporting clergy and their congregations and would compromise the more pressing task of soul-saving. Anyway, it was the job of the churches to provide the detailed teaching once the evangelist had stimulated the interest.

Televangelists are even more influenced by the same considerations. Doctrinal detail leads to doctrinal disputes and that reduces the audience. Although urban revivalism was often called 'mass' evangelism, the audience which the televangelist wishes (or needs) to attract is bigger and hence less homogeneous than that which Moody or Sunday tried to influence. TV is also far more expensive than urban revivalism and there is hence an even more pressing need to be popular. The result is a constant pressure to be 'middle of the road'. The CBN officials who train their telephone counsellors ackowledge that one of their first tasks is to persuade the volunteers to give up their own sectarian preferences: 'We are constantly having to say "Don't do this" and "Don't say that". We don't want them to get on the phone and turn first-time callers off by preaching extreme beliefs at them' (quoted in Hoover 1988: 84).

The need to attract large audiences is one reason for avoiding doctrinal detail, but audience expectations of stimulation move producers in the same direction. In the first great awakening, Edwards read sermons that lasted more than two hours. In the second revival of the frontier camps and in the preaching of 1857-8, the audience sat through long dissertations. The modern television audience has a very short attention span. Although still shown on Eternal Word television, we can be sure that the half-hour talks of Bishop Sheen would not be as widely popular now as they were in the 1950s. We live in the world of the 'sound bite' (to use a term coined during the 1988 presidential election campaigns); everything important is condensed into a 20-second snippet which attracts the viewer's attention and encapsulates the speaker's appeal. With the notable exception of Jimmy Swaggart, the most popular televangelists are those with fast-moving formats and brief hortatory presentations.

Most televangelists, like their urban revivalist predecessors, are well aware that they are preaching only a very small part of what has traditionally been regarded as the Christian gospel. Schuller said: 'I've learned that the first step has to be simple and easy. Once they understand that Christians really care about them, they're willing to listen to the deeper, harder parts of the message' (quoted in Armstrong 1979: 113). The procedure is justified on the grounds that, once the viewers' appetites have been whetted they can get detailed Christian teaching in the local church of their choice. They also point to the division of labour of clerical roles. Others can do the teaching; they are best at eliciting an initial interest. Like the urban revivalists, they offer a pragmatic justification for their lack of interest in theology: soul-winning is the important thing. When the Bakkers stood down from the PTL network and show, they asked Jerry Falwell to step in. Pentecostalists were concerned that Falwell, an orthodox fundamentalist who had often denounced pentecostalism, would change the nature of the programme. Fundamentalists were worried that he would fail to purge PTL of un-biblical conceits. He promised that the show would continue to be pentecostal and defended his actions to his core constituency by saying that conservative Protestant unity in the face of its detractors was more important than quarrelling over details of theology. The mission was to produce Christian television shows which would interest the heathen who could then learn the details of their new found faith at a local church.

In practice, it does not work like that. The viewers are either already church members or they are not. If they are not, they are unlikely to become members because of being drawn to a television programme. As Horsfield's research shows, even those shows which claim a good record in referring inquirers to local churches do very little of it.[2] This is not surprising given that encouraging a viewer to become involved in a local church may result in them re-directing their 'sacrificial giving' to that church.

To be fair to religious broadcasters, there is not a lot of doctrine in the churches. Although the process has affected liberal churches more than conservative ones, there has been a general 'internal secularization' of American Protestantism. The contrast is a caricature, of course but there is a good deal of truth in the observation that in Europe, religion died away as people ceased to go to church. In America, the churches retained popular support while abandoning large parts of what made them distinctive (Wilson 1968). To an extent this has been exaggerated by the considerable pentecostal influence on televangelism. Although pentecostalism usually shares many of the doctrines of fundamentalism, the stress on the gifts of the Spirit means that belief and dogma may take second place to emotional states, which opens a 'second front' to internal secularization. If the doctrinal under-pinnings collapse, one is left with the diffuse therapy of what David Martin once rather cruelly called 'touchy-feely' religion.

RATIONALIZATION OF THE FAITH

Given that one of the strongest images of fundamentalism is William Jennings Bryan announcing during the Scopes evolution trial in Little Rock, Arkansas, that if science said one thing and the Bible said another, then he would believe the Bible, it is not surprising that conservative Protestants are seen as intellectual reactionaries, dismissing rational thought for faith in the supernatural. However, this would be a misleading picture. It is worth noting that, in so far as fundamentalists are found in such enterprises as higher education, it is as natural scientists and engineers rather than as social scientists and students of the arts and humanities. In British student Protestant movements, conserv-ative evangelicals have their strongest base in medicine and the natural sciences (Bruce 1984b: Ch. 8). As I will suggest, fundamentalists may dislike some of the propositions of natural science but they generally find the methods and assumptions of mundane (as opposed to pioneering) science congenial.

Although this sounds counter-intuitive, it makes sense if one goes back to the central images that the two streams of Protest-antism have about authoritative knowledge. Conservatives believe that there is one truth, that there is one empirical reality, that the Bible is the Word of God, and that, give or take the odd difficulty, the words of the Bible mean what they say they mean. Although there are various epistemologies within conservative Protest-antism, what they have in common can readily be seen in the contrast with the *relativism* of liberal Protestantism. Liberals allow that there is a difficulty of interpretation, that there are a number of worlds, that God's message is by no means clear, that the words of the Bible can mean different things to different people, in different cultures at different times.

Conservatives have a realistic view of the world. There are facts out there to be collected. Once one has enough facts, one develops a theory to explain them. Then one collects more facts to test the theory. Enough supporting facts and the theory becomes a law.

There is no sense of a hermeneutic or interpretative problem; no sense that what we see in the world might be a reflection of our interests and ideologies rather than the facts of the matter; no sense of the idea that knowledge might be socially constructed. In that sense conservatives are naive scientists after the fashion of Francis Bacon.

The fundamentalist view can be criticized from an extreme relativist position that sees even hard 'science' as being a social construction, a cultural artefact permeated by the ethnocentric assumptions of our time and place. Even scientific knowledge is ideologically informed. There is no such thing as 'factual' knowledge. But many who would not go that far still have trouble with the fundamentalist position because they want to retain a division between the natural and supernatural world. Most moderate Christians are Baconians when it comes to stories about the natural world but they slide into the relativist hermeneutic camp when it comes to accounts of the supernatural; in this world, a fact is a fact but when we talk of the other world, then apparently contradictory propositions can be simultaneously true. Absolute truth is replaced by a variety of truths.

Understanding that point, allows us to see what is unusual about the fundamentalist epistemology. It applies a naïve Baconian 'fact is a fact' view to both the natural and supernatural worlds. In fact, it denies any significant difference between the two. Thus Bill Bright (founder of the very large, popular, and influential Campus Crusade for Christ) can say in his *The Four Spiritual Laws*: 'just as there are physical laws that govern the physical universe, so are there spiritual laws which govern your relationship with God' (quoted in Hunter 1983: 76).

A further element of important background can be introduced here. We live in a world dominated by what Peter Berger and his associates call 'technological consciousness' (1973). To simplify their account, automated mechanical mass production implies certain assumptions about the nature of the world which it manipulates. It presupposes that complex tasks and objects can be broken down into simple, infinitely reproducible acts or elements. That is, the combination adds nothing to the elements. It assumes regularity; an act performed the same way tomorrow will have the same effect as it did when performed today. It assumes the existence of technical solutions. If we wish to perform some hitherto unknown feat (such as getting oil out of frozen shale), we rationally examine our present resources, work out what is missing, conduct research to improve our knowledge, build prototypes, test them, and eventually we get out the oil. There is no mystery and no awe. We take it for granted that examination and rational thought and experimentation will reveal the presently hidden. The attitude characteristic of technological consciousness is 'problem-solving inventiveness'.

The various ideas and assumptions implicit in technological mass production are further elaborated by Berger *et al.* but their general thrust seems unexceptionable: societies which use this form of production will come to be dominated by the subtle styles of thought of technological consciousness. Note that this is not a story about the ratiocinations of scientists or the intellectual elites. Nor is it suggested that ordinary people have such notions as reproducibility and componentiality at the front of their minds often. The point is that technological consciousness permeates the culture so that certain ways of thinking seem more 'natural' than others.

Books of instruction were one of the earliest forms of literature and have remained one of the most common but there has been a considerable increase in the number of such works and in their scope. In particular, modern societies have a vast literature of what Dylan called 'road maps for the soul', manuals of self- improvement. The point will be elaborated below. Here I want to establish two connections: the first between science and conservative Protestant epistemology and the second between technological consciousness and contemporary fundamentalist thinking. In contrast to liberal Protestantism, the conservative variety is well-suited to the *codification* of spiritual knowledge and its present-ation in manuals, a process which James Davison Hunter appro-priately calls 'the rationalization of spirituality' (1983: 73-83). Bill Bright's pamphlet tells the reader that conversion (essential to salvation) follows from acknowledging the four spiritual laws:

Law One. God loves you, and offers a wonderful plan for your life.
Law Two. Man is sinful and separated from God. Therefore, he cannot know and experience God's love and plan for his life.

Law Three. Jesus Christ is God's only provision for man's sin. Through him you can know and experience God's love and plan for your life.

Law Four. We must individually receive Jesus Christ as Savior and Lord; then we can know and experience God's love and plan for our lives. ... Receiving Christ involves turning to God from self (repentance) and trusting Christ to come into our lives to forgive our sins and to make us the kind of people He wants us to be.

(Bright 1965)

Note that it is not only the reader who is supposed to have a plan; even God has a plan!

There seems no reason to suppose that the compression (reduction is too evaluative a term) of the saving faith into a number of 'easy to remember' principles is a consequence of the media of radio and television. Its roots are more plausibly suggested by the observation that pre-literate cultures often made knowledge easier to remember and teach by expressing it in rhyming couplets, alliterative phrases, or mnemonic devices. I would suggest that what we see here (as in the down-playing of theology) is democratization. Why should the ill-educated masses be excluded from the Christian message? Liturgical religions have no problem because they teach people simple responses or rituals. Protestantism, with its stress on right belief, has to find ways of teaching the masses the Word in ways they can absorb and recall. The compressions and simplifications of 'Four Laws' and 'Three Ways to Christ' may offend the reading classes but they are a vital part of popular Protestantism.

THE ENJOYMENT OF WEALTH

One only had to view the *PTL Club* or *Oral Roberts and You* to realize that the gospel of the televangelist does not promote asceticism. There is little renunciation of material wealth evident here. The hosts and the guests are all expensively dressed and the sets are extravagantly furnished.

As in all religious traditions, the pastor is offered as a role model, as an exemplar of whatever that religious culture regards as virtuous. In the case of televangelism, the wealth of the pastor is not only defended as necessary to the proper fulfilment of his functions (Falwell's explanation for his private jet and pilot) but as proper acknowledgement of the pastor's position as the representative of God. As Jim Bakker put it in one of his many televised defences of what all but the most besotted supporter regarded as an extravagant lifestyle:

> I think we ought to want the best for our pastors. I believe a pastor should live at least, at least, as good as the wealthiest member of the congregation. When you bless the man in the pulpit, you will be blessed!

Note that 'bless' here is being used as a synonymn for 'give lots of money to'. Falwell said 'material wealth is God's way of blessing people who put him first' (quoted in Horsfield 1984: 49).

Although the Bakkers are a little extreme, they do illustrate the deep desire among many fundamentalists and pentecostalists to demonstrate their arrival in the mainstream of American life by acquiring the possessions previously denied to their class. When the Bakkers were in their twenties, they moved to Portsmouth, Virginia. Rather than looking for an apartment in a neighbourhood they could afford, they went to a high-rise block in an expensive area. They found a bedsit on the seventh floor that rented for a fifth of the price of the better apartments.

> We never told anyone the apartment didn't have a bedroom. With so many doors opening off the huge living room, everybody probably thought the door leading to the furnace was our bedroom. We purchased a comfortable hide-a-bed and that worked out fine until the Lord could perform another miracle with accommodations.
>
> (Quoted in Barnhart 1988: 105)

One day, when Tammy was in the lift, a society matron asked what floor she lived on. When Tammy said 'The seventh', the matron announced that she lived on the eighteenth floor, which was the most expensive in the block. Within a year, the Bakkers' finances improved enough for them to move to the eighteenth floor. Writing about it twenty years later, Jim Bakker with no sense of anything but pride added: 'Then when the society matron would ask Tammy, "What floor do you live on?" she could say "Praise God, we've gone to the eighteenth".'

Oral Roberts grew up in extreme poverty in the 1930s. For most of his childhood his only clothes were a single set of dungarees. When he graduated from elementary school he was elected 'King of the Class'. He had saved money from a paper round to buy a new pair of dungarees so that he would be well dressed to escort the girl elected Queen. She turned up in a white satin evening gown. The teacher told Oral he had time to go home and put on his best clothes (Harrell 1985: 28-9). In young adulthood, as his career as a preacher developed and he travelled increasingly widely, his frustration with grinding poverty increased. In that context, his discovery of what later became 'prosperity theology' in the text of 'I wish above all things that thou mayest prosper and be in health, even as thy soul prospereth' (3rd John, v. 2) is understandable.

In legitimating the enjoyment of wealth, televangelists were simply following a major shift in popular culture. In a 1944 study of biographies in popular magazines, Lowenthal argued that the idols of production – men and women celebrated for economic, technical, or industrial achievement – had since the 1920s been replaced by idols of consumption (Lowenthal 1944; Janowitz 1978: 338). In advanced industrial societies, it is consumption which is king and televangelists fully endorse consumerist values. There was a time when conservative Protestants denounced a degree of material comfort which they could not afford but slowly, as the standard of living of the people who formed the bulk of fund-amentalism and pentecostalism rose to allow conspicuous consumption, the prohibitions were relaxed. Now wealth is positively endorsed as proof of God's blessing.

THE ENJOYMENT OF GLAMOUR

It is not just that money is now good instead of bad; spending it on personal adornment is now acceptable. The most obvious difference between the dramatis personae of televangelism shows and of tent meetings in the 1930s is the former's *glamour*. It is not just that the clothes are made of better material, are brighter, and are more expertly cut; there is also more attention to hair style and, for the women, make-up is common. In the extent to which they are self-consciously attractive there is no difference between the choir of young people on the Oral Roberts show and on a secular music programme.

In his rambling but insightful account of the career of the Bakkers, Joe Barnhart makes an interesting point:

> Ironically, it was male evangelists and ministers who unwittingly led the way in this reform. Pentecostal ministers began sporting colorful ties, artful tie clasps, and trendy suits and shoes. Some of them drove shiny cars and wore fashionable overcoats. It did not take some of the women long to realize that the preachers seemed increasingly concerned with their own outward appearance even as they delivered sanctimonious sermons to women about inward beauty. It was not uncommon to see a Pentecostal husband decked out in stylish clothes while his wife looked as if she was wearing a flour sack.
>
> (Barnhart 1988: 106)

Ministers and travelling evangelists not only had more money than the average member of their audience but they also had more contact with the cosmopolitan centre; they brought the glamour of cities to the rural towns and villages.

The impression that being sexually attractive and active is now acceptable in many fundamentalist circles is reinforced by recent currents in conservative Protestant literature. Tim and Beverley La Haye, leading Californian fundamentalists, have published a Christian sex book which encourages 'elegant variation' in coupling (underneath the dining table is recommended) and views sexual intercourse as a great gift from God to be enjoyed for its own values (within marriage, of course). Mirabel Morgan's best selling *Total Woman*, while conservative in its general view of the subordinate role for women, is frankly aggressive about sexuality. Sex is a pleasure and it is the woman's job to keep her man interested in her body. (For a review of thirteen recent evangelical sex books, see Lewis and Blisset 1986.)

James Davison Hunter's survey of attitudes among young evangelical students shows considerable change in views on sex. In 1963, almost half said that 'casual petting' was always wrong; in 1982 less than a quarter held that view. In 1963, 81 per cent thought that 'heavy petting' was always wrong but by 1982 only 45 per cent thought that (Hunter 1987: 58).

Hunter's survey confirms a similar shift across a range of behaviours which the cold war fundamentalist world would have regarded as loose or worldly living. The 1951 and 1961 surveys which Hunter builds on asked about attitudes towards watching 'Hollywood-type' films. In 1951, 46 per cent and in 1961 14 per cent thought it was always morally wrong. When Hunter asked his students in 1982, he found that only 7 per cent thought that attending an R-rated movie (age-restricted because of sex, violence, or profanity) was always wrong. The figures for those who thought similarly about smoking for 1951, 1961, and 1982 were 93 per cent, 70 per cent, and 51 per cent; concerning alcohol they were 98 per cent, 78 per cent, and 17 per cent (Hunter 1987: 59).

Dancing has often been the subject of puritan prohibition. For a long time 'sacred' music was suspect. Secular music was even worse. But dancing, which brought the warm bodies of men and women together in circumstances where the rhythms inflamed the passions and aroused the lusts, was taboo. A Texas Southern Baptist told me the following joke: Q: 'Why don't Baptists make love standing up?'; A: 'Because if God's watching he might think they're dancing'. In 1951, 91 per cent of a sample of young evangelicals thought that tangoing and waltzing were always morally wrong. By 1961, the percentage had fallen to 61. When Hunter repeated the question in his interviews with evangelical students he found that *none* regarded dancing as a sin. He offers as representative the female student who said: 'These things could be sinful if they become an obsession but they are not intrinsically wrong' (1987: 58). Both the direction and the extent of the changes are neatly described by Hunter when he says that 'the words *worldly* and *worldliness* have, within a generation, lost most of their traditional meaning' (1987: 63).

There are, of course, differences between televangelists. The Bakkers and Roberts probably went further than most in changing conservative Protestant attitudes to pleasure. Swaggart's preaching (although, as we shall see, not his own practice) remains orthodox in its denunciation of fun, as does Falwell's.

The explanation for these changes is complex but the centre piece is increasing affluence. Many pre-war conservative Protestants were dirt poor and could not afford good clothes, dancing, or make-up. Being unable to satisfy their appetites, they kept them under control by denouncing them. Having a good time was not only something they could not afford to do; it was something they did not want to do and those who did it were clearly destined for hell. But fundamentalists can now afford the clothes, the stereo-systems, the nights out, the make-up; freed by contraception from the burden of large families and liberated by their increasing prosperity from the drudgery which ages, fundamentalists can now see sex as a pleasurable leisure activity rather than as some demo-nic spirit which tempts and then destroys those who fall prey to the temptation. Licit sex need no longer be a chore; it can be fun.

I do not want to suggest that beliefs are impotent to control appetites. It is clearly possible for people who feel strongly opposed to some practice to avoid it even when the barrier of poverty is removed.[5] However, it is important to remember that a large part of fundamentalism was not a movement of deliberate choice but of cultural survival. Fundamentalists (and this was even more the case for pentecostalists who had a generally lower socio-economic status) were not people who had dallied among the bright lights of the modern big city and deliberately turned their backs on them. They were people who were relatively untouched by the rewards of the modern industrial urban society and who countered the pain of yearning by condemning. Once those rewards became theirs, the costs of asceticism were propor-tionately raised. Before they had been giving up what were at best aspirations and were more often sources of frustration; now they would be giving up actual consumer products and the manifold satisfactions which advertising promised accompanied such pro-ducts. Slowly many were won over to accept the benefits which their new prosperity offered, although the transition could be painful. Tammy Faye Bakker talks of her acquaintance with movies:

> One time my mother and father were going to see the movie *The Ten Commandments.* I told mother if she went to that movie I'd leave home and never return. I thought it would keep her from backsliding. They went, and I cried and cried. I saw my very first movie after I was married. I'll never forget it. It was *White Christmas* with Bing Crosby.
>
> (Quoted in Barnhart 1988: 87)

Going to the movies was a public violation of pentecostal morals. Other more rigorous believers could see the behaviour and register their disapproval. The spread of radio and television, stereos and cheap cassette players all made private unsupervised entertainment possible and thus permitted a gradual shift. One could go from denouncing the Babylon of Hollywood to movie-going via the half-way house of watching films on television at home. In every respect, increased affluence allows greater privacy and thus reduces social pressure to conform.

The liberating effects of freedom from poverty were neatly encapsulated by a young Bible Baptist who told Hunter:

> For my Dad, the most important thing in the world was to provide for his family financially. Until about two years ago, he worked two to three jobs all of the time. Since my basic needs have been taken care of, I can pursue what I find fulfilling, which is different than just financial security.
>
> (Quoted Hunter in 1987: 68)

In so far as a section of American Protestantism has not yet abandoned its puritanism, it is because it remains poor. In her small study of watchers of the *PTL Club* in a town in south-eastern Ohio, Bourgault notes that most members of the small United Pentecostal church were 'economically disaffected, with most of the household heads unemployed or working seasonally at menial occupations' (Bourgault 1985: 135). It was in this group of viewers that one found unanimous disapproval of the worldly appearance of Tammy Faye Bakker and most of her female 'born again' guests. As one put it: 'I think Tammy should take her wigs off, take off her mascara, her lipstick and rouge, and put on some decent-looking clothes'.

SUPER-PATRIOTISM

Fundamentalists are American jingoes. The thousands who travelled to spend the Fourth of July with Jerry Falwell at his *I Love America* rally where he happily asserted that America was 'the greatest freest democracy in the world' and he could not think who came second, were in complete agreement. In the general formulae used to describe the more politically active fundamentalists, 'pro-family, pro-life, and pro-moral' are often accompanied by 'pro-America'.

There is nothing new in conservative Protestant Americanism. From the first puritan settlement, conservative Protestants have entangled the fate of America and the fulfilment of God's will. But there has been a marked change. When the puritans of Salem and Massachusetts asserted the link between their City on a Hill and the kingdom of God, they had a firm image (based on criticism of contemporary worlds) of what the kingdom of God on earth would look like and were determined to re-make the material world in God's image. Gradually the emphasis shifted so that modern American fundamentalism, instead of having a vision of a new earth from which to judge this one, simply endorsed what presently obtained.

Billy Sunday was a transitional figure. At the start of his career he was, like William Jennings Bryan, a populist, critical of such features of modern capitalism as robber baron capitalists and 'trusts'. Towards the end of his ministry, social problems had been individualized to character defects and being in thrall to the booze trade. But such problems as he did allow himself to perceive were small beer. God had 'kept this country hid from the greedy eyes of monarchs 3,000 miles away' until it could be settled by God-fearing people (quoted in McLoughlin 1955: 131). He reckoned that the discovery of America and the establishment of free government were two of the four greatest events in world history (the birth of Christ and the Reformation were the other two).

Such views were fundamentalist orthodoxy by the time of the cold war. Billy Graham prayed in Congress:

> Our father, we give Thee thanks for this greatest nation in the world. We thank Thee for the Stars and Stripes that wave above the land of the free and home of the brave. We thank Thee for the highest standard of living in the world ...
>
> (Quoted in Frady 1979: 240)

In explaining why from early days in his career, wealthy and powerful figures entertained him, Graham suggested:

> They are beginning to realize that evangelism's a tremendous factor, not only politically but from the moral and spiritual point of view, which will make a contribution to the country. Because the Communists are dedicated to Com-

munism, and we need the same dedication to the principles on which this country was founded.

(Quoted in Frady 1979: 242)

More aggressive than Graham,[4] Billy James Hargis and Carl McIntire saw the world in the same stark conflict terms (see below, pp. 164–7). There was America and there was the Soviet Union; God's own country and Godless atheism. Any criticism of the former was tacit support for the latter and was to be denounced. These preachers were so concerned with promoting 'one hundred per cent Americanism' that they offended many even in the conservative Protestant milieu, but a less outspoken version of their views, which confined itself to the frequent assertion that America was divinely blessed and stopped short of attacking liberal churchmen, was conservative Protestant orthodoxy during the cold war.

Graham had his fingers burnt with his too public support for Richard Nixon and has since been critical of those who try to link the fortunes of the Christian gospel with the political fortunes of America but Robertson, Robison, and Falwell remain 'super-patriots'.

THE THERAPEUTIC ETHOS

For many people, affluent democratic societies have solved most of the problems which previously demanded their attention; responding to physical attack and collecting food no longer take as much of our energy or time as they once did. Compared to our ancestors, we have excellent health, a negligible infant mortality rate, peace, prosperity, and personal security. No doubt we could all do with more of these things but we all have far more of them than any previous civilization. This allows us the luxury of being concerned with the self and the psychic states described by such terms as 'personal fulfilment' and 'human growth'. This is a major re-orientation of what Max Weber neatly termed 'theodicy': the explanation of why God permits bad things. In the past theodicies have been concerned with the explanation and justification of war, pestilence, and fatal illness against which there seemed to be no protection. Now, when innocents are less often snatched away from us for no apparent reason, our theodicies have shifted to more nebulous concerns of self-realization. Janowitz makes a telling point when he adds a third layer to Lowenthal's observations about idols of consumption replacing idols of production in popular culture; 'Themes of consumption still exceeded those of production ... [but] the new element deals with the strategies human beings use to handle ... personal and emotional problems' (1978: 338-9). The mass media now have a considerable interest in themes of interpersonal relationships and their management.

In an excellent essay on the development of a consumer culture between 1880 and 1930, Lears details the way in which the previous concern with the objective condition of 'being saved' was displaced by the subjective notion of human growth and potential. This hedonism first affected liberal Protestants, who tried to reconcile Christianity with the therapeutic ethos by psychologizing the key parts of the Christian faith. Thus for Harry Emerson Fosdick, the starting point of Christianity was not an objective faith but faith in human personality: 'Not an outward temple, but the inward shrine of man's personality, with all its possibilities and powers is . . . infinitely sacred' (quoted in Lears 1983: 14). Religion and life had been drifting apart and as a result 'multitudes of people are living not bad but frittered lives – split, scattered, uncoordinated'. The solution was a religion which 'will furnish an inward spiritual dynamic for radiant and triumphant living' and such a religion had to pass the following test: 'First, is it intelligently defensible; second, does it contribute to man's abundant life?' As Lears puts it: 'The problem, in other words, was not morality but morale. Like other religious leaders, Fosdick unwittingly transformed Protestant Christianity into a form of abundance therapy' (Lears 1983: 14).

Although thoroughly secularized, this sort of human potential promotion was quite prescriptive and proscriptive. But by the 1960s, it was being replaced, even in *soi-disant* Protestant circles by almost entirely *laissez faire* notions of growth. There was no longer any one direction in which one developed, any one measure of what counted as abundant life. 'If it feels good, do it' and 'Do your own thing' were the slogans adopted from secular culture by churchmen, as always too late, when they are already passé.

A second set of reasons for psychologizing the gospel came from the felt need to respond to secular knowledge. One way of viewing liberal theology is to see it as an attempt to save the Christian gospel from refutation by restructuring its propositions so that they no longer apply to the world out there (where they appeared to have been proved wrong) but refer instead to the internal mental and emotional world of the individual where, of course, they are incontestable. Thus the objective external and historically real Devil is replaced by some weakness or character defect internal to us all. The expulsion from the Garden of Eden is turned from a real event in the historical world into a psychodrama; man becoming alienated from his true nature. Whether Christ really died for our sins becomes secondary to the placebo effect of our *believing* that Christ died for our sins. Genesis 1-12 is not really a (false) account of the origins of the world but a story told by God to a simple people who would not have been able to understand the truth any other way. It is not that the Bible makes claims about the world which are false; rather God's message was revealed to different cultures in terms which each could understand. The miracle stories were educational for the people of Israel but we do not need them because God has revealed his majesty to us through allowing us to understand science.

Psychologizing the gospel makes it immune to refutation by secularists. It also removes the necessity for Christians of different persuasions (indeed, believers of different religions) to argue with each other. If the truth of the message depends on its internal impact, then there can be a number of 'truths'; what is true for you and what is true for me may well be apparently different things.

Peale and Fuller

There were a number of ways in which this internalizing, relativizing, and psychologizing of the gospel could be pursued. One was the existential philosophy of Rudolf Bultmann which was popular with European intellectuals. Another was most fully developed in Norman Vincent Peale's 'power of positive thinking'. The Christian message is reduced first to a Manichean dichotomy: human life is a struggle between the two forces good and evil. But good and evil are no longer external to us. Evil, that which holds us back and stops us from being happy and successful, is now a lack of self-confidence. Good becomes 'positive thinking'. Those people who think positively (while conforming to the moral and ethical codes of middle-class suburban America) will be successful; this is salvation. Those who do not will be damned; that is, they will be unhappy and unsuccessful.

In the 1950s Everett Parker led a major team survey of the impact of religious broadcasting in New Haven. As well as studying the audience, the team developed methods for recording and statistically describing the content of the most popular programmes. The following is a résumé of a Norman Vincent Peale broadcast:

> There is an infinite perfectibility about human nature. If you get firmly fixed in your mind the dynamic of change and will apply faith to your mental attitude, whatever your defect is, it can be corrected. Many of us have defects of the emotions of personality. Another type of defect is a moral defect. This, too, can be corrected. It is a fact that there is no change that cannot take place in a human being, none whatsoever, provided that individual wants to change and provided he will believe.
>
> (Parker *et al.* 1955: 144)

Although Peale was the most prominent spokesman for this approach and, with the title of his best selling book *The Power of Positive Thinking*, in both senses 'christened' it, he was not its sole representative. A similar psychologizing of sin and salvation can be found in the sermons of more mainstream stars of religious radio of the period: Ralph Sockman, for example.

Conservative Protestants have been the most vociferous critics of such internalizing. They reasonably point out that if God had meant that sort of thing, he would have said it in the first place. A useful technique of content analysis used by the New Haven study is keyword counting. Although there is more to understanding than adding up the number of times words appear, the frequency of certain sorts of words can illustrate the tenor, tone, and content of a piece of speech. In particular, we can get a measure of the degree of optimism in the speaker's attitude to the world by comparing the number of positive or favourable references and comparing them with the number of condemnatory, pessimistic, critical, and unfavourable mentions. In six sermons in 1952, Ralph Sockman used positive or favourable keywords 966 times and unfavourable words only 297 times. A similar ratio is found in

Peale's talks: 1,103 favourable words or concepts to 329 unfavourable ones. In contrast, fundamentalist Charles E. Fuller in his *Old Fashioned Revival Hour* had 1,091 unfavourable to 372 favourable words or concepts. The extent to which Fuller's concerns differed from Peale's can be seen from the breakdown of each man's most frequently referred to 'undesirable' conditions or objectionable qualities. For Peale, the most frequently cited undesirables were 'defects', 'unhappiness', 'wrong', 'problems', 'troubles', and 'worries'. For Fuller, the undesirables were 'death', 'darkness', 'alienated', 'Satan' (who appears three times as often in Fuller's talks than in Peale's), 'world', and 'blind'. Even greater difference can be seen in the things of which they spoke favourably. Peale's most common desirables were 'happy(iness)', 'pray(er)', 'Jesus Christ', 'peace of mind', 'wonderful', 'simplicity', and in seventh place, 'God'. The greater conservatism of Fuller's theology is evidenced in his 'God', 'Christ', and 'Bible texts' being his three most frequently cited desirables, followed by 'gift of grace', 'believer', 'spiritual', and 'body of Christ'.

For Peale the forces of evil are internalized as defects, frustrations, and personal failures. God is a benign force who can be called on to help you overcome troubles and live to your full potential. Fuller wants his audience to realize that they are in danger of eternal damnation and need to be born again to avoid the fate.

Thus in the mid-1950s we have the most popular fundamentalist preacher clearly setting himself against the psychologizing of the gospel.

Robert Schuller

Although an exception as the one televangelist who is not, and who has never claimed to be, a fundamentalist, Robert Schuller is one of the most popular. His *Hour of Power* show is watched by about 2.5 per cent of American households with a television and is the second most popular of the weekly shows, with around 2.7 million viewers.

His books *You Can Become the Person You Want to Be* and *Self-esteem: The New Reformation* have massive circulations. The latter places his 'possibility thinking' – for which he frankly acknowledges his debt to Peale, also a Reformed Church minister – in its theological context. He believes that the Protestant Reformation was good as far as it went but had a flawed psychology at its base: it was not a 'well-rounded, full-orbed, honestly-interrelated theology system' (1983: 146). It made a mistake in seeing sin as rebellion against God when it should have been seen as a lack of self-esteem and self-worth. To be saved then is to be freed from a lack of self-esteem and allowed to appreciate the

> God-glorifying, need-meeting, constructive and creative consequences of conversion. . . . To be saved is to know that Christ forgives me and now I dare to believe that I am somebody and I can do something for God and my fellow human beings.
>
> (Schuller 1983: 99)

Put in its broader context, the main problem with the modern world is that: 'many human beings don't realize who they are. And if we don't know who we are and where we have come from, we will never become what we are meant to be' (1983: 66).

The conservative response

Conservative Protestant reaction has developed in step with the rise of the therapeutic ethos and its permeation of Protestantism. The first reaction was to denounce it out of hand and, as we saw in the talks of Charles Fuller, to stress the old agenda of sin and repentance, morality and asceticism, and bending to God's will (which normally coincided with the morality of small town America). But the same imperatives that drove Fosdick and Peale, and now Schuller to produce their banal 'feel good' religion have now come to influence conservatives.

As early as 1955, there was evidence of the impress of the therapeutic image on evangelicalism. In Billy Graham's New York crusade of that year, the largest proportion of 'decision cards' – the cards completed by people who came forward for further counselling and which included, if the neophyte had a preference, the name of a church – were for the Marble Collegiate Church of Norman Vincent Peale. Some of that is explained, of course, by simple name recognition. But one may assume that a lot of the Graham converts knew the name because they listened to Peale on the radio and read his books and liked what they heard and read.

I have already suggested that pentecostalism, with its stress on the personal experience of the second blessing of the power of the Holy Spirit, offered a 'second front' for secularization. Through the 1940s and early 1950s, Oral Roberts was just the best known of a very large number of popular faith healers who ministered to millions in the small towns and villages of rural America (Harrell 1975). Perhaps because the clientele were increasing in wealth, the demand for the signs and wonders of physical healing fell away and there was a shift from the cure of the body to the cure of the personality.

In the last twenty years there has been a considerable growth in interest in Christian counselling. Initially the counselling movement presented itself as a conservative Protestant alternative to the dominant ethos of secular and liberal Protestant counselling. Where the secular version eschewed judging and directing patients, preferring to help them find out what was right for them, the conservative Protestant variety saw personal problems as the product of sin and the purpose of counselling as the eradication of sin through conversion. Problems were overcome by getting right with God. The Christian counsellor was really only the Christian evangelist with a more detailed interest in particular biographies and with a skill for discerning just which sin was causing the problem.

Conservative Protestant counselling could be just a technique of holding the template of the saved Christian against the actual biography of the person with problems and showing them what they have to change in order to resolve the problems. One may note that even in its most radical form, this already involves a degree of accommodation with the modern world in that it is conceding the private nature of religion. In so far as religion has a secondary purpose, unlike the puritan vision with its *social* templates, the modern Christian counselling movement sees that role as the improvement of the inner person.

If the ethos of counselling itself is a product of modern secular influence, the version of it which informs much televangelism is even more thoroughly secularized in that it seems to involve little behavioural challenge to the individual. Although it may initially seem a little perverse to describe it as psychologizing, a major element of internalizing is the Bakkers' or Roberts' use of the devil in explaining one's fortunes. At first hearing, the frequent talk of the devil sounds like old fashioned revival preaching but this devil is no longer an identifiable objective force in the world. Instead he has become synonymous with personal failure and internal character defects. the problem for all religions which want to have an all-powerful and a just God is to explain why bad things happen to good people. Why did God not make everybody happy? The orthodox Calvinist answer – that, for reasons we can never hope to understand, he did not want you to be happy – is out of fashion.

The Bakker and Roberts syllogism (and it is common to many modern pentecostalists) goes like this:

(a) God is good and wants you to be happy and successful.
(b) If you are not happy and successful, it must be because you have given in to the devil, who does not want you to be happy and successful.
(c) Your problems are caused by your weakness, lack of faith, or lack of sacrificial giving.

If God has provided you with all that you need to be devil-resistant and you are not, the fault must be yours. The devil is reduced to a lack of will power. He is now 'failure to pray enough' or 'failure to give enough'. Joe Barnhart makes the point that while the Bakkers had relieved themselves and others from their back- ground in poor pentecostal churches from the need to feel guilty about enjoying the material rewards of this world, they had created a new source of guilt from personal failure. After this smooth reversal, those who previously had felt deprived but righteous now had to feel deprived and guilty.

To summarize this section, my point is a simple one. A number of factors combine to privatize religion in the modern world. One form of this is the psychologizing of key elements of the gospel. It was first promoted enthusiastically by liberal Protestants and rejected by conservatives but now televangelists have followed Fosdick and Peale down the road which they so vocally scorned in the pre-war period.

THE TRADITIONAL FAMILY

American televangelism is socially conservative. Among many other things, its spokesmen oppose abortion, homosexuality, sex education, and the Equal Rights for women Amendment to the constitution (ERA). The core of televangelism's socio-moral platform is the importance of the 'traditional' nuclear family. Very often the Christian message is advertised for what it can do to 'heal troubled families' (and there are specialized family ministeries). So far in discussing the format of religious television and its key ideas, I have said nothing about its tone. Most American televangelism is sentimental and at times mawkish to the point of being nauseating. No heart string is left untugged. As an example, the following is a testimony offered from the pulpit of Thomas Road Baptist Church on *The Old Time Gospel Hour*. Doug Oldham is an extremely fat but talented gospel soloist. Although reared in a Christian home, he had 'never had a personal relationship with Jesus Christ'. While not yet truly saved he took a job as a Minister of Music in an evangelical church:

> Life became frustrating and confusing for Doug: the incon-sistencies in his own life with the gospel songs he sang hardened his heart and made him difficult to get along with. As Doug stood before the masses at Thomas Road and looked into the television camera, he brushed a tear from his eye and indicated that he began attending places he shouldn't, and was sold out to the love of money. He treated his family terribly. . . . Doug had been on national radio and television for another denomination but at home his wife, Laura Lee, knew that he was a hypocrite. After nine years of pressure, tension and argument, she made her decision to leave Doug and try to evaluate the problems that filled their marriage.
>
> When Laura Lee left Doug, he found himself with nothing. The home was lost, the big car was gone, and he ended up living in small room in the back of a friend's house. One clear night as Doug drove in southern Ohio, the full impact of his problems crashed upon him. He prayed, 'Lord, if you're up there, give me something worth living for'. Doug points to this incident as the time he came to know Jesus Christ as Saviour from sin. His family were reunited and they have spent ten wonderful years together.
>
> (Towns 1973: 54)

Shortly after the reunion, Doug took one of his daughters to the old house to clean it up. After he had been sweeping for a while, he noticed that the girl was missing. He found her hiding. She remembering the beatings and the arguments, and with fear in her eyes, she said 'Daddy, I don't like this house.'

While Doug is relating this tale to the cameras (and finding it so moving that, even after ten years, he still cries about it), the organist is slowly building up to the opening of a moving ballad, and Doug sings:

> Today I went back to the place where I used to go
> Today I saw the same old crowd I knew before
> When they asked me what had happened, I tried to tell them
> Thanks to Calvary, I don't come here anymore.

And the final verse recapitulates the story:

> Thanks to Calvary, I am not the dad I used to be
> Thanks to Calvary, things are different than before
> While the tears ran down my face, I tried to tell her
> Thanks to Calvary, we don't live here anymore.

CHRISTIAN SERVICE

What, according to televangelists, is the consequence of being born again? What changes should occur in the lives of those who have experienced redemption? I have already suggested that even the limited degree of asceticism and personal renunciation advocated by Billy Sunday or Charles Fuller has been severely attenuated. What then is left? The main answer is evangelism. The primary duty of the Christian is to spread the Word. It is the responsibility of every Christian to maintain a Christian witness in his or her life. In addition, he or she should support missionary work, if they are not called to engage in it themselves.

But Brother Jim or Brother Oral is already working hard, and efficiently, at spreading the gospel and with his electronic technology can reach places and numbers that you cannot. He needs your money to continue his work, to make sure that his soul-saving broadcasts continue to reach as many people as possible. You can help him in this by sending your money to him now. Thus the highest Christian service is giving money to the Lord via his servant the televangelist.

MIRACLES

A theme of this chapter has been the accommodation of conservative Protestantism to the modern world. Some elements – the legitimation of wealth or the adoption of 'worldly' attitudes to sexuality – represent a coming to terms with the behavioural standards of the secular world. Others – the rationalization of the faith and its reconstruction as plans and codes in manuals, for example – represent changes at the level of the plausibility of ideas and assumptions about the nature and order of the world. I would like to return to this second type of accommodation in talking about miracles.

At first flush, the frequent claiming of miracles might seem a rejection of a key assumption of secular thinking: that things happen in the world because of other things in the world and not because of intervention by supernatural forces. But close inspection shows the extent to which, in the world of televangelism, miracles have become routinized. Most things hailed as miracles are not even surprising, let alone miraculous. No coincidence is too small to be claimed as a miracle. An unemployed man getting a job, a son giving up drinking in response to his mother's pleas, a fund-raising financial target having been met, a viewer getting promoted, house hunters finding a suitable property; all of these are hailed as miracles.

Physical healing has been down-played in the last thirty years. None of the major televangelists now practices healing on screen or makes grand claims to having healed ailments. Oral Roberts no longer stresses miraculous cures and prefers to raise funds for his medical school where more this-worldly cures will be developed. Only relative small fry such as the extravagantly toupéed Ernest Angeley still claim to heal and present the testimonies of those so helped.

Another evidence of the presence of the supernatural – speaking in tongues – has also been removed from the repertoire of televangelism's miracles. The Bakkers, Swaggart, and Robertson are all pentecostalists but they do not speak in tongues on the air, nor do they broadcast members of the audience doing so.

Finally, miracles have not only been trivialized, they have been domesticated. The moving of the Spirit is no longer mysterious; it follows sending a gift to Oral or Jim or Pat. In promoting the miraculous consequences which follow blessing the Lord, the televangelist effectively takes the uncertainty out of God's response to man. God's positive response to our actions is so far from being speculative that its certainty frequently calls forth banking metaphors: Rex Humbard offered viewers a book called *Your Key to God's Bank: How to Cash your Check for Spiritual Power, Physical Healing, Financial Success.*

CONCLUSION

Although it involves considerable simplification, a useful way of describing the evolution of one strand of American Protestantism is in terms of the rise of man. Although nowhere near the paranoid depressives they are now painted, the puritans and their Calvinist heirs were overawed by the majesty of God and the weakness and sinfulness of man. With the shift to the Arminian view of man's positive part in the process of salvation, there is a gradual increase in the supposed capacity of humanity to redeem itself. This is still not a' religion of works; that which redeems, the atonement of Christ, was a gift of grace freely given. Nonetheless, salvation is *chosen* by man. The drift to perfectionism and pentecostalism took this even further. The right religious exercises could encourage the indwelling of the Holy Spirit; humans can become holy.

What the above discussion of the ideological content of televangelism shows is that the religion one would acquire from watching most American religious broadcasting offers very little challenge to the values and practices of the modern secular world. There is a considerable stress on being 'Bible believing' but little sense that this should make one's life very different from that of other fairly conservative, lower middle-class, small-town Americans.

It should of course be remembered that most members of the audience for televangelism have other sources of religious ideas and other outlets for religious activities. As a study of CBN supporters shows, religious television is only a part (and for some a small part) of their religious lives (Hoover 1988). But it seems unlikely that the ideas conveyed in this medium are drastically at variance with the notions and practices implied in other parts of the typical viewer's religious world (although they are certainly a selection of that wider world). That the religion is being promoted on television, rather than in print or in a crusade tent, has had little obvious impact. And we know from other sources that much of what has been said above about televangelism could equally well have been said about white conservative Protestantism generally (Hunter 1983; 1986; Wilson 1968). The theme will be returned to in the final chapter but for brevity we can describe what has happened to evangelicalism and fundamentalism in the last fifty years as partial secularization. Although some distinctive religious beliefs (for example concerning the genesis and age of the earth or the status of the Bible) and some conservative socio-moral positions have been retained, much that was once constitutive of fundamentalism has been attenuated and some things which were subliminal (the therapeutic ethos, for example) have become a visible part of the package. Asceticism has disappeared as has service. Restraint has gone with the constraint of poverty. Accommodating to the values and logic of the modern world is both cause and consequence of success. It simplifies, of course, but we can see in the evolution of American conservative Protestantism the next stage in the journey from Calvinism to Arminianism to perfectionist pentecostalism to secularity.

Chapter Five

THE AUDIENCE

By and large television audiences are not terribly selective in what they watch nor do they divide radically in their preferences. Contrary to what sociologists might expect, class is not a strong predictor of viewing patterns beyond the general point that less well-educated people do more viewing. Even when one examines the audience for 'demanding' programmes, one does not find major social divisions (Barwise and Ehrenburg 1988: 26). The two sorts of broadcasting which are clear exceptions are minority language programmes and religious programmes. For a very obvious reason in the case of the former, these two types of output attract a very different response to normal television or radio programming. Instead of the 'mass' audience which shows little loyalty, there is a very small audience which consumes a lot of that product (Barwise and Ehrenburg 1988: 71).

This chapter is concerned with identifying the audience for religious television. How many people watch Oral Roberts, Jerry Farewell, and Pat Robertson? What sorts of people are they?

AUDIENCE SIZE

Consider the following media estimates for the popularity of one prime-time preacher:

> Playboy reported that 'each week as many as 30,000,000 Americans tuned in to Jerry Falwell's *Old Time Gospel Hour*'. Jimmy Breslin whittled Falwell's audience down to 25 million; the *Today Show* and Billy Moyers gave him only 20 million; and Joseph Sullivan and Anthony Lewis, of the *New*

York Times, various reporters at *Newsweek,* and the Knight-Ridder newspapers seemed finally to settle on 18 million as the appropriate estimate.

(Martin 1981: 9)

Falwell himself repeatedly claimed that his *The Old Time Gospel Hour* was watched by 25 million (Hadden and Swann 1981: 47). A setting where his influence would depend on the size of his television audience brought Falwell to a new appreciation of his popularity and at the 1980 Republican National Convention in Detroit, he told reporters that *The Old Time Gospel Hour* was seen by 50 million viewers (Hadden and Shupe 1988: 146). He was soon challenged on figures which, from his mail and income, he must have known were a very long way from the mark. He learnt to handle the potential embarrassment by joking about his inflated statistics with the distancing asides 'ministerially speaking' and 'evangelistically speaking'. Nonetheless, the preachers and their spokesmen continue to claim vague but always very large numbers for their audience size and some liberal critics, keen to mobilize against television preachers who use their air-waves to press political messages, are happy to see their wolves as very big wolves and collude in this inflation.

As one would expect, the first stage in the response to these claims was debunking and Hadden and Swann, and William Martin published reports of audience size based respectively on Arbitron and Nielsen rating data which showed the audiences to be con- siderably smaller than had been claimed. Martin concluded that the audience for the top ten religious television programmes in November 1980 was 13.8 million. Hadden and Swann estimated that 20.5 million people watched the 66 syndicated religious programmes while the top ten had an audience of 14.9 million (under 7 per cent of the population).

The televangelists were, hardly surprisingly, not impressed by this news and although their private claims were lower than their public ones, they were still markedly higher than Hadden and Swann, or Martin were prepared to allow. After much argument, the mainstream churches, the National Religious Broadcasters association, and leading televangelists agreed to jointly fund research which would determine the audience size and answer other topical questions about television evangelism (Hadden and

Frankl 1987a, 1987b). Annenberg School of Communications co-ordinated the project, part of which involved analysing Arbitron ratings data and part of which was a Gallup nationwide survey of religious television viewing habits. Unfortunately, for reasons which will be explained below, the two parts produced quite different results and little or no effort was made to reconcile or explain the differences. The Annenberg use of Arbitron data produced a final audience of 13.3 million viewers. William Fore, a mainstream church critic of televangelism, using apparently reasonable adjustment assumptions, managed to work the total figure down to between 7.2 and 9.2 million (Fore 1987: 103).[1] In contrast, the Gallup survey, which asked people if they had watched a religious TV programme in the previous month, produced 70 million viewers (approximately 32 per cent of the population).

Technical issues of audience measurement

Many of the reasons for such disagreements in estimating the size of the audience for television religious programmes are technical and will be explained in a brief description of the construction of such statistics.

Polls such as those conducted by Gallup have the innate advantage that they can only count each individual once and so do not have a problem of duplication. However, like all research based on *self-report*, they have the problem that some people may wish to appear more respectable or more cultured than they really are and give what they feel to be flattering rather than accurate answers.[2] They also have the weakness that respondents define what is a religious programme. When asked to name the programmes they watched, people may cite a film with a religious theme such as *The Ten Commandments*. Hoover reports that over 10 per cent of the responses in the Annenberg study were 'unclassifiable' and were probably not what we would think of as religious television (Hoover 1987: 141).

Because television companies can charge higher rates for advertising during popular programmes, there is a demand for information more reliable than that provided by polls. Two companies – Arbitron and Nielsen – provide a variety of indices of programme popularity. Until recently, the main sources of information were *diaries* kept by a sample of viewers. Arbitron and Nielsen select between 200 and 2,000 households in each of the 200 local television markets into which the networks divide the United States, the size of the sample depending on the size of the market. To keep costs down, samples are kept as small as is compatible with persuading the purchasers of the information that they are in some sense reliable. A household is in the sample for only a week and four separate samples are drawn for the four weeks of the 'sweep' months of November, February, May, and July (Clark and Virts 1985: 5). People in each household are asked to keep a diary of what they watch.

Data collection is designed to produce information about individual television markets (the unit preferred by advertisers) and not about the country as a whole. Each sample is constructed to be representative of its market. To produce national data – the sort used to describe the televangelism audience – the local market figures are aggregated. However valid or reliable each set of data is for its local area, the different sample sizes may, when aggregated, produce invalidity and unreliablity for the country as a whole.

On the accuracy of the diaries themselves, there are a number of obvious difficulties. People may forget to complete them at the time of viewing and later suppose they have watched their 'usual' programmes or their usual station. This may under-estimate the audience for newer independent stations (which are those used by many religious programmes). In the other direction, we might suppose that the committed viewer of religious television may well have a proselytizing interest in accurately recording support for such programmes.

Only just over half of the households initially contacted actually participate in the survey and they tend to be those which watch most television. Responses are lower among lower income and lower education families (and, as we will see below, the audience for televangelism is strong in precisely those categories). If this might lead to underestimating the televangelism audience, another characteristic of the diary method will over-estimate it: failure to complete the diary is not randomly distributed but concentrated among the young. The viewers most likely to complete the forms conscientiously are also those most likely to watch religious broadcasting.

With all these weaknesses, one may wonder why anyone uses

diaries as a basis for ratings. The explanation is that the alternatives are more expensive, have their own drawbacks, or both.
The best method for surveying viewing habits – 'telephone coin-
cidentals' – involves phoning households during the airing of the
programme one is interested in and asking who, if anybody, is
watching the television and what they are watching. Although
simple and effective, this is far too expensive for most operators
and advertisers to use often.

An alternative is to 'meter' the set. A sample of television sets
are fitted with meters which record if the set is on and what it is
tuned to. The flaw is that metering does not tell us who, if anybody,
is actually watching the set.[3]

The only initially nationwide audience estimates (as distinct
from those aggregated from local samples) are produced by
Nielsen who meter 1,700 randomly selected households. Of these
900 subscribe to cable and both broadcast and cable are metered.
Nielsen also try to compensate for the weaknesses of the meter
method by having a sample of 2,600 households, a third of whom
keep a diary during any given week. The households stay in the
sample for as long as three years.

To improve the chances of the diaries being completed at the
time of viewing, a green light on the set flashes every quarter of an
hour as a reminder to complete the forms. The meter records the
total number of hours the set is switched on. Nielsen then compare
the hours described in the diary and the hours metered and
eliminate households whose diary figures differ significantly from
the meter reading.[4]

The final technical issue which has to be discussed before the
results of the CBN/Nielsen study are outlined is the description of
the data. There are a number of different ways in which an
audience can be measured and described. One can report the
average number of sets tuned to a programme in each quarter of
an hour of the programme (but one must set some lower limit for
how long the set must be on that channel in the fifteen minute
period to avoid counting people zapping by). This 'average
audience' is the most commonly cited figure. One can report the
frequency with which a household watches a particular programme
within a given period (in the case of the CBN/Nielsen data the
period was a month). One can also add up the number of
households which have tuned in during a given period and present

a cumulative total (or 'cume'). Given that different programmes have a different pattern of appearance, for some a cume is a better representation of appeal than the average quarter-hour audience.

> *Oral Roberts and You*, for example, is a thirty-minute program, while the *700 Club* airs ninety minutes a day, five days a week, with reruns on Saturday and Sunday in some markets. In terms of average quarter-hour audiences, Oral Roberts has a much larger audience than the *700 Club* but his cumulative audience is much smaller, because the *700 Club* has fifteen times more airtime per week.
>
> (Hadden and Shupe 1988: 153)

Such differences must be borne in mind when comparing the popularity of a variety of programmes.

So what does the CBN data show? Taking the average quarter-hour audience first, the highest rated show – *Jimmy Swaggart* – was watched by 3.1 per cent of households, Schuller's *Hour of Power* was next with 2.5 per cent, then came Oral Robert's *Expect a Miracle* with 2.4 per cent, and Pat Robertson's *700 Club* with 1.7 of TV households (Clark and Virts 1985). As one would expect, the order changes when one considers monthly cumes. Robertson, whose *700 Club* is shown at least once and sometimes twice daily on CBN, moves to first place with 19.1 per cent of households. *Jimmy Swaggart* has a cume of 10.9 per cent, followed closely by Schuller's *Hour of Power* with 9 per cent. Because it was shown daily on a large number of broadcast stations, the *Jim Bakker Show* comes in fourth place with 6.8 per cent of households.

These data begin to allow us to answer the simple question of how many people consume televangelism. Using the conventional diary method, Nielsen produced the following results. The top ten programmes had a combined average quarter-hour audience of just under 8 million. The cume for a week was 27 million and for a month 68 million. But, when they used the meter and diary method and included cable, the average quarter-hour audience for the *700 Club* went from 424,000 to 1,443,000 – what Hadden and Shupe (1988: 156) gushingly call 'an amazing 340 percent increase'. For Falwell's show the audience size went from 594,000 to 1,358,000. Taking the top ten programmes, the meter and diary method produced an audience size on average 82 per cent higher than the conventional diary method.

101

On loyalty, Clark and Virts say: 'Of all those households that viewed one of these programs during the month, each household viewed on the average 4.1 episodes of one of the programs' (1985: 18). Additionally, these data do not include details of viewing on non-commercial cable networks such as PTL and Trinity or of the audience for some 50 or so less popular religious television programmes.

To summarize the gross results, Clark and Virts claim that the *700 Club* attracts an audience of around 4.4 million people a day. Jimmy Swaggart is watched by 3.6 million people per week, 2.7 million watch Robert Schuller's *Hour of Power*, and *Expect a Miracle* with Oral Roberts is seen by 2.5 million in a week. The unduplicated cume for the top ten programmes in a month is 34.1 million households. On average, according to the CBN data, 40 per cent of the 85 million TV households watched at least one segment of religious television in February 1985.

Although at first sight the CBN study appears to have produced the data to settle the arguments, this is far from the case. Fore, with some reason, accuses CBN of giving a misleading impression;

> it measured the percent of viewers who were viewing at the time the top-ten programs were on the air – periods such as early Sunday mornings when the total number of viewers is very small. The 40.2% turned out to be a percentage of only 33 million viewers.
>
> (Fore 1987: 104)

But Fore is himself a little disingenuous. It is not true that the 40.2 per cent turned out to be a 'percentage of only 33 million viewers'; 40.2 is a percentage of a very small *sample*. The question is whether one should generalize from that sample to the total number of TV households or only to the number of viewers typically attracted to *any* programming in fringe and 'deep fringe' times (about a third of the normal audience). Should 40.2 per cent of the sample be turned into a total audience of 40 million viewers (the CBN implication) or only 13.3 million (the Annenberg/Fore position)? Should one generalize at all given that the behaviour being studied is so infrequent that contamination from sampling error is a real possibility?

Furthermore, the CBN study uses a very weak measure of viewing; it counts any set which was tuned for six minutes or more. So the grand-sounding 40.2 per cent (whatever it is a percentage of) tells us only that 40.2 per cent watched six minutes or more in a month. We need to be clear that the CBN figure refers to the audience for, not a single show, but for a whole *genre* of television. And it is a genre which is well supplied. If one followed the same method for 'sports programmes' or 'crime dramas' one would get an audience penetration of nearly 100 per cent! The aggregate weekly rating figure for 'religious viewing' (whether duplicated or not) is a percentage not only of the total audience available at that slot but of all possible audiences during that week. 'Seen in that light, the figures often reported represent a miniscule percentage of total viewing opportunities by all television households' (Hoover 1987: 142). The confusion of this issue is massively compounded when people make the entirely inappropriate comparison of the total audience for any religious broadcasting and the audience for any single popular non-religious programme. The relevant comparison would be with the totals watching six or more minutes of any 'comedy' or any 'crime drama' in a month and those totals would be 'almost everybody'.

The conclusion of this tortuous discussion of technical problems must be that we are still some way from a definitive estimate of the size of the audience of religious television. This is not really surprising given that the methodology has been designed to assess gross choices within a very popular activity. It is simply not sensitive enough to tell us about the audience for a genre of limited popularity, where viewing is a relatively rare occurrence.

In the end there is little option but to agree with Hadden and Shupe that we do not know how many people watch religious television programmes beyond saying that the weekly audience is not less than 13.3 million and may well be more. The highest figure for which any good evidence is presented is around 25 million (the CBN figure for households, assuming 1.4 viewers per household) but it requires a very weak measure of viewing. If one picks the number 15 million (for no better reason than that it is easy to remember) this is sizeable, but only some 8 per cent of the total viewing population.

RELATIVE POPULARITY

Although there are enormous difficulties in using ratings to produce an estimate of the total audience size and in comparing religious and secular television, there are fewer problems in using them as an index of relative popularity of religious broadcasters. The following Arbitron figures for broadcast programmes are crude but, remembering to allow for the different lengths and patterns of airing of the programmes, they are still useful for rough comparisons of popularity. Table 2 is a good guide to standing in 1980.

Table 2 Arbitron ratings (in millions): top fourteen shows in February 1980

Oral Roberts and You	2.72
Rex Humbard	2.41
Hour of Power (Schuller)	2.07
Jimmy Swaggart	1.99
The Day of Discovery (De Haan)	1.52
The Old Time Gospel Hour (Falwell)	1.45
Gospel Singing Jubilee	.94
Davey and Goliath	.68
The PTL Club (Bakker)	.67
Insight	.48
James Robison	.46
700 Club	.38
Ernest Angeley	.32
Kenneth Copeland	.24

Source: Hadden and Swann 1981: 51

Table 3 Nielsen ratings (in millions): top eleven shows in November 1986

Hour of Power (Schuller)	1.91
Jimmy Swaggart	1.56
Oral Roberts	1.22
The World Tomorrow (Armstrong)[5]	.84
The Day of Discovery (De Haan)	.66
The Old Time Gospel Hour	.66
Kenneth Copeland	.55
Dr James Kennedy	.54
700 Club	.46
A Study in the Word (Swaggart)	.39
Jim Bakker	.33

Source: Fore 1987: 84

It is worth noting that three of the top ten are not televangelist programmes. *Gospel Singing Jubilee* is what it sounds like, *Davey and Goliath* is a children's programme produced by the Lutheran Church of America, and *Insight* is a drama show produced by the Roman Catholic Paulist Fathers. As Table 3 shows, by November 1986, the ranking had changed, most spectacularly with the retirement of Rex Humbard and the slipping of Oral Roberts.

A further point, which is important for a later discussion of potential political power, is that the most publicly political preachers were a long way from being the most popular. Robert Schuller, who conspicuously maintained his distance from the new Christian right, was by far and away the most popular with his 'possibility thinking' and the 'prosperity theology' of Oral Roberts, for all his problems in re-launching a new format to fight off the challenge from Swaggart, remained far more popular than, for example, Jerry Falwell's politicized fundamentalism.

WATCHING TELEVISION

Given that audience size is often taken as an index of influence, a number of obvious but important points should be made about interpreting ratings. The first is that one should not automatically take audience size as an indication of active support for the televangelism message. Audience and programme are not immediately linked by a *demand* relationship. A proportion of the American population will watch whatever is on the television set. Those programmes which are aired most often must attract sufficient funds to cover their greater costs but they acquire a good part of their increased audience simply by virtue of being on the air. That is, audience size is in part a supply-side phenomenon.

A second obvious point is that not all the television sets which are switched on are being watched and not all of those 'watching' are concentrating. That someone is sitting in front of a set does not mean that the programmes being aired are given any serious attention. People knit, eat, converse, clean, cook, sleep, and even make love while the television illuminates one corner of the room. Regardless of what size of audience we agree to impute to Falwell or Roberts, we should not assume that such numbers represent attentive viewers.

Finally, it would be a mistake to suppose that, because most religious television has a clear ideological purpose, all or most of its audience agree entirely with even their favourite televangelists. Bourgault's study of regular *PTL Club* viewers (1985) and Hoover's study of *700 Club* 'partners' (1988) show that the audience is selective and critical. They watch these programmes because they like some, perhaps many, of their features but they are quite willing and able to criticize things in the shows they do not like. Indeed, some of Bourgault's *PTL Club* regulars seemed to use the show to clarify those elements of their own beliefs which most obviously clashed with the views of the Bakkers. In assessing the likely impact of televangelism, it is important to remember that some members of the audience watch because they are generally interested in religion or in country gospel music, or because they like the celebrity interviews. Not all viewers are true believers.

IS THE AUDIENCE GROWING?

Although we are still a long way from a reliable estimate of the size of the television evangelism audience, we can ask whether it is growing. We certainly know that the budgets of televangelistic organizations have expanded massively. Almost everyone who writes about televangelism assumes that the audience has mushroomed and hence is a cause for either concern or rejoicing. The conventional wisdom is that popularity has been increasing steadily since the late 1950s with the sharpest growth in the last decade. Hadden and Shupe (1988: 156) suggest even more recent growth when they compare the 1987 Gallup survey results of 25 per cent having watched some religious programme in the previous week with the 1983 figure for the same question of 18 per cent.[6]

That the audience for religious broadcasting has grown in absolute terms is obviously true, if only because the number of television sets have increased steadily since the 1950s as has the amount of television of any sort that is watched. However, supporters and critics alike usually mean something more with their claims of increasing popularity. Hadden and Shupe, for example, construct their whole book around the assumption that televangelism and the culture it represents is becoming more powerful because it is relatively, as well as absolutely, more popular; that is, it is displacing other forms of programming because the beliefs and values which it expresses are displacing other sorts of beliefs and values. For Hadden and Shupe, the rise of televangelism is a change which needs explaining and which is of tremendous significance for the future.

There is undoubtedly something in such a notion but we should be careful. In the first place we have no data for previous periods which is comparable to the above in accuracy and hence we cannot establish the extent of recent growth. The only good data from the early days of religious broadcasting is from the Parker *et al.* survey of New Haven in 1952 and that showed that, 'In spite of the shortage of religious programs available, 57 per cent of all households with television sets watched at least one religious program regularly' (1955: 200).

If this figure is at all reliable[7] then the change from the immediate post-war period to now could be described as one of relative *decline* in the audience for religious television. In 1978 71 per cent of a sample said they watched absolutely no religious television (Gaddy 1984). Of course other things have changed. Almost all Americans now have televisions but that would mean an expansion, not contraction, of that part of the potential audience most likely to watch religion on television as sets became more common among the lower classes and in the south, where conservative religion is more common. Total church membership has declined only slightly since the 1950s so that cannot explain the decline.

WHO WATCHES RELIGIOUS TELEVANGELISM?

A little easier to answer than the 'how many' question is 'who'. While television audiences are not usually especially selective, people who are attracted to religious broadcasting do seem to differ markedly from any random collection of 'couch potatoes' in the following respects.

Gender

The first demographic characteristic in which the religious broadcast audience differs from the American TV audience at large is gender. In a survey of white Americans in Dallas-Fort Worth suburbs, Stacey and Shupe (1982) found a significant link between gender and support for televangelism: 38 per cent of women but only 27.9 per cent of men scored above the median on their index of 'media religiosity'. In Buddenbaum's Indianapolis survey of televangelism, women were twice as likely as men to say that they 'almost always watched' and 44 per cent of women but 68 per cent of men said they almost never watched (Buddenbaum 1981: 269; see also Mobley 1984). Hadden and Swann report some Arbitron data which makes the same point even more strongly: for the top ten programmes, the percentage of watchers who are women ranges from a low of 60 per cent for *Gospel Singing Jubilee* to a high of 73 per cent for the *PTL Club* (1981: 61-2).

The CBN/Nielsen data confirm the picture while adding some detail. The gender imbalance varies from programme to programme. The audience for the *700 Club* was 59 per cent female and 22 per cent male (the rest were children). For *Jimmy Swaggart* it divided 43 and 37 per cent. Falwell's *The Old Time Gospel Hour* attracted a high proportion of children (30 per cent) and the adults divided 43 per cent women and 25 per cent men.

These gender variations are amplifications of the differences already present in the conservative Protestant milieu. Men and women are almost balanced in the total population (48 to 52 per cent) but among 'evangelicals' men are rarer than women: 40 as against 60 per cent (Hunter 1983: 51). That the difference in the audience for television religion is greater is almost certainly explained by the imbalance in television watching; women watch significantly more television, especially day-time television, than do men.

Age

The religious broadcasting audience has a distinct age profile. In the Dallas-Fort Worth sample 38.8 per cent of the over-35 year olds but only 26.4 per cent among those younger than 35 scored above the median for watching 'holy roller' shows. Again Hadden and Swann's Arbitron data makes the same point more forcefully. In that sample, 'all the syndicated programs have audiences of which two-thirds to three-quarters are fifty years of age or over' (1981: 61). We know that evangelical Protestants tend to be older than average: a mean of 48.4 against a mean of 43.9 (Hunter 1983: 51).[8]

Secondly, old people are more likely to suffer from infirmities and to have trouble in travelling to church. One of televangelism's self-advertised virtues is that it provides religious offices for 'shut-ins'. A third point, which critics of televangelism would advertise, is that the old are often irredeemably ill. As one ages the likelihood of degenerative and incurable illness increases. One of the services offered by many televangelists (early Oral Roberts and Pat Robertson and now Kenneth Copeland explicitly; Robert Schuller implicitly) is the cure of the body. The old, because they are immobile or ill, are thus in the greatest need of what televangelism offers and, because they are theologically conservative, most likely to find it plausible.

One attempt to untangle the link with age and church attendance gives some idea of how complex are such relationships. Tamney and Johnson's (1984) study of the religious television viewing habits of a sample of residents of Muncie, Indiana (the 'Middletown' of the Lynds' research) suggests that the relationship between age, religiosity, and viewing religious television itself changes with age. Among the young, those who did not attend church also did not watch religious television. Among the old, those who did not attend church did watch religious television. For both age groups, frequent church attenders were also heavy religious television watchers but this relationship is stronger for the older group. For the old, the two principles cancel out: both those who do not go to church and those who do go to church watch religious television. Tamney and Johnson conclude that old people watch more religious television than young people because (a) they have greater trouble attending church and (b) because they are more involved in all religious activities (1984: 311).

Education and occupation

The consumers of televangelism are less well-educated than average. In the Dallas-Fort Worth sample, those who consumed most religious broadcasting were also those with least formal education. Half of those with less than high school education were above the median in their religious television watching while only 28.2 per cent of college graduates were keen consumers (Stacey and Shupe 1982: 296). In Buddenbaum's Indianapolis sample, 34 per cent of those with only elementary school education, 15 per cent of high school graduates, and only 8 per cent of college graduates said they 'almost always' watched (see also Gaddy and Pritchard 1985).

Not surprisingly, the socio-economic status of the televangelism audience, as measured by occupation, both reflects and amplifies the education bias. Almost a third of manual workers (30.4 per cent) and a quarter of housewives and 'unclassifiables' (25.3 per cent) but only 5.3 per cent of professionals in the Indianapolis group frequently watched religious television.

Region

In a country as large and with as varied a culture as the United States, regional variations are always liable to be interesting. Not surprising given its theological complexion, the electronic church is still a largely southern phenomenon. If we divide the United States into the four regions of east, midwest, south, and west, while the eastern region of the United States contains almost a quarter of the population, the electronic churches draw only 11 per cent of their audience from that part of America. Over half of Jimmy Swaggart's viewers live in the south. The midwest (28.3 per cent) is his second most fertile region. The western states (14.2 per cent) and the east (11.5) are nowhere near as taken with his pentecostal preaching (Hadden and Swann 1981: 60). Of all the major televangelists, only Robert Schuller, the one preacher who is a minister of a mainstream denomination (the Reformed Church) and whose programmes are furthest from conservative evangelicalism or fundamentalism, is equally popular in the east, the midwest, and the south.

POLARIZATION

It is worth noting that the quality of appealing disproportionately to some social groups is relatively new. The 1952 New Haven study went to immense pains (far more than modern surveys would) to discover differences between the viewers and non-viewers of religious broadcasting and concluded:

Insofar as these data can be said to measure the taste for religious programs, therefore, it is important to note that this taste has a marked universality. Whether we divide our sample by social class, religious affiliation, church attendance, occupation, age of adults, education, income or type of

110

household, we find an audience for religious radio and television representing, in the great majority of cases, over half of any given group.

(Parker *et al.* 1955: 205)

Two small studies in the early 1960s (Dennis 1962; Robinson 1964) showed the emergence of the sort of pattern which Gaddy and Pritchard neatly describe when they say: 'watching religious television is positively related to living in a small town ... and in the south, having a lower income, having had less education, being unemployed or retired' (1985: 127).[9]

Dennis and Robinson explain polarization as a consequence of the declining novelty of television. As people became more blasé about TV they became more selective in their viewing and different sorts of people selected different things. This is possible but unlikely, given what we know about the lack of selectivity (Barwise and Ehrenburg 1988: 26). A more plausible explanation is already suggested in the detail of the New Haven study. When one moves from religious broadcasting as a whole to the audience for specific programmes one does find some hint of the patterns which later emerged. Billy Graham's *Hour of Decision* and Charles E. Fuller's *Old Fashioned Revival Hour* appealed especially to older working-class Protestants, while the more liberal *National Radio Pulpit* of Methodist pastor Ralph W. Sockman drew an audience of 'church members of high educational level' (Parker *et al.* 1955: 220). Nearly a quarter of the television audience was made up of viewers of Bishop Sheen's commercially sponsored show. What appears to have happened is that, as the programmes of the mainstream denominations and ecumenical councils have been squeezed out by the product of the independent 'holy roller' televangelists, so the general population's reponse to religious broadcasting has become more polarized. Certain social groups are attracted to it and consume considerable amounts of it while others find the programmes repellent. Sheen was sufficiently popular for his talks to be the subject of general and sympathetic discussion at work the next day; it is difficult to imagine any of the present major broadcasters being received in that way.

The most obvious reason why none of the televangelists of the 1980s can hope to attain the market penetration of Sheen is that, despite the attenuation of distinctive doctrine I described in the previous chapter, they more narrowly represent a particular theological position. The theology of the prime-time preachers is reflected in the religious disposition of their audiences. By far the best predictor of religious television viewing habits is religious conservativism. Taking denominational affiliation, the largest groups of viewers are independent fundamentalist Baptists (21 per cent). Second are Southern Baptists (19 per cent). A group describing themselves as 'charismatic Christians' is third at 10.5 per cent, followed closely by Catholics (10 per cent), United Methodists (8.3 per cent), and other Methodists (7.1 per cent). Mainstream Presbyterians, Lutherans, Disciples of Christ, United Church of Christ members, and Episcopalians each make up less than 2 per cent of the audience.

> Heavy viewers are much more likely than nonviewers to read the Bible, pray frequently, take the Bible literally, believe 'that Jesus Christ will return to earth someday', report having been 'born again', believe in miracles and favor 'speaking in tongues'.
>
> (Fore 1984: 711)

Thus, not only is the audience drawn disproportionately from particularly conservative Protestant traditions but, within any denomination, it is the most conservative members who will be the most frequent watchers (see also Buddenbaum 1981; Stacey and Shupe 1982; Gaddy and Pritchard 1985).[10]

CONCLUSION

One of the main reasons for such new programming styles as those used by Robertson's *700 Club* was to attract a wider, less religiously homogeneous audience. The aim was to break out of the Sunday morning ghetto and out of providing religious programmes for religious people. The new confidence of televangelists in the last decade stemmed in part from the belief that they were reaching a more representative audience. Clark and Virts do their best to find evidence that the new formats and scheduling have had the desired effect but the furthest they can go in that direction is to point out that, for women:

the spread between the two age groups [divided at age 55] is more nearly equal for 'The 700 Club' (55% to 45%) and 'The Old Time Gospel Hour' (56% to 44%) than for the other programs where there is a two or three to one ratio in favour of older women.

(Clark and Virts 1985: 21)

But one of the two shows with the most representative profile is Falwell's *The Old Time Gospel Hour* which, in broadcasting a church service, has one of the most conservative formats of all the religious television programmes. Hoover, drawing on the extensive data of the Annenberg study, concludes that contemporary religious television still draws on the same narrow audience:

in spite of their much-touted new formats, technological sophistication, and prominence in the 'secular' world, the audience for religious television today is ... older, less educated, more rural, and more conventionally religious than its non-religious-viewing cohort. There is little reason to believe that many outside of the traditional audience are actually viewing.

(Hoover 1988: 69)

And most of the programmes remain anchored in the ghetto time slots despite the arrival of Christian networks providing all-day programming. On CBN there is three hours of religion on Sunday morning – James Kennedy, Kenneth Copeland, and Jimmy Swaggart – and then it is repeats of *Alias Smith and Jones* and *Wagon Train*.

Chapter Six

THE IMPACT OF
TELEVANGELISM

The description of the demographic characteristics of the televangelism audience presented in the previous chapter is a good
place to start an analysis of the role of paid-time religious
broadcasting but it is only a start. We need to consider what people
do with such programmes and what such programmes do with
people. Chapter Eight will consider the political impact of televangelism; here I want to look at the extent to which it succeeds in
its manifest or primary purpose of 'spreading the gospel'. In order
to establish a context which will help explain the impact of
televangelism, I will look briefly at the religious impact of mass
revivalism and at the influence of television generally before
evaluating the combination of the two elements in religious
broadcasting.

MASS EVANGELISM

While the great urban revivalists – Moody, Torrey, Sunday, and
Graham – preached to very large numbers of people, they did very
little to expand Christendom by converting the ungodly. In an
attempt to suggest otherwise, Horatio Bonar, a leading Scottish
Presbyterian evangelical, said of Moody's campaigns in Edinburgh
in 1873:

> The spiritual influence (contagion some call it) has struck
> into every rank and circle. . . . This movement has not only
> reached the great houses of Moray Place and the west end of
> town but has penetrated to the lowest depths of iniquity in
> the Cowgate, Canongate and Grassmarket.
>
> (Quoted in McLoughlin 1959: 200)

In an attempt to reach the denizens of the 'lowest depths of iniquity', Moody held a meeting for men only at the Corn Exchange, near the slums of Grassmarket. At the end of a rally attended by 6,000 people, Moody asked those who wished further conversation with him about their souls to follow him to the Free Church Assembly Hall. According to Bonar: 'Six hundred of the Grassmarket men streamed up from the Corn Exchange and into the Assembly Hall and falling on their knees gave themselves to God'.

Another minister who assisted at the meetings challenged Bonar:

> What a pity that Christians should exaggerate like that and give the enemy cause to ask incredulously 'Where were your 600 Corn Exchange converts when the converts' farewell meeting was held?' . . . A similar band of men, 400 strong, came up from the Corn Exchange on a subsequent Sunday evening, and filled the body of the Assembly Hall; and to an outsider and onlooker they would have appeared to be 400 anxious inquirers, but on being tested at the close (as was done) they were found to be mostly Christian men – many of them helpers in the work; and it turned out that there was not a score of anxious souls amongst them.
>
> (Quoted in McLoughlin 1959: 205)

So little were 'ranks and circles' outside those who were regular church members affected by what was a tremendously popular and well-attended series of meetings that even ministers sympathetic to the cause of urban revivalism later recorded that the crusade had made very little or absolutely no difference to their membership. Bonar himself three months after the meetings admitted: 'This work has been not so much among the profane and godless as among the children of godly parents' (quoted in McLoughlin 1959: 206).

Exactly the same could be said about the evangelistic efforts of Billy Sunday at the start of this century or of the preaching of Billy Graham in the 1950s and 1960s. Billy Sunday made extravagant use of statistics to demonstrate the importance of his work but could only make such claims because he was extremely inclusive in his appeal at the close of his meetings. Because he asked those 'who stood with' him or some similarly general formulation to show it by coming to the front of the tent, he could give the impression of having made large numbers of converts when most of those who stepped forward to shake his hand were already converted Christians.

The Billy Graham organization uses the much narrower formula of asking those who can 'make a decision for Christ' or who 'want to accept Jesus into their hearts' to come forward and it recognizes that over 60 per cent of the 'decisions for Christ' which it records are made by people who are already church members. Researchers who interviewed those who signed decision cards at a rally in Greensboro, North Carolina, concluded that 'Every "convert" interviewed had previously had connections of some sort with the churches' (McLoughlin 1959: 516).

One might explain the apparent failure of Moody in Scotland or Graham in North Carolina to affect the unregenerate by noting that church membership was high in nineteenth-century Scotland or the post-war Carolinas; with very few people outside the churches, any method of trying to contact them would appear to be unsuccessful. The same explanation would not work for England in the mid-1950s.

A great deal of publicity attended Graham's 1954 rallies in London. The London *Evening News* tried to assess the impact of the crusade by interviewing ministers who had received decision cards from the Billy Graham Evangelistic Association about the subsequent careers of their new contacts. Of 336 decision card signers, 226 had been members or regular attenders of the church before the crusade. Of the remaining 110, only 35 were still attending the churches eight months after the crusade. The staunchly evangelical *British Weekly*, convinced that this assessment was misleading or malicious, commissioned its own survey using a larger sample of churches; the results were only slightly more impressive.

Many other studies of Graham crusades have come to the same conclusion (Clelland *et al.* 1974; Ward 1980). For example, of two 1957 New York samples of deciders, 63 per cent and 87 per cent were regular churchgoers at the time of decision (Whitam 1968).

In addition to the survey and follow-up types of research, there is the interesting study of Altheide and Johnson (1977) who arranged for planted 'inquirers' to go forward at the end of Graham crusade meetings and present themselves to a counsellor.

After having twelve individuals go forward, they had the plants go forward in pairs.

> This second approach required one of the researchers to bring his 'friend' to the altar call. The first would tell the counsellor that he has already 'accepted Jesus Christ into his life' and that his friend was on the verge of doing so as well.
> (Altheide and Johnson 1977: 327)

Counsellors, in addition to counselling, perform the bureaucratic task of ticking one of three boxes on a decision card: (1) Acceptance of Christ as Savior and Lord; (2) Assurance of Salvation; or (3) Rededication. The cards form the basis for the statistical claims which the Billy Graham Evangelistic Association later makes about its crusades. Altheide and Johnson found that, despite the researchers' best efforts to present accounts which should have led to them being classified as (2) or (3), all of them were ticked as (1). That is, irrespective of what biography was presented to them, the counsellors recorded all inquirers as 'converts'. One is back to the Sunday position where such a flexible notion of conversion is used, and there is such a premium on showing the enterprise a success that it is enough for a member of the audience to show any interest for him or her to be scored and publicized as a 'convert'. From all that we now know it is clear that mass evangelism is not responsible for the conversion of significant numbers of the heathen. Its services are consumed almost entirely by committed church activists. What is presented as conversion is actually much closer to the first communion or confirmation service of other Christian traditions (Ward 1980; Bruce 1984b). Young people who have been thoroughly socialized into evangelicalism use the revival event as an opportunity to signal to the world their personal commitment to what is literally 'the faith of their fathers'.

THE IMPACT OF TELEVISION

The power of television is a curious phenomenon. Most people are convinced that the medium is extremely powerful and many worry that showing violence, for example, on the small screen will cause people to be more violent. But when asked if watching violence on television makes them more violent, such people always deny that it has an effect on *them*. It is always someone else who is supposedly

117

moved in this manner. We seem torn between our own self-knowledge that television has little effect and the plausible supposition that anything which people watch that much must be doing something.

There are immense difficulties in thinking critically about media effects. Early media researchers supposed three sorts of effect – cognitive, affective, and behavioural – and supposed a temporal sequence. First knowledge and opinions change, then feelings, and finally behaviour changes. Some idea why such a simple schema was soon abandoned is given by McQuail's listing of six possible effects: the media might produce the major change it intends; produce some unintended major change; stimulate a minor change; facilitate some change; reinforce what already exists; or prevent some change that would otherwise have occurred (McQuail 1983: 170-92). When one adds the possibility that any effects may be long-term and cumulative, one can appreciate the difficulty of even conceptualizing what is to be studied.

There are also considerable practical difficulties in constructing measures. There are so many causes of any individual's actions that it is unrealistic to suppose we can devise ways of isolating what part in any change in the actions of large numbers of people may be due to stimuli from one medium, especially when that medium conveys a very large array of different sorts of 'products' and when single products may be presented in so many different media. The problem can be simplified by creating laboratory experiments but they only tell us how people appear to respond to television stimuli in artificially simple laboratory settings and there is no warrant for generalizing from such research to the real world. Furthermore, such experiments do not produce consistent results, which probably reflects the absence of discrete effects rather than poor research design.

In so far as there is a consensus among researchers about the effect of television, it involves the following. First, television does not have a strong independent causal effect.[1] Like all mass media, it is too easily ignored, talked over, or switched off to transform people's attitudes and beliefs. People perceive *selectively*. They see and hear those things which tend to confirm their present world-view; they pass over or filter out information which does not have its assigned place in their mental cupboards. Consequently, the main impact of television is *confirmatory*. If it presents images

118

which fit with what people already believe, it bolsters those views; if what it presents clashes, it is ignored or explained away.

Second, and following from that, television messages only influence the sympathetic viewer. Only people who are already disposed to see the world or some issue in a particular light respond positively to attempts to influence them in that direction.

Third, what little behavioural change effect television messages do have, they have only if the new idea is reinforced by some opportunity to act out the new belief, value, or attitude.

However, the research consensus changes a little if one moves from considering specific stimuli (such as a campaign) or specific responses (such as increased aggression) to thinking about the long-term cumulative effects of television. Harold Laswell, a pioneer of mass media research, accepted that members of the audience might have powerful resistance to particular media appeals but nonetheless thought them to have considerable long-term effects (see also Seymour-Ure 1974). Contemporary researchers stress the artificiality of the 'mythic' world presented by American television (Gerbner *et al.* 1980). In the TV world half to two-thirds of the important roles are played by male, unmarried, middle-class Americans in the prime of life. It must be stressed there is no evidence that this misleading selection of images *causes* anything; the concern of liberals is based on the intuitive feeling that, with so much of it being consumed for so long, it ought to have some impact. But we are back to the violence problem. It is always some other group of people, not us, who are fooled by this and just as Hitler, Stalin, and Genghis Khan managed their atrocities without the benefit of television (Barwise and Ehrenburg 1988: 139) so male domination precedes television's replication of it.

DOES ADVERTISING WORK?

An obvious parallel for the ideological campaign is commercial advertising and the efficacy of the selling campaign has been extensively considered. Hostility to its work has left the advertising industry in the awkward position of telling its employers that it is very persuasive while assuring its critics that it cannot lead people astray. Not just when defending its campaigns on behalf of such now-unpopular products as tobacco and alcohol, the industry argues that it has little impact beyond stimulating interest in new products and in 'defensive propaganda' by brand-name producers against each other (Leiss, Kline, and Jhally 1986: 39). Critics such as Packard, who stated his thesis in the title of his best-known work, *The Hidden Persuaders: An Introduction to the Techniques of Mass Persuasion Through the Unconscious*, believe that advertising agencies have the power to fool people into buying things they do not want or need. He actually had little or no evidence for this claim. A more measured study of the same period was ironically and unsuspectingly self-refuting. As his centre-piece case study in the course of a long presentation about the value for industry of advertising, Meyer (1958) focuses on the planning and work that went into the campaign to promote the Ford Edsel, the disaster of a car which nearly bankrupted the Ford motor company. Unfortunately Meyer finished his book before the fate of the Edsel had become clear enough to undermine his theme. A recent survey of research on advertising concludes:

> We regard advertising as a weak influence on people's attitudes and behavior rather than as strongly persuasive. It can help to create awareness and interest in a new brand, possibly help to lead to a first or trial purchase, and (especially for established brands) reawaken awareness and help to reinforce feelings of satisfaction after use.
>
> (Barwise and Ehrenburg 1988: 173)

Particular attention has been given to political advertising. In theory one has a neater problem: the extent to which people change their voting intentions as a result of a campaign. The problem is that measures of exposure to commercials are often suspect because (a) most people cannot recall with confidence how many commercials they have seen and (b) the number is usually in the narrow range of 3 to 5. When there is a high chance that the people who think they were exposed to 3 were really exposed to 4, it is very difficult to talk confidently about the cumulative effects of repeated exposure.

The relationships are weak but Atkin and Heald concluded from a study of advertising in a congressional election that:

> a well-designed and well-financed political advertising campaign in the broadcast media can serve to (1) increase

the electorate's level of knowledge about the candidate and his featured issue positions, (2) elevate emphasized issues and attributes higher on the voters' agenda of decisional criteria, (3) stimulate the electorate's interest in the campaign, produce more positive affect toward the candidate as a person, and (5) intensify polarization of evaluations.

(Atkin and Heald 1976: 228)

These effects suggest that political advertising is moderately worthwhile. Even if no Democrat is made Republican by watching the Republican's slots, the ability to set an agenda may be useful. Most candidates look good on some things and weak on others. It is in each candidate's interest to have the election focus on those points of his platform which are most popular. A candidate for an incumbent party in a weak economy would rather voters thought about foreign policy or socio-moral issues than about taxes, inflation, and unemployment. It is certainly worth considering if religious broadcasting has a similar ability to influence a public agenda.

To summarize, the conclusion of most researchers is that the mass media in general, and television in particular, are not very good at promoting deliberate change. In so far as television is thought to be an agent for change as well as an expression of it, its power is held to lie in the long-term consequences of a repetitious endorsement of certain values or patterns of behaviour. It is so easy to perceive selectively or to tune out unwelcome information that the active promotion of a particular ideology – propaganda, if you like – is largely pointless. If that seems over-stated consider the enormous sustained effort that Marxist governments have put into making their peoples into loyal Marxists – and the success they have had! There are considerable doubts about the impact of advertisements for consumer goods or services about which people do not have strong feelings. When the product being offered is something which most viewers will already have a view about, it seems sensible to conclude with Katz that: 'More than the mass media are able to convert, they reinforce ... intentions and the basic loyalties underlying them' (Katz 1971: 308). As a study of the politicizing role of television summarized: 'The nearly universal conclusion of media research is that mass communication generally has a reinforcing effect. Each program selects its audience and

121

consequently reinforces opinions and interests rather than changes or creates them' (Johnson 1973: 474).

THE RELIGIOUS IMPACT OF TELEVANGELISM

Has television evangelism been any more successful in reaching and influencing the heathen than its urban revival forbear? Has it been any more influential than other sorts of television programme? Does it sell its product more successfully than secular advertising sells its? All three questions must be answered in the negative. The same circular pattern of the churches putting on events which are attended only by the churched obtains here. The most obvious shared characteristic of viewers of televangelism is that they do not need it: they are already Christians. The figures vary slightly from one study to another but the conclusion of Stacey and Shupe's Dallas study can stand for them all: '[televangelism] preaches to the converted who are already predisposed or self-selected, to seek out its message. These are persons who are members of fundamentalist congregations and/or persons with highly orthodox religious beliefs' (1982: 299).

Although not terribly likely, it could be that they had achieved this condition with the help of television: the apparent circularity of the enterprise could represent its very success. To eliminate that possibility we must discover how and where the viewers who are born again Christians came into that status. Hoover's study of a large number of *700 Club* partners suggests that, even taking a broad view of conversion, very few were converted as a result of their watching the programme. Furthermore, a large number of studies of conservative Protestant conversion experiences in a variety of contexts repeatedly show that most evangelicals are evangelicals because they were socialized into that faith by their parents (Bruce 1984b: Ch. 5). The most significant parts of early religious experience concern *personal* relationships. Very few evangelicals attribute their conversion to mass media and (importantly for the theory of personal influence I will advance shortly) when they do, the media is almost always itself 'mediated' by a personal contact. In the rare cases of people who claim to have been converted through a radio or television programme (and they are rare), one usually finds that the convert was coaxed into listening by a friend who was already a believer and who was present at the time, adding their own reinforcements to the message coming through the mass medium (Gerlach and Hine 1968).

This makes it very likely that the large part of the televangelism audience which describes itself as 'born again' and church-going is these things independent of watching religious television. In fact, despite justifying the expense of television evangelism by its supposed ability to reach the unchurched, televangelists themselves normally assume that their viewers are already believers. In their sermons, they take it for granted that their viewers accept the authority of the scriptures, believe in miracles, believe in the power of prayer, and have no problem believing that the devil is responsible for personal problems. Although at the close of most sermons, preachers explicitly turn to the unsaved, for most of the time they use inclusive language when talking to their television audience; 'we' is used a lot.

The tension between the avowed purpose of televangelism and the assumption that the audience is already saved will be explored shortly but first I want to explain why televangelism is no more successful in saving souls than the mass evangelism it has largely superseded.

PERSONAL INFLUENCE

If we brutally summarize the evidence into the proposition that televangelism fails in its manifest purpose, should we have expected anything different? I will argue that the failure of religious broadcasting to have any major impact on the heathen is entirely predictable given what is known about patterns of influence in a variety of other fields. There is not the space here to elaborate a full blown theory of why people change from seeing the world in one way to seeing it in another but I will briefly review what is known about the diffusion of innovations and recent work on religious conversions and suggest some simple principles of influence which make sense of both the impact and the strategies of the televangelists.

In so far as they thought about these things, the first students of the impact of mass media worked with an atomistic 'mass society' model of the relationship between media as the sources of message and individuals as the recipients. The media had their effect (in so far as they had any) through the direct stimuli on every individual 'receiver'. As Katz puts it in discussing early studies of campaigns:

> [society] was conceived of as aggregates of age, sex, social class and the like, but little thought was given to the relationships implied thereby or to more informal relationships. The point is not that the student of mass communication was unaware that members of the audience have families and friends but that he did not believe that they might affect the outcome of the campaign; informal interpersonal relationships, thus, were considered irrelevant to the institutions of modern society.
>
> (Katz 1960: 436)

In their study of the impact of media on the 1940 presidential election, Lazarsfeld *et al.* found that, instead of the media having a direct impact, ideas flowed in a 'two-step' pattern 'from radio and print to the opinion leaders and from them to the less active section of the population' (1948: 151). Rather than a passive audience, influenced by the media as is appropriate for their position and interests (defined by such categories as race, sex, class, and education), one had a much more realistic image of people in relationships, some of whom deferred to others and looked to others for a lead in thinking about particular topics.

Quite independent of this change in the approach of media effect studies, rural sociologists had been coming to some related conclusions in their research on the speed and pattern of the diffusion of technical innovations. They were interested in trying to work out what sorts of considerations affected the speed with which different sorts of farmers would adopt an innovation; in the best known studies, it was a new hybrid variety of seed corn. Responding to this body of research Katz and his associates studied the pattern of the spread of physicians' use of a new drug. The sociologically interesting results of the considerable body of work which followed can be briefly summarized as follows:

1. Even in the case of apparently incontrovertibly superior innovations, simply knowing about the new product did not induce adoption.

2. Personal experimentation was crucial. As Ryan and Gross said of their farmers: 'however clearly the advantages of

hybrid corn had been demonstrated by community experience, most farmers insisted upon personal experimentation before they would adopt the innovation completely' (quoted in Rogers 1962: 85).

3. If the adoption of an innovation is divided into a five-stage process of awareness, interest, evaluation, trial, and adoption, sources of information differ in their influence at various stages; for example, 'impersonal information sources are most important at the awareness stage, and personal sources are most important at the evaluation stage in the adoption process' (Rogers 1962: 99).

There is one major difference between technical and ideological innovations. Generally the technical innovations studied have been obviously worthwhile. An objective measure of yield can be agreed and all interested parties could measure the yields of different sorts of seeds. Although there might be minor quibbles about other aspects of technique or soil fertility, it should be relatively easy to determine whether the new corn is or is not more productive than the old. This is usually not the case with ideological innovations. We cannot in this life know if we must be born again to enter the kingdom of heaven. Even more mundane promises – getting right with Jesus will improve your marriage – are hardly susceptible to objective or inter-subjective evaluation when what counts as 'improving your marriage' is so clearly a matter of social construction – of how one feels about it.

However, this difference actually increases the relevance of the diffusion of innovation research. It might be possible to say with regard to some technical innovation that social relationships and personal influence were, in the long run, unimportant. Finally even the most obdurate stick-in-the-mud would have agreed that the yield was higher with the new corn and would have adopted it. The same cannot be said of a new religion or a new politics. Here belief, rather than knowledge, is the key.[2] Because there is no way to 'test' the suggested innovation, the persuasiveness of the source of information is a vital element in how one feels about, in what one thinks about, the new ideas. When the message cannot itself be tested, *the plausibility of the medium is the plausibility of the message.*

Although conversion to a new religious perspective can very obviously be viewed as an innovation, almost no student of religious conversion has noticed the parallel with the work of Katz and his students. None the less, the development of the research traditions has been remarkably similar. Before the 1960s, religious conversions and the spread of new religions were often explained in terms of the social locations, structural characteristics, and material interests of individuals. Whether or not a new religion was 'adopted' was seen as a matter of the fit between the new product and the pre-existing 'needs' (which could be seen either as rational responses or as anxious reactions to social strains) of an aggregate of individuals. Little thought was given to communication or to explaining why the number of people who converted to a new religion was always incomparably smaller than the total number of people possessing the social characteristics which were offered as explaining susceptibility to that sort of thing.

Out of interactionist studies of new religious movements came a revived interest in the role which personal relationships play in making a new religious perspective more or less plausible. John Lofland's study of an early Moonie group on the west coast was especially influential (Lofland and Stark 1965; Lofland 1966). He argued that conversion to what he called 'the Divine Precepts' was most likely when there was a pre-existing friendship or kinship bond. When such a bond did not exist then first the semblance and then the reality had to be created before the ideological message could be successfully transmitted.

Although, like the two-step flow of communication idea, Lofland's observations may now seem banal, they were a useful corrective to a discipline famous for pursuing the appearance of science at the price of missing the obvious. In discussing the role of opinion leaders, Katz and Lazarsfeld separated the relay from the reinforcement function:

> Some individuals seem to serve as personal transmitters for others. Without these relay individuals, messages originating from the mass media might not reach otherwise unexposed people. This, of course, is the major part of the opinion-leader idea; we call it the *relay function* of interpersonal relations. . . . Furthermore, personal influence seems to be singularly effective. When a mass-media influence-attempt coincides with an interpersonal communication, it appears

to have much greater chance of success. We call this the *reinforcment function.*

(Katz and Lazarsfeld 1955: 82-83)

Katz and Lazarsfeld rather miss the point of their observations in seeing reinforcement as a result of two things – mass media and personal contact – coinciding. Although they recognize that mass media messages are most effective when accompanied by personal communication, they seem to see the conjunction as effective simply because it doubles the strength of the message. I think they are missing the point.

Although the topic is obviously immensely complex, I would like briefly to suggest that 'facticity' and 'authority' are alternative sources of plausibility. Some things seem concrete enough and close enough to us to be tested by our own experience; they have high 'facticity'. The constitution of the next world is very low on facticity and propositions about it have to be taken on trust. Where we cannot 'experiment' or call on personal experience, we fall back on the word of others. We rely on external authorities. For some things, we vest authority in impersonal bodies and the credentials they validate. Thus in matters of medicine we still, for all our recently increased scepticism, tend to defer to properly qualified doctors. But for the particularly numinous, and where the innovation is presented as having personal psychological properties, how we feel about the product will be heavily influenced by how we feel about the person offering it to us. In an initial consideration of competing second-hand cars I am more likely to listen to my friend than to a stranger but if I move beyond the interest stage to evaluation, I can perform the required test drives for myself. In responding to a new religion, where such tests are difficult, my relationship with the source of information will be a major consideration, not just in developing an interest but also in evaluation. What is clear from detailed and close studies of conversion is that many neophytes do their best to 'test' the innovation. They begin tentatively, playing the part of a Moonie or whatever with a degree of 'role distance' and only as they become more and more comfortable with the role do they allow themselves to become absorbed by it to the point where instead of playing the part of a Moonie, they actually are Moonies (Bromley and Shupe

127

1979). But even in such experiments, relationships of influence are important because one needs to learn to interpret one's experience in a positive rather than a negative way. For example, the first time a new evangelical goes out to spread the Word and finds rejection and hostility, he needs to be persuaded to see this in terms of Christ's warning that the faithful will be scorned rather than as evidence that his new faith is implausible.[3]

So much more could be said but I have done enough to illustrate the main point: researchers in a variety of fields concerned with opinion change have come to the conclusion that impersonal sources are weaker and less influential than personal sources. The affective bond between two people is a major source of plausibility. We are more willing to listen to those whom we know and have previously and successfully trusted than we are to strangers. The personal channel of communication is important not just as a means of transmitting information but also as a means of *vouchsafing* it. The medium may not be the message but it has impact on whether or not the message is believed. When mass media are the source of information and ideas, such content is most likely to influence the audience when it is mediated through personal relationships. Thus in the Gerlach and Hine study (1968) of pentecostal conversions, the message of the radio evangelist is vouchsafed and reinforced by the legitimating and supporting comment of the personal friend who acts as host and sponsor.

To return to mass evangelism, we can now understand why it is not particularly successful in converting the ungodly and why most evangelicals have either been socialized into their faith by their parents or have been converted through the agency of a personal relationship with a believer. We can also see why it is that those organizations which have put most effort into personal 'door to door' work (such as the Jehovah's Witnesses and the Mormons) have the highest recruitment rate. Although introducing oneself to thousands of strangers and attempting to create some sort of personal bond with them is time-consuming and personally wearing, it is much more likely to have the desired result than hiring billboards, newspaper pages, or even air-time to broadcast a message.

Turning points and world-views

Any successful theory of influence has to incorporate a second important principle: the basic conservatism of human beings. We are incapable of deciding everything anew all the time. If every morning, every action must be the product of fresh ratiocination, we could never leave the house. Humans are pattern-forming animals; we fill the huge gaps left in our lives by the absence of the severe straitjacket of instincts with habits.[4] Although we allow ourselves some small areas of our lives where we put a premium on novelty and experimentation (usually safely contained within the frame of 'holiday': Cohen and Taylor 1976), we tend to do today what we did yesterday that worked. The start of any response to a set of circumstances is to find the previous set of circumstances most similar and do what we did then. Only when we find ourselves in trouble do we consciously attend to our actions.

There is a similar inertial effect for belief systems. We have ways of thinking about the world, assumptions about the way things are, and about who we are. We may have a world-view with a supernatural element which is sufficiently well elaborated and codified to be a 'religion'. Provided the ideas and beliefs which we use to interpret our experiences and to frame our responses 'work' for us, we do not examine them too closely and we are not in the market for changing them.

This explains why a lot of people are recruited to new religions or new politics at crucial junctures or turning points in their lives: adolescence, moving from university to the world of work, or getting married. The individual confronted by new problems and new circumstances may well be interested in a new set of ideas to make sense of the changes.

But I have already argued that, outside the world of hybrid seed corn, what counts as working may itself involve considerable interpretation. It is precisely this which gives the ideology salesmen hope. They see the possibility of persuading me that, although I used to think my world and its accompanying world-view was working just fine, I actually have major problems, that the sound which I thought was my life ticking over nicely is instead a bomb counting down to explosion. Here we finally see the interactive nature of the relationship between persuasion, source, and belief. In ideology as in most else, there is a great deal of inertia. Only when our world-view fails are most of us in the market for a new one. Major social dislocations, such as mass migrations or the destruction of an economic structure may put a large number of people in the market for a new vision. In a relatively stable situation, the source of the message about the innovation must try to persuade us that our world-view has indeed failed and that the innovation represents a superior model. The chances of us being so persuaded are clearly higher the more we already feel receptive to new ideas. The same could have been said of any medium of new ideas, but a summary of research on television's ability to produce attitudinal change rather inelegantly but reasonably concluded: 'Radical change of attitudes may also take place when existing attitudes are no longer adequate to satisfy the related need-state of the viewer' (Horsfield 1984: 135). But whether our existing attitudes are no longer adequate is itself a matter of belief which may be altered by persuasion.[5]

PARAPERSONAL COMMUNICATION

Televangelists know all about the importance of personal relationships and have done as much as is possible to either change or disguise the nature of their communications. In a contrast with personal interaction, McQuail describes mass media communications in the following way:

> the source is not a single person but a formal organization, and the 'sender' is often a professional communicator. The message is not unique, variable and unpredictable but often 'manufactured', standardized, always 'multiplied' in some way. It is also a product of work and a commodity with an exchange value as well as being a symbolic reference with a 'use value'. The relationship between sender and receiver is one-directional and rarely interactional, it is necessarily impersonal.
>
> (McQuail 1983: 34)

But as Horton and Wohl perceptively noted in 1956, electronic mass media have the advantage over print of giving the illusion of face-to-face interaction: 'The conditions of response to the performer are analogous to those in a primary group. The most remote and illustrious men are met *as if* they were in the circle of one's peers' (Horton and Wohl 1956: 215). The new media allow a type of relations which Horton and Wohl call 'para-social interaction' and which later commentators called 'parapersonal communication'. The evangelists who have done best on television are those who have been able to either mute or disguise the mass characteristics of the medium. Thus, although the programmes are designed and produced by large bureaucratic organizations, the evangelists have built the programmes around their own personalities. Some are avowedly personality shows with the evangelist's name in the title. But even those which have a slightly more impersonal format – Falwell's *The Old Time Gospel Hour* for example – feature the personality at the start and the end of the programme and have him deliver the central sermon and usually the money pitches. When the evangelist invites the audience to write or phone, it is not to the organization, but 'to me, Jerry Falwell, at . . .'.

The mass media evangelists are all highly skilled broadcasters who devote considerable energy to appearing otherwise. In a medium which normally accords great prestige to those who display 'coolness' and maintain face under stress, where the hero is the newscaster who continues competently to read the news while protestors break into the studio, religious broadcasters allow themselves frequent displays of emotion. The Bakkers, Oral Roberts, Jimmy Swaggart, and 'early' Pat Robertson were all often moved to tears on screen.

The wives and children of the evangelist are used for additional intimacy. They may appear on screen and play a part in the shows. Mrs Vincent Peale sometimes read listeners' letters and commented on them but she was present as more of a co-host than as spouse. The wives of modern religious broadcasters are shamelessly used to create the impression of informality. Falwell will often break a fluid performance to camera to deliver an apparently impromptu aside to his wife. The home life of the Bakkers always played a major part in their shows.

> Jim's personal struggle with ambition, his sometimes-ecstatic-sometimes-whiney approach, Tammy Faye's incredibly open on-air discussions of their marital difficulties . . . have always been right there for viewers to see. Sometimes the Bakkers' problems were so overwhelming that one or both of them

had to get away for a few days. And when they did, there often was no attempt to hide their emotional and spiritual exhaustion. All of these are elements of real people opening their lives to public examination in ways that we see in soap operas but rarely in real life.

(Hadden and Shupe 1988: 129)

Televangelists encourage viewers to think of themselves as intimates by 'sharing' with the cameras thoughts which would normally seem out of place in public and by letting down their guard in ways that suggest that they are not really acting in front of millions but are sitting in your front room. They also develop the appearance of intimacy in the other direction, by claiming personal knowledge of, and interest in, individual viewers.

In describing the operations of the typical televangelism organization, I pointed to the irony of the most advanced and impersonal technology – the computer – being used to simulate personal communication. When Oral Roberts says that he prays over your personal problems and prayer requests, what he means is that he prays over a computer printout of the names of those who have written to him but he is able to tell his correspondents that he prays about their letters, as if he not only read them and replied to them but also invested emotional capital in his responses.

The letter-writing machines produce the semblance of a unique personal communication between the evangelist and the individual audience member who writes in. The letter refers to the reader by name, mentions his problem, assures him that Jim or Oral or Pat is praying for him, and often has a line or two in a facsimile of the evangelist's hand. The substance of the letter continues the fiction with the evangelist pretending a great personal interest in every recipient of a mass produced document. Peter Horsfield reprints a marvellous example of the genre, a circular from Oral Roberts:

Dear Brother Horsfield,
I must tell you an almost overwhelming feeling has come over me about you. I don't know if there's something I don't know about. It may be something that is happening or is about to happen. But something inside me says that you are hurting in some way spiritually . . . or physically . . . or

132

emotionally . . . or financially. I tell you I feel this, there's a problem.

I guess you have a right to say, 'Well, Oral, if you don't know what it is you feel I'm hurting with, why write me?' I can't answer that except I'm very sensitive to God and to you as my partner. You see, you have a different relationship with me: I feel closer to you and I believe you feel closer to me.

(Horsfield 1984: 31–2)

What we have here is a potent combination of attitude and technology. It requires a certain way of thinking to bring oneself to make claims which are, to put it bluntly, fraudulent, but it also needs a certain level of technological sophistication. And it is not only in solicitation that a machine has been able to introduce the semblance of the personal. The television picture and sound technology is itself important. There is no doubt that the viewers of television evangelism are 'closer' to the preacher than was the audience for urban revivalism. Modern equipment can reproduce sound and vision in a degree of detail not available beyond the first rows of a large church.[6]

There are also the prayer phone lines that allow members of the audience to call up and talk to, not the evangelist himself, but at least a member of the staff. The staff members' responses will be the automatic responses of bureaucrats performing a narrowly specified role for which they have been trained but there is a degree of interaction between the audience member and the 'sender' which is not characteristic of the archetypically 'mass' medium.

SUMMARY: INFLUENCE, PERSUASION, AND CIRCULARITY

'Parapersonal communication' neatly describes the end product of using high technology and a certain degree of obfuscation to modify or appear to modify what is fundamentally an impersonal medium; a form of contact which lies between genuinely personal interaction and the entirely impersonal mass media. In its persuasiveness, televangelism conforms to what we would expect from previous research on conversion and influence. It develops a considerable loyalty between members of the audience and the evangelist, whom many feel they know as well as or better than they know people whom they meet in the flesh. But it does not have the degree of 'plausibility' which will cause unbelievers to become believers, critics to become supporters. There is enough influence for people who already like conservative Protestantism to be convinced that they like *this brand* but there is not enough to shift people the greater distance from mainstream Protestantism to fundamentalism or from unbelief to Christianity. In this respect televangelism is not very different to the mass evangelism which it has largely replaced but it does have the important advantage for *claiming* to be influential that its audience is invisible. Statistics were vital for crusade evangelism. It laboured and labours still under the double handicap of costing a lot and being criticized by many in the mainstream of Christian church life for theological and spiritual shallowness. While acknowledging these observations, mass evangelists defend their activity on the grounds that it reaches a 'mass'; that is, it is efficient and productive. As early as Jonathan Edwards, the justification for 'new measures' was that they *worked*. The early itinerant evangelists simply made grandiose claims about the vast numbers of people who had heard the Word through their ministry and left the arguments about accuracy to their critics and supporters.

The problem with claiming merit on the grounds of the large numbers addressed is that critics will argue (usually reasonably) that, because the largest part of the audience consists of the thoroughly churched, this is less evangelism than a large Sunday service. This invites the next stage in using statistics to demonstrate value for money, which is the Graham method of keeping records of 'inquirers' and their spiritual state. But to keep records of this sort is to invite outsiders to inspect them and test their fit with some reality outside the rhetoric of the evangelistic organization. As we have seen, the results of such tests are disappointing. In explaining why they continue with such an unproductive exercise, evangelists fall back on seed-sowing analogies. It is not their job to convert people; God does that. Although not many decided for Christ here, who knows what seeds might have been planted in hearts and how many will bear fruit later?

At first sight electronic evangelists have similar problems with justifying their work. They admit the expense of mass media and most of them also recognize that the Christian message suffers somewhat in the forms in which it must be presented over the air if it is to attract an audience. But they are preaching the gospel to millions. Although most televangelists do not sell advertising time in their programmes, they are in a similar position to conventional programme-makers in the relationship between audience size and income. NBC needs a big audience so that it can charge advertisers lots of money for slots. Jerry Falwell needs a big audience so that he can use the number of people he reaches with the gospel message as a *reason* why the section of that audience which is already Christian should give him lots of money: audience size equals income.

Mass media evangelists have a major advantage over their urban revivalist progenitors; because their audience is usually invisible they can make any claim they like about its size with very little chance of having that claim refuted. Empty seats in crusade halls are a very public evidence of failure. In reality, falling revenues are a much sharper threat to the televangelist with his high costs than they were to the mass evangelist. As Rex Humbard discovered, a sudden fall in income can mean the abrupt end of a long career. But the difficulty of knowing the actual size of the television audience means that the televangelist can for a long time maintain an illusory world. Provided income can be brought in and air-time bought on stations, preferably slightly more stations every year, then the total possible audience can be claimed as the number of people one is reaching with God's Word. 'Faith partners' can be asked to give more money to buy more time to 'reach more people with God's Word' and the promise is fulfilled, not because the gospel is actually heard and attended to by more people (although it might be) but simply because more air-time has been bought. An increase in supply is passed off as an increase in demand.

Although mass evangelism fails in its primary purpose, it may have important secondary consequences. First, it offers good clean entertainment and Christian education for believers; it makes a welcome addition to the normal round of church-related activities. Just as a touring orchestra does for provincial music lovers, crusade evangelism gives believers a chance to hear a new and often famous voice. Second, it offers an opportunity for young conservatives who have been socialized in the faith of their parents to have their own conversion experience and announce their faith publicly. Third, the preaching of the crusade with its radical division of the world into the saved and the unsaved, its stress on the virtues of being among the former, and its climax in the call to 'decide for Christ', reinforces the shared beliefs of the audience and unites them as a believing community temporarily distinct from the world. Especially through its depictions of the horrors that await those who are not saved, evangelical preaching brings Durkheim's 'upright consciences' together in a manner which presumably reinforces their faith and makes it more likely that, through personal 'witnessing', these believers will bring in more stray sheep.

Finally, the organization of a large crusade strengthens the faithful by offering them opportunities for short-term but intensive involvement in the Lord's work. There are choirs to be sung in, buses to be driven, church prayer groups to be led, and publicity to be arranged. Two or three hundred volunteers will be given training in personal evangelism and used to counsel those who come forward. Such involvement reinforces commitment and, if the newly zealous do more personal witnessing, it may indirectly contribute to the growth of conservative Protestantism.

Does televangelism have the same potential for secondary effects? Religious television is certainly attractive as a source of entertainment and 'spiritual nourishment'. Evangelicals and fundamentalists who want to hear good gospel music or listen to a celebrity talk about her religious conversion and her campaign against homosexuality can now turn to their favourite show. Those people who like talk shows can indulge in their secular pleasures without missing 'added value' religion by watching the *700 Club*. In the sense of expanding the resources of the conservative Protestant milieu, religious broadcasting is as important as Christian schools, colleges, publishing houses, or film companies.

The televangelism audience sees it as not only entertaining and spiritually up-lifting but also as being informative in a secular sense. In a complex way, this is linked to the conservative Protestant sense of cultural and educational inferiority. Although fundamentalists and pentecostals present their low status as a source of pride, their disparagement of credentials and secular authority contains a large element of insecurity and envy. The sense that comes very clearly through some of Hoover's interviews with *700 Club* partners is their pleasure that there are now people who think like them but who have status in the world. As one 'partner' described his visit to CBN:

136

Humility is important but here you could tell by the people
and the way they talked, the vocabulary and everything else,
the things they expressed, and their spirituality. I like
dedicated hearts, and people with degrees, who can say and
believe these things. I was at Wheaton College when Billy
Graham was there, and his wife was there and both of them
were walking around and dealing with people ... wow.
And here to listen to a consecrated woman [with] a college
degree ... I get a blessing from people with degrees, top
people who are servants. I love people with degrees, consecrated.

(Quoted in Hoover 1988: 184)

For this viewer and others what is impressive about the *700 Club* is
that it is not just some good ole boy in a bri-nylon shirt healing the
sick in a tent or belting out 'heart-felt, Holy Ghost, heaven-sent,
devil-chasing, sin-killing, true-blue, red-hot, blood-bought,
God-given singing of the gospel' (Swaggart, quoted in Barnhart
1988: 128). It is a professional programme in which serious matters
of foreign policy and domestic politics are discussed by people who
appear to know what they are talking about.

We're very proud of Christian programming. We use it ourselves, in our witnessing, we're very proud that instead of just
'Bible thumping' as it used to be in the old days on TV –
which was mostly embarassing, really not that great content,
it was mostly the salvation message and nothing much more,
or something negative, something out of touch with society –
now we're not ashamed because now there is excellent
Christian programming that is very much contemporary, and
in touch with society, and not afraid to discuss controversial
issues. Hollywood and Madison Avenue will still try and make
us look like a bunch of Elmer Gantrys and weirdoes in
general, but basically speaking, people think it's OK.

(Quoted in Hoover 1988: 182)

This was specifically a reflection on the appeal of Pat Robertson's
CBN but a similar point could be made about most religious
television. Thirty years ago conservative Protestants compensated
for their lack of this-worldly wealth and status by exalting in their
next-worldly superiority. They have now acquired wealth and

137

status and want cultural products which are as good as those enjoyed by the ungodly. They want education and information about parts of the world of which they were previously ignorant. Much televangelism has the added value that it provides a quality cultural product of which fundamentalists can feel proud and which, by reflecting their new position in the world, reinforces their commitment to fundamentalism.

To a limited degree, televangelism creates a sense of fellowship or communion among its viewers[7] but it is still an impersonal medium and the vital stimulation of actually being part of the mass, the crowd, the living community which in unison sings 'Just as I am' or some such gospel anthem, is missing. In particular it gives little or no opportunity for people to exhibit their conversion experiences and to have them endorsed by the community. Televangelism also gives little opportunity for lay participation in gospel work. Despite all the rhetoric of 'faith partners' and 'prayer partners', there is little room for anything other than giving money. For all its attempts to modify its 'mass media' nature, like conventional television, religious television has a passive audience. It may be that, by allowing supporters to mistakenly take the total possible audience as the number of people influenced by the programmes, televangelists free their supporters from the possibility of the disappointments of the half empty rows of seats in a damp crusade tent but they also deprive them of the possibility of active involvement.

Does televangelism have any secondary effects which are not found with crusade evangelism? The Annenberg study of televangelism, not surprisingly given that he was the director, took up George Gerbner's general point that television has a persistent and long-term conservative effect because it presents a distorted view of the social world in which too much attention is given to both the 'top' and 'bottom'; the rich, prestigious, and powerful on the one hand, and deviants, troublemakers, and criminals on the other are massively over-represented in all forms of television programming (McQuail 1983). Neuendorf and Abelman (1987) provide data which illuminate the question. At the end of a detailed and sophisticated analysis of the content of a range of religious television programmes, they concluded that: 'Men initiated the majority of verbal interaction and were involved in 95.8% of all interactions. When women interacted with others, receiving direction and accepting the direction of others were their primary mode of verbal behaviour' (Neuendorf and Ableman 1987: 191). The elderly and the young were similarly underrepresented and appeared only in a very narrow range of roles and relationships. Despite claims of healing power, the halt and the lame rarely figured. Racial and ethnic minorities were vastly underrepresented.

Although it is impossible to measure the impact, it seems highly likely that continued exposure to partial representations of the world confirms the socio-political beliefs which created such images. But a white, male-dominated world is exactly the world of conservative Protestantism and religious television is no different to either the religion in any other medium or the television with any other sort of programme. Televangelism *per se* has no effect here other than the general one of representing what evangelicals, fundamentalists, and pentecostals already believe in an additional medium.[8]

I am suggesting that beyond the narrow effect of religious conversion (at which it is not terribly good), televangelism may have some useful secondary effects of reinforcing the faith of those who are already believers and of confirming the social stereotypes common to the evangelical world. As Wuthnow says, it offers 'entertainment, inspiration, music, worship and spiritual growth' (Wuthnow 1987: 128). Critics and some neutral commentators have wanted to see more than this in the communications role of televangelism. The case that televangelism provides the base for the rise of a powerful social movement will be the focus of Chapter Eight.

Chapter Seven

GOD AND MAMMON

In the 1870s, Moody and Sankey were accused of profiteering from the sales of Sankey's revival hymn book. Billy Sunday was often accused of using donations to fund an excessively luxurious standard of living. Usually he ignored such carping but was once sufficiently stung by it to give the offering from his 1917 New York crusade (about $120,500) to the Red Cross, YMCA, and YWCA (McLoughlin 1955: xxviii). The prologue to a ghastly hatchet job on Billy Graham was entitled 'The preacher and the pay-off' (Ashman 1977). And this was before religious television became so expensive that the Rex Humbard organization in 1979 had to spend 35 per cent of its budget on fund-raising. In the early 1980s, Falwell estimated that he needed an income of $4 million a month to pay his 2,000 employees and to maintain his operations; he spends about 24 per cent of his income on raising more (Horsfield 1984: 28). This chapter will describe some of the ways in which televangelists raise money and consider the attitudes towards work and wealth which are either implied or promoted by the mass media evangelists.

FUND-RAISING

Apart from a narrow range of exceptions, the rulings of the Federal Communications Commission prohibit people using the air-waves to ask for money. Religious programming is one of those exceptions. Some – the programmes of the Bob Jones family and those on the new Southern Baptist Convention cable network, for example – make a principle of never soliciting on the air. The rest seem to do little else. On average 11 per cent of air-time is spent asking for money which is either a lot or not much depending on the comparison. It is far more time than would be given to soliciting in an ordinary church service but it is less than the 20 per cent of any hour of ordinary television which is taken up with advertisements (*Washington Times* 3 April 1987; Frankl 1987: 134).

In some programmes, financial appeals (especially if they are for a special project) are presented as discrete spot items, like commercial breaks in a secular show. But often the preacher delivers the sales pitch himself, as part of the general flow of the service or entertainment, depending on the format. Frankl breaks down the 782 appeals she observed into three types: appeals to some personal need of the viewer; appeals to support the television ministry; and appeals to a sense of Christian altruism. Taking them in reverse order, appeals to altruism – asking for money to save souls and to engage in moral crusades or political activities – account for 16 per cent of all requests for money. Surprisingly, given the claims which televangelists make about their manifest purposes, of the total number of pitches Frankl observed, only 10 per cent asked for money to convert the unsaved.[1]

The second most common category of appeal – for money to support the ministry – accounted for 21 per cent of all pitches. An important point about these appeals is that more than a third concerned a special project. Most televangelists are committed to extravagant schemes; Falwell, Roberts, Robertson, and Swaggart have their colleges and the Bakkers had Heritage USA. Bricks and mortar projects are more glamorous than paying the television station bills. There is no end to the costs for air-time and little sense of progress to be had from just meeting the bills. Asking for money just to air the show comes a little too close to admitting the circular nature of the enterprise but colleges and hospitals are tangible and impressive additions to God's plant.

When the routine costs are used in fund-raising appeals, it is often in the context of impending doom. Televangelists live in a world in which crises do constant battle with miracles. When Falwell founded the Moral Majority to campaign on socio-moral issues, he was motivated to do so by the fear that America was incurring God's wrath and was on the point of being irrevocably damned. Yet if God's people just came out of the closet (to use James Robison's memorable phrase) then America would be turned round. Oral Roberts' claim in 1986 that unless he got the

$9 million he needed for his medical school, God would call him home, was regarded even by other televangelists as having crossed some line of good taste in impending doom-saying but he was merely extending slightly a time-honoured technique. Jim Bakker had only recently joined Pat Robertson's CBN when he went on the air just before the scheduled close and told the audience:

> Our entire purpose has been to serve the Lord Jesus Christ through radio and television. But we've fallen short. We need $10,000 a month to stay on the air, and we're far short of that. Frankly, we're on the verge of bankruptcy and just don't have the money to pay our bills.

Bakker started to cry and the cameraman held the camera on him as the tears rolled. According to Pat Robertson:

> Immediately the phones in the studio started ringing until all the lines were jammed. Those tears touched the hearts of people all over the state. People called in weeping . . . By 2.30 A.M. we had raised $105,000.
>
> (Quoted in Hadden and Swann 1981: 114)

The 'going out of business' sale is commonplace; television evangelists are forever on the point of having to stop airing their programme 'in your area' unless the viewer rushes them large sums of money. As a result of signing the visitor's book at Thomas Road Baptist Church, I was the recipient of a series of dire appeals. On 1 December 1983, Falwell's computer wrote to me and a million others:

> I told you recently that December is also a crucial month for us. I told you I have established a *Survival Fund* to save our television and radio ministry.
> *We are several months behind in paying most of our television and radio stations.* These station managers have been most gracious – but they must *now* be paid.
> And I am saddened to tell you we have now been forced to borrow $3 million in order to prevent being cut off many stations in the next several days.
> What am I saying?
> *I am saying that by God's grace we must pay all our TV and radio accounts up-to-date by December 31 – and we must also pay back this*

$3 million loan in early January.

My back is to the wall. I have talked to the Lord about this need, and even though it is almost Christmas, I must now ask you about it again.

Dr. Bruce, your gift of $100 is so important right now.

Televangelists frequently claim that Satan, or more prosaically, secular humanists, are working hard to stop the airing of their shows. Jim Bakker often responded to stories of his financial improprieties in the *Charlotte Observer* by accusing the paper of conducting a vendetta. This view is sufficiently widely shared that when Bourgault began her study of the attitudes of Appalachian pentecostalists to the *PTL Club*, her respondents were initially loath to criticize the programme because they thought she was collecting evidence to 'have it stopped' (Bourgault 1985). In his letter, Falwell deploys the same tactic when he explains that Larry Flynt, the publisher of the pornographic magazine *Hustler*, and Norman Lear, the founder of the liberal campaigning organization People for the American Way, wanted to silence *The Old Time Gospel Hour*, as did Satan, and that only my donation would prevent this fate.

I know I am asking a lot of you — but perhaps you can find a way to make this sacrifice before this year comes to a close in the next few days.

Our TV and radio network can only survive now with God's grace and the generous gifts of good friends like you.

The response was clearly not enough. Two weeks later, Falwell's computer wrote to me again:

This letter is being mailed to you from my office — a little ahead of Christmas. I want you to receive it as close to Christmas Day as possible — and certainly before New Year's Day, 1984.

Why, because, Dr Bruce, *I want you to have the most current report possible on the status of The Old Time Gospel Hour Survival Fund.*

And further I want you to have time to make a last minute Survival Gift of $50 and have it postmarked before midnight Saturday, December 31st — New Year's Eve.

The middle section of the letter again told me that *The Old Time*

Gospel Hour is a major instrument in God's fight against sin and that it could spark a revival so that '(1) convenience abortions could be outlawed in this land, (2) prayer would be returned to our schools, and (3) moral and traditional family values would again become prevalent in our society'. Unfortunately Satan was coming close to silencing Falwell.

> I am pouring out my heart to you. Please do what you can. So much is at stake. Your $50 gift, or whatever you can give, will be such a help.
> You should make your tax deductible gift payable to the Old Time Gospel Hour.

Notice the spurious personal relationship implied in these letters. I didn't give but presumably others did; *The Old Time Gospel Hour* is still on the air.

With what was, as it turned out, better reason, Rex Humbard also used the closing down sale technique. The following is from a letter sent out in April 1980:

> I've got some very bad news. My heart is broken and I have not been able to eat or sleep. For today I had to do something that wars against every fiber in my being. . . . I had to take the first step to remove our program from the TV stations in your area. . . . Eternal souls are at stake. For if our program goes off the air – there are men, women, boys and girls who will spend eternity in hell. People will miss heaven because I lost God's call to your city.
>
> (Quoted in Horsfield 1984: 32)

Gifts and intimacy

One commonly used appeal involves an element of self-interest; the preacher offers the viewer some personal service or tangible object. The goods given in return for a donation (they are rarely 'sold') are usually fairly mundane: Bibles, calendars, paperback books, greetings cards. But radio evangelist Bill Beeny offered his listeners a riot pack consisting of a stove, five fuel cans, a rescue gun, a radio, and the Defender, a weapon that covers an attacker with dye thus making him an easy target for the police:

> Ten dollars will buy a blue-steel, pearl-handled, tear-gas

pistol, plus the informative and inspirational Truth-Pac 4. Or, for the same price, evangelist Beeny will send his own album of eighteen songs about heaven, together with the Paralyzer, 'made by the famous Mace Company'.

(Martin 1970: 3)

Radio evangelists with a less apocalyptic view offer their books and records without throwing in a canister of Mace gas. Jimmy Swaggart, who like his cousin Jerry Lee Lewis is a genuinely talented singer, makes a large proportion of his income from selling his records.

The pitch is not a straightforward commercial transaction. The theme is always one of an exchange of gifts. God has given us the gift of salvation. We should give God our gifts. As we cannot give them directly to God, we should give them to the televangelist. When items are offered, they are always worth considerably less than the asked-for donation, gift, or 'love offering'. For example, Falwell offered a boxed set of 'the seven books that have most influenced my life' to anyone who gave $100 to his college. The books were cheap paperbacks and worth far less than $100 but presumably donors knew that and were knowingly taking part in an exchange of gifts between friends rather than a market transaction.

The ambition of fund-raisers is to stabilize the close relationship between televangelist and viewer by enlisting the viewer as a partner in the enterprise through some sort of membership scheme. In the following pitch, Falwell is promoting a new reward of Faith Partnership:

Now if you call me and call for the passport and join as a Faith Partner, this passport, number one, will mean that when you come as much as 50 miles or more to visit with us on a Sunday and show this passport there'll be reserved seats for you. That's a very valuable thing around Thomas Road. Getting a reserved seat is something nobody gets. Beyond that we'll have you in a reserved tour of Liberty Mountain. You will also have dinner with Macel and me. My wife and I – I tell you about that, honey? We're going to eat with all the Faith Partners – when the Faith Partners come to town and my wife

145

and I, our family, will have dinner with you and this passport
will ensure that for you.

(Morning Service 12 February 1979)

Note what is being sold: intimacy with the preacher. You don't
phone the organization; you phone Jerry. Note also the folksy
technique for presenting himself as being just like anyone else.
Just like any ordinary husband, he has forgotten to tell his wife
about some people he has invited to dinner! Always the
consummate professional broadcaster, Falwell contrives to appear
amateurish by breaking off in the middle of a formal 'piece to
camera' to turn to his wife and deliver a joking personal aside.

Oral Roberts also has his Prayer Partners. Pat Robertson has his
700 Club members. Rex Humbard had his Prayer Key Family. Jim
Bakker told his prospective PTL members:

[you] will receive your PTL partner card, PTL lapel pin and
a special edition of 'Action magazine'. Every month, you will
receive my letter and either 'Action Magazine' or 'Action
Update' detailing what God is doing through your support.

(Quoted in Horsfield 1984: 32)

The most succesful appeals are those which offer the viewer a
chance to participate in the enterprise and a touch of immortality.
Bricks and mortar projects can be funded by promising donors
that their contributions will be recorded in the structure of the
projects themselves. In 1976 Falwell promised to engrave the
names of all those who gave to his university project on a 'Liberty
Bell monument' to be erected in the centre of the campus. The
great European cathedrals were built with the donations of the
very rich and money raised by various forms of general taxation. It
is symbolically appropriate for a modern democracy that much of
the money for Robert Schuller's Crystal Cathedral came from the
10,000 people who gave $500 to have their names engraved on one
of that number of mirrored glass panes. Patrons can read their
names – with the help of a powerful pair of binoculars.

MONEY TROUBLES

Televangelists have an almost unique position of freedom from
financial scrutiny. Investigations by the Internal Revenue Service
can be deflected by claiming that they are government infringe-

ment of the constitutional right to the 'free exercise' of religion. Even state attorneys generally have had to work hard to establish a right to investigate the use of funds collected for religious purposes. None the less, there is extensive interest in how the very large sums raised are spent and outsiders such as the journalists of the *Charlotte Observer* (who reported the financial scandals of PTL for ten years before Bakker's sexual indiscretion interested the rest of the media) have created difficulties for some televangelists.

In particular there have been embarrassments arising from straying into the well-policed business of selling stocks and bonds. In 1973 a federal court permanently enjoined Thomas Road Baptist Church from using the mails or other interstate means to obtain money or other property by making untrue statements concerning its finances. This instruction not to lie about money was a response to a report by the Securities Exchange Commission (SEC) that the church had made 'false and misleading' statements about its property. In 1972 Falwell's organization had contracted with Houston-based Cooperative Church Finance to sell $2.5 million worth of bonds. Unfortunately the SEC was actively interested in church bonds. It had just discovered that 'the head of the Baptist Foundation of America had linked up with organized crime to sell $26 million in worthless church paper' (Davis and Volkman 1982a: 64). The SEC investigator discovered that the Thomas Road financial statements printed in the bond offer circular were out-of-date and:

> that the church claimed to own 25,000 shares of Virginia International Corporation worth $1.1 million – when in fact, it owned none at the time of offering in 1972. .... He also discovered that, in addition to the $2.5 million offering, the church had already sold more than $5.2 million in general obligation bonds, in large part to Falwell's television audience, on the basis of a three-page brochure that disclosed little more than the interest rate.
>
> (Davis and Volkman 1982a: 66)

Furthermore, the books were in such a mess it was impossible to tell if funds were being misappropriated. There were vast debts and no reserves existed to pay off the general obligation bonds. Although the church was eventually cleared of deliberate wrong-doing, it had to pay considerable costs.

In the early 1970s, Rex Humbard similarly found himself being investigated by the Ohio Commerce Department over the sale of 'securities' to finance his ambitious building projects and he abandoned the schemes. When his popularity collapsed a decade later, Humbard explained the decline in his income as a direct result of lacking an extravagant project to market.

Although they attract funding, special projects also attract the suspicion of 'bait and switch': money is raised for one purpose and then diverted to another, less popular cause. In 1980, *The Old Time Gospel Hour* was raising money for missionary work with heart-rending film of Cambodian refugees and 'boat people'. But the budget of the missions department showed that of $2,037,500, only half went to missionaries and projects abroad. $400,000 went to pay the overheads of staff at Thomas Road Baptist Church. $450,000 went to expanding facilities on Liberty Mountain for 300 missionary students; that is, went to improving Liberty University plant. Finally, $37,500 was spent buying air-time to broadcast *The Old Time Gospel Hour* to Haiti, Puerto Rico, the Bahamas, and the Virgin Islands, not normally places one thinks of as being in need of Christian missionaries (Davis and Volkman 1982b: 182).[2]

In December 1986, the State Department withdrew 'private voluntary organization' status from the body which Falwell had set up to channel funds to famine victims in the Sudan because the proper financial records had not been submitted. Although the Sudanese government refused him permission to operate in the Sudan, Falwell continued to raise money using such phrases as 'Our food and medical supplies are running low. . .' which implied that relief work was actually in progress (*US News and World Report* 6 April 1987: 60).

In 1979, PTL was in similar trouble with the Justice Department over allegations that money raised for foreign missions had been used on overheads (Haught 1980).

Although I do not want to suggest that the major televangelists are guilty of peculation (with the exception of the Bakkers, see Chapter Ten) or that most professional evangelists are corrupt, it should be noted that the inability of many believers to think badly of people claiming to be ministers means that the milieu is highly vulnerable to sharks. Oklahoma evangelist James Roy Whitby was convicted in 1978 of swindling an old lady out of $25,000. In 1979, the California Attorney General filed suit against Herbert W. Armstrong, the founder and publisher of *The Plain Truth*, for misusing over $1 million of church money. LeRoy Jenkins of South Carolina made an emergency appeal for $300,000 to pay church debts and a fortnight later paid $250,000 for a house!

Most outrageous of all was the Revd Hakeem Abdul Rasheed who peddled an extravagant form of 'seed faith' in California. He offered to make those members of his congregation who donated $300 'ministers of increase' and promised that God would repay them many times over. Periodically he would call them to the front of his church and give them sums of around $2,000 dollars each. This level of return – a truly heavenly investment – seemed so good that many followers handed over much greater sums. Of course, they got nothing back. The plan was a 'Ponzi' scam: some of the capital of the later investors was given as apparent 'dividends' to the first investors.[3]

Offering the cheap or the trivial – Falwell's Jesus First tie stick pins – is safe. So is selling the intangible; although sceptics might wish that people who sell 'prayer cloths' be prosecuted for false pretences, the courts wisely decide that the efficacy of a prayer cloth is not something they want to get entangled in.

NAME IT AND CLAIM IT

An element of the pitch is an appeal to obligation. One radio evangelist is very explicit about this:

> You've got God's money in your wallet, you old stingy Christian. No wonder we've got all these problems. You want to know how you can pay God what you owe? God is speaking through me. God said 'Inasmuch as you do it unto one of these you do it to me'. God said 'Give all you have for the gospel's sake'. My address is Brother Glenn, Paragould, Arkansas.
>
> (Quoted in Martin 1970: 4)

The prime-time preachers are more sophisticated and more subtle but there is still the implication that what we have we hold in stewardship for God and that some of it should be given back to the Lord's work. Most conservative Protestants will be well acquainted with this expectation and many follow the pattern of 'tithing' - giving a tenth of their income to the church.

There is much fun to be derived from studying 'holy roller' fund-raising but there is also a very serious point about the product, about the sort of theology being presented. In appealing to a sense of obligation, the televangelist suggests that *because* God gave you money, you should give some back to God. But many deploy the same connection in reverse order: you should give to God in order that he give to you. This is the 'seed faith' of Oral Roberts or Pat Robertson's 'Kingdom Principles'. Robertson believes that these 'Principles' are 'as valid for our lives as the laws of thermodynamics or the law of gravity'. One of the laws is God's reciprocity:

> If we want to release the superabundance of the kingdom of heaven, we first give. . . . I am certain of this as of anything in my life. If you are in financial trouble, the smartest thing you can do is to start giving money away. . . . Your return, poured into your lap, will be great, pressed down and running over.
>
> (Quoted in Hadden and Shupe 1988: 131)

As an aside, note the presence here of two of the modernity themes discussed in Chapter Four. In the talk of 'laws', we have the Baconian view of the order and regularity of the world and in the word 'superabundance' we have the clearest illustration of the secularization of perfectionism. Where conservative Protestants rebuked Fosdick and Peale for trivializing the gospel, Robertson has the *Abundant Life* (also the title of Oral Robert's magazine) reduced to more cash.

The following is the back page of *Daily Blessing*, a pamphlet produced by the Oral Roberts Evangelistic Association:

> What is your need? Is it spiritual? Is it for finances? Is it for a loved one? Is it for your body? Is it for harmony in your home? Whatever it is, God knows all about it and He wants to meet it by His miracle power. I challenge you to enter into a Blessing Pact with God, for I believe that it will change your life. It's so scriptural and practical. It's not magic; it's just God working miracles as we release our faith to Him.
>
> Fill in the attached Blessing Pact enrolment Card and mail it to me. When I receive it, I will mail you your free copy of

the 'Miracle Catch' painting and the Blessing Pact Covenant book. Each month I will write you a personal letter and share with you from God's Word how to trust God and how to apply the Blessing Pact Scriptures to your actual needs. We will be partners together in our Blessing Pact with the Lord.

The enrolment card on the reverse allows one to indicate how deep one can go in giving to the Lord.

Although one finds shades of such thinking in most religious broadcasting, the belief that giving money to God will cause God to reciprocate is promoted most obviously by those television evangelists on the charismatic wing of pentecostalism (as distinct from the more traditional stance of Jimmy Swaggart): Robertson, Bakker, Roberts, and Kenneth Copeland. It is also a key concept in a popular religious movement within American conservative Protestantism known to its supporters as the 'faith movement' or the 'Word movement' and to its detractors as 'Name it and Claim it' and 'the gospel of prosperity' (Barron 1987; McConnell 1988; Hollinger 1989).

In addition to the common currency of conservative Protestantism, the health and wealth gospel has three distinctive emphases. The first is a revival of the classic pentecostal belief in spiritual healing of physical ailments. The second is a stress on material prosperity, legitimated by the text the discovery of which so affected Oral Roberts in the late 1940s: 'Beloved, I wish above all things that thou mayest prosper and be in health, even as thy soul prospereth' (3rd John 2). Instead of some nebulous expectation of 'improvement', one has a very specific promise taken from a reading of Mark 10, verses 28-30:

> Then Peter began to say unto him, Lo, we have left all, and have followed thee.
>
> And Jesus answered and said, Verily I say unto you, There is no man that hath left house, or brethren, or sisters, or father, or mother, or wife, or children, or lands, for my sake, and the gospels,
>
> But he shall receive an hundredfold now in this time, houses, and brethren, and sisters, and mothers, and children...

As Kenneth Copeland puts it: 'Do you want a hundredfold return

151

on your money? Give and let God multiply it back to you' (quoted in Hollinger 1989: 7).

The third defining belief of the health and wealth movement is 'positive confession'. Initially this was developed in pentecostal circles in connection with healing. Rather than ask to be healed, one was supposed to pray that one was healed and believe it, even if the symptoms of the illness appeared to persist. According to Romans 10, verse 10: 'For with the heart man believeth unto righteousness; and with the mouth confession is made unto salvation.' The other favoured text is Mark 11, verses 23-24:

> For verily I say unto you, That whosoever shall say unto this mountain, be thou removed, and be cast into the sea; and shall not doubt in his heart, but shall believe that those things which he saith shall come to pass; he shall have whatsoever he saith.

> Therefore I say unto you, What things soever ye desire, when ye pray, believe that ye receive them, and ye shall have them.

Through Christ, God has promised that we can have what we say or, as the critics put it, 'Name it and claim it'.[4]

The plausibility of health and wealth gospel

Discussions of fund-raising by promising considerable material gains for those who give to God's work are usually couched in terms of the honesty of televangelists. Critics ask if Oral Roberts or Kenneth Copeland really believe that Christ's reply to Peter's complaining was a promise of vast riches in this life. Without engaging in that debate, it is worth noting that many televangelists have a very good reason to believe their own pitch: it worked for them. Oral Roberts was seriously ill as a teenager and appears to have had a faith cure. Kenneth Hagin, the doyen of the contemporary health and wealth movement was born weighing only two pounds and with a congenital heart defect:

> His physicians said that he didn't have a chance in a million to live a long life. Hagin's physical incapacities were compounded by his father's desertion of the family at age six and the subsequent nervous breakdown of his mother. At age

sixteen, after being essentially an invalid his whole life, Kenneth experienced a miraculous healing.

(Hollinger 1989: 11)

Because the gospel they have preached has been attractive to many Americans, the health and wealth preachers have seen their churches grow, their broadcasts attract increasing audiences, and their books sell in vast quantities; all evidence of God keeping his promises and answering prayers.

More particularly, the leading televangelists have seen in their own careers God's willingness to respond to their acts of faith. Most gambled outrageously, committing themselves to buying air-time they could not afford and then begging the audience to pay their debts. In the early days of PTL, Jim Bakker mailed a cheque on Friday knowing that it could not be covered. By Monday enough money had come to meet it. The next Friday he had another cheque delivered even though he knew that PTL could not pay. Again the money came in (Barnhart 1988: 19). The television preachers started building projects without the money to get to the end of the first month's work and then cried on the screen about their financial problems; the viewers sent in the money. As a response to his 1973 troubles with the Securities Exchange Commission, Falwell established a committee of respectable Lynchburg businessmen to help sort out his tangled financial affairs. Their suggested way of dealing with unpaid air-time bills was to *increase* media exposure in the hope of raising more money from donations (Davis and Volkman 1982a). It worked. Six years later, when the construction costs of the university on Liberty Mountain were escalating, Falwell called a temporary halt to building but added fifty TV stations to his broadcast schedule and bought time to show three specially produced shows (Fitzgerald 1981: 95). Again, it worked: the bread cast upon the waters was increased ten-fold. Oral Roberts may have over-reached himself with his medical school but generally televangelists have every reason to believe in miracles.

An overlooked but significant point is that many members of the audience may have less spectacular but similar good reasons to believe in 'seed faith'. I do not mean that the numerous stories of prayers answered are true (although they might be) or convincing (although they might be). I mean that most of the audience, although they will rarely reflect on it, will have shared an experience which should dispose them to believe in miracles: a rising standard of living.[5] The average American is significantly better off now than in 1945. Although the core religious television audience has a socio-economic profile which American researchers quaintly describe as 'downscale', their income has increased considerably in the last two decades and with that has gone a major improvement in health. Many viewers will have had (a) their support of televangelists and (b) a considerable increase in standard of living *coincide*. For the person inclined to fundamentalism, it is a relatively short step to suppose that the former has caused the latter. The smart suits, large houses, and affluent lifestyle of televangelists are admired by their audience as a token of what they too might hope to enjoy if they just accept Jim Bakker's reading of Philippians 4: 19 – 'But my God shall supply all your need according to his riches in glory by Jesus Christ' – but that hope is made reasonable by the experience of living in a growing economy.

THE PROTESTANT WORK ETHIC AND FUNDAMENTALISM

In discussing the ways in which the values represented by much religious television represent, not a reaction against, but an accommodation to, modernity, I described the easy attitude towards enjoying wealth. Now I want to make some general points as to what the fund-raising pitches tell us about attitudes to wealth-acquisition.

The first concerns the 'opportunity structure' of their world. Liberal critics make fun of the constant selling of the televangelists and forget that there is a long tradition in revivalist and fundamentalist circles of supposing that the Christian message is flattered rather than insulted by being linked in metaphor with commerce and selling. In the 1820s Charles Finney may have described himself as a lawyer evangelist but Dwight L. Moody and Billy Sunday – straddling the turn of the century – saw themselves as God's *salesmen*. And they appealed to businessmen and the clerks of business houses who hoped to step up in the world through salesmanship. Billy Graham was, briefly, a door-to-door salesman for Fuller Brushes. The core televangelism audience appreciates the fund-raising pitches. After all, this is what many of them do for a living or aspire to do. An examination of the content of non-religious advertisements in a number of fundamentalist and Moral Majority-type papers and magazines shows a high number of dealerships and franchising and direct selling opportunities. Given their class position, the best hope most fundamentalists have of becoming their own master is through retailing, preferably of some commodity which requires very little start-up capital and a lot of hard work.

A particularly American form of selling is the direct selling organization (or DSO) of which Mary Kay Cosmetics, Tupperware, and Amway are well known examples (Biggart 1989). In the network DSO, each distributor not only retails the products but recruits others to do likewise until one has a very large pyramid shaped structure. Distributors are not employed by the DSO. They are independent contractors who make money from the difference between wholesale and resale price. Those who have recruited lots of others will also make money from sizeable discounts on the volume purchases of goods they make to supply their recruits. They may also earn a royalty on the amount of product shifted by their recruits. Although most distributors do not make enough to give up their main jobs, the apparently close tie between effort and earnings means that failure to acquire the promised motor home (for some reason Amway distributors are obsessed with motor homes) an expensive car is seen as a lack of will-power and not as evidence that the dream of financial independence is unattainable through Amway (Buttterfield 1986).

The founders of Amway, Richard De Vos and Jay Van Andel, have been highly active supporters of conservative religious, socio-moral, and political values and movements and many Amway dealers are conservative Protestants. In the eyes of some critics the close relationship between a self-consciously entrepreneurial and individualistic commercial enterprise, fundamentalism, and political conservatism represents some sort of sinister conspiracy which should be exposed. A more reasonable approach would be to note the consonance of values embedded in conservative Protestantism and an enterprise such as Amway where material rewards are democratically offered to anyone who is prepared to work hard to better themselves.[6] As one DSO worker put it:

[The founders of this business made it] possible for anybody, no matter whether they had education, no matter what race they were, no matter if they had money or not, there were no criteria that would prevent them from having the American dream. And it sounds corny to a lot of people, but I felt very much that way because I never had the opportunity of an education.

(Quoted in Biggart 1989: 107)

There is no doubt that the Protestant Reformation pioneered new attitudes to work.[7] Luther criticized the monastic system and the high doctrine of the clergy because the limited view of a 'religious calling' they embodied inadvertently promoted a division of religious labour. Those people who had a vocation retreated from the world and became religious virtuosi. The bulk of the population sat very lightly to its religious obligations and in many cases confined them to supporting the religious virtuosi. Luther's solution was to extend the notion of calling so that any work, any honest occupation followed diligently was pleasing to God. The English puritan divine Matthew Perkins (1558-1602) held that in addition to a general calling there were a vast number of 'particular callings' or kinds of lives imposed on men by God for the common good. If one were a bricklayer, then the appropriate response to a sense of religious vocation was to continue to be a bricklayer (for that was probably one's calling):

Whatsoever is not done within the compass of calling is not faith . . . [and] every man must do the duties of his calling with diligence. [There are] two damnable sins that are contrary to this diligence. The first is idleness, whereby the duties of our callings and the occasions of glorifying God are neglected or omitted. The second is slothfulness, whereby they are performed slackly or carelessly.

(Perkins quoted in Lessnoff 1981: 5)

The Calvinist puritans believed that work glorified God, that honest secular labour could be a vocation, and that hard work provided a discipline which reduced the opportunities for sins of the flesh. There was also a more subtle satisfaction. Calvinists believed that, even before their birth, some had been chosen for heaven and some for hell. Given that heaven and hell were very real, they had a pressing interest in knowing their spiritual state.

156

They had no hope that hard work would *earn* them salvation; a god impressed by the labours of sinful man was hardly a god. But they could reason that the Lord would not be so perverse as to materially bless scoundrels and the unregenerate. If one worked diligently and prospered, this might be a sign that one was part of the elect. As Perkins put it: 'If thou wouldst have signs and tokens of thy election and salvation, thou must fetch them from the constant practice of thy two callings' (quoted in Lessnoff 1981: 6). One worked in order to glorify God and enjoyed the fruits of one's work as a sign of God's blessing.

The specifically Calvinist element had only very limited impact on American Protestantism which, since the first and second 'great awakenings', has been dominated by the Arminianism of the Methodist and Baptist movements. None the less the American tradition retained the notion that diligent labour was pleasing to God and continued to stress another Reformation theme: responsibility. The reformers were highly critical of what they saw as the 'something for nothing' attitude in the Catholic practices of praying for the souls of the dead and offering absolution to people who did nothing by way of repentance other than repeat a stock formula. The extension of this objection into the secular world was the opposition to the gambling for which nineteenth century urban Catholics were well known. Traditionally, Protestants have held that people should not squander their money and then hope that luck will give them lots in return. They should work hard and save. Even if the improvident did hit the jackpot, this was still not to be condoned because they had done nothing to earn that reward.

Conservative Protestants have always been keen on personal responsibility. In Chapter One, I described the way in which modern conservative Protestantism became thoroughly *individualistic*. All except the most radical Protestants have always been individualistic in matters of salvational status. Each of us faces God alone and gives his own account. But since the division at the end of the nineteenth century between social gospellers and fundamentalists, conservative Protestants have also been individualistic in social analysis. Although they are not consistent in this, they often deny that there is such a thing as a 'society' or even an 'economy' which to any extent forms or constrains the actions of individuals. In the depression of 1914-15, Mrs Billy Sunday was saying:

I haven't got any patience for a man who can't find a job. . . . He has usually wasted his strength and his brain through drink or cigarettes or women. . . . [If an unemployed man gets converted] and shows by his actions that he is trying to do good and live cleanly, the well-off Christians in that town will help him. . . . I say that a Christian can always buy his own shirt no matter how poor he has been. . . . I've seen thousands and thousands of people get converted and begin to make money right away.

(McLoughlin 1955: 252)

The Christian in the above contrast is applauded for being self-sufficient and looking after his family *by getting a job.* But in the world of televangelism, there has been a partial displacement of the self-help reliance embodied in the capitalism of Amway. In Mrs Sunday's rather cruel formulation, the key to making money is to get converted, get the right attitude, go out and get a job, and work diligently. The Holy Spirit provides money by (a) producing the right attitude in the convert and (b) creating the cultural climate in which Christians will be willing to employ a convert. Although the latter has an element of undeservedness about it, it can be seen as giving the opportunity to the convert to display his new character; the advantage has in some sense been earned by the conversion.

In franchises and DSOs, there is still the implied connection between hard work and income; people who put in the hours will benefit their families. Work is a sign of character and determination and success is the appropriate reward. But in the illustration of the miracles which fill Roberts's magazine *Abundant Life*, one sees something quite different, something which is exaggerated by the fund-raising techniques of the televangelists but which is found in the pentecostal wing of conservative Protestantism more widely: money for conversion. The corrupt pre-reformed Christian church asked for this-worldly goods and promised rewards in the next life. The post-Reformation church demanded this-worldly asceticism as a sign of the elect status which guaranteed rewards in the next life. In its first transformation, this gave way to the notion that one's this-worldly rewards were the product of this-worldly effort. Some elements of the electronic church have produced a further secularization of the Protestant ethic. It promises that those who get saved will be rewarded *in this life* with health and wealth. And being rich is not only a good thing but it can come painlessly, without the effort of diligently striving. If you need something, just write it on the back of your Blessing Pact card and send it with your donation to Oral Roberts or make it one of your Seven Lifetime Prayer requests and accompany it by a suitably large donation and Pat Robertson will place it with thousands of others in a column in a prayer room in CBN headquarters where it will be promoted daily by the prayers of CBN employees until the Lord returns.

The decline of the 'Protestant ethic' with its asceticism, its striving, and its rationality is clearly too complex a phenomenon to be explained here and there are still no good studies of just what sorts of people are attracted to the modern health and wealth teachings but a few general points can be made. What Max Weber neatly described as 'this-worldly asceticism' obviously fits best with the material interests of a social class which has the opportunity to better itself by diligence and such opportunities are not universally distributed. American blacks, for example, have been systematically denied opportunities and this is half of the explanation for the popularity of miracles in black pentecostalism. The other half is the greater presence in black Christianity of the expectation of miracles (see MacRobert 1988). One can appreciate why many poor whites would feel similarly unmoved by an ethos tailored to the situation of small businessmen, small farmers, or independent craftsmen.

It also fits best with a culture of *production*. As commentators of various political hues have noted, modern industrial societies laud heroes of consumption but even had the world of production remained an important source of images of prestige, it would not have been informed by the sort of direct connection between effort and reward envisaged by Mrs Sunday. As C. Wright Mills's *White Collar* (1956) and W.H. Whyte's *The Organization Man* (1960), classic sociological studies of the 1950s, noted, the growth in the post-war period of large bureaucracies had subordinated many individuals to the organization.

In the absence of good empirical material one is forced back on informed speculation but there seems little doubt that the health and wealth gospel and its slightly more moderate televangelism cousin appeals primarily to the working class and the lower middle class. Although it has rightly been criticized for failing to live up to its author's expectations of providing a general explanation of crime and deviance, Robert K. Merton's seminal 'Social structure and anomie' essay (1957) does point us in the right direction for understanding the appeal of prosperity theology to a particular section of the population who are already disposed to conservative Protestantism. The core of his essay is the simple but important point that there is a disjuncture at the heart of modern democracies. All members of our societies are encouraged to want and expect the same 'good things' out of life. That is, the goals are distributed universalistically. But the means to achieve these goals legitimately are not equally distributed. Some people have a long head start and others are patently handicapped. The result is a strong sense for many people of being *relatively deprived.*

One might also note Durkheim's comments about the role which limited expectations play in producing contentment. Unlike many other animals, our desires are not confined by a set of genetically given instincts. Left to our own devices there is no intrinsic limit to our desires. Satisfaction is produced by our culture convincing us that what we have is what we deserve. Such an equilibrium existed for 'downscale' conservative Protestants when they reconciled themselves to a low standard of living by denouncing as ungodly and 'worldly' the pleasures which they could not afford. For many, the balance of expectations and circumstances was destroyed by an improvement in their standard of living undermining their commitment to the previously orthodox asceticism. As Durkheim put it at the turn of the century:

> as the conditions of life are changed, the standard according to which needs are regulated can no longer remain the same. . . . With increased prosperity desires increase. At the very moment when traditional rules have lost their authority, the richer prize offered these appetites stimulates them and makes them more exigent and impatient of control.
>
> (1970: 252-3)

And of course, it is made all the worse by two things. As Meyrowitz argues in his excellent discussion of the long-term impact of the electronic media, we are all much better informed about the lives (and material comforts) of our social superiors. The social distance which to some extent kept us in ignorance of what we were missing has gone. And producers and the advertisers they pay are in the business of encouraging us to believe we deserve more and better. To return to Merton, the result is a sense of relative deprivation which clearly bears down on all of us but which effects some groups – essentially those with least – more than others.

To simplify, there are two possible responses to relative deprivation. For a section of those people who are excluded from such conventional channels of social mobility as education, the response is the instrumental one of working ever harder, taking a second job, often in a DSO. Organizations such as Tupperware and Amway have a strong affinity with conservative Protestantism in two ways; indirectly in that the entrepreneurial ideology of DSOs is itself a 'secularized' form of some elements of the conservative Protestant tradition and directly in that the values found in conservative Protestant religion and in the direct selling economy combine to reinforce each other. But for reasons which are not yet clear (but which almost certainly stem from their position in the economy) some people do not produce that instrumental response but fall back instead on the magical promises of prosperity theology and 'name it and claim it'. The success in fund-raising of those television evangelists who make such promises demonstrates the demand, the need, which exists for miraculous solutions to socio-economic problems.

However, this should not be taken, as it is by Stark and Bainbridge in their grand theory of religion (1985), as an explanation of why some people are attracted to religious belief. Where they argue that the persistence of needs that cannot be met in this world explains why people believe in a next world, I would argue (see Wallis and Bruce 1986: 47-80) that the faith comes first. It is because they are already disposed to believe that the Bible is the word of God, that there is a God who takes a direct interest in our lives, and that prayer works, that some people come to see solutions to their economic problems in religious activities.

Chapter Eight

TELEVANGELISM AND POLITICAL CAMPAIGNS

If evangelical and fundamentalist religious broadcasting was only a complementary source of spiritual gratifications for conservative Protestants, there would be little interest in it beyond the circles of those who like it and those who deplore it. What explains the public interest in televangelism is the belief, suspicion, or fear that religion on American radio and television is being used to mobilize a powerful socio-political movement. Before the appearance on the political stage of Jerry Falwell and the Moral Majority, prime-time preachers only featured in the secular media for the occasional witty traveller's tale about the oddities of snake-handling cult religious life in the deep south. In so far as there was a consistent theme in such reports it was 'How can people believe this sort of thing?' But since the new Christian right commanded the attention of journalists, televangelists have been examined with new respect.

This chapter will look at the history of political involvement of religious broadcasters before turning to a description of the new Christian right and an evaluation of its importance. Finally, it will examine in some detail the campaign of Pat Robertson for the Republican nomination for the 1988 presidential election. The next chapter will offer a general assessment of the political power of the prime-time preachers.

SMALL TOWN CRANKS AND COLD WARRIORS

Many of the very first radio evangelists were involved in politics but the weakness of their transmitters and the absence of the technology and the social organization for an efficient syndicating system meant that their interests, like their audience, tended to be parochial. They could only be heard over small areas and confined themselves to fighting personal feuds with their rivals and with local political big-wigs. 'Fighting Bob' Shuller's campaigns against public officials of Los Angeles in the 1920s were an example. He annoyed enough powerful people for his radio licence to be withdrawn! (Orbison 1977; Schultze 1988a).

Father Coughlin

The first radio preacher consistently to offer political messages to a significant audience was Father Charles Coughlin who began regular broadcasting on religious topics in October 1926 (Brown 1980). From 1930, when he secured a place on a national network, his talks became increasingly political (Barnouw 1968: 44-7). Initially he was a radical monetary reformer but like many economic populists he gradually moved from criticising bankers to being thoroughly anti-semitic. He supported F.D. Roosevelt during his first years in office but turned against him in 1935. His National Union for Social Justice organization first got involved in democratic primaries and then joined two other populist move-ments – Gerald L.K. Smith's Share-Our-Wealth (which had been founded by Huey Long) and Dr Francis Townsend's Old Age Movement – in the Union Party. Unable to agree which of the three should run against Roosevelt, they supported little-known Representative William Lemke of North Dakota (Lipset and Raab 1978: 170). Like Pat Robertson in 1988, Coughlin supposed that his radio popularity could be turned into votes. He claimed 5 million members for his National Union; his radio audiences were certainly in the millions but his candidate polled only 900,000 votes nationally.

Coughlin's reaction to his political impotence was to become increasingly fascist. He supported Franco, Mussolini, and Hitler, attacked governors who would not use troops to break strikes, accused everyone with whom he disagreed of communism and after war had broken out, vehemently opposed any attempt to assist the allies. The larger radio stations refused to renew his contracts and he cancelled his 1940-41 series. The following year, the Postmaster-General prevented his magazine *Social Justice* being distributed by mail on the grounds that it was seditious. To prevent a trial for sedition, the Attorney-General asked the Archbishop of Detroit to stop Coughlin broadcasting. Father Coughlin accepted his Archbishop's instruction and his career as a radio demagogue was over (Lipset and Raab 1978: 150-208).

Carl McIntire

For conservative Protestants, the most formidable cold war broadcaster was Carl McIntire. McIntire built a career on schism. As a student at Princeton Theological Seminary, he walked out of the Presbyterian Church in the split led by J. Gresham Machen and enrolled at Machen's new Westminster College. For a short time he was a minister in Machen's Presbyterian Church of America but he wanted pre-millennialism made an essential doctrine and a more vigorously separatist stand. In 1938 the PCA divided into Machen's orthodox Presbyterians and McIntire's Bible Presbyterians (Clabaugh 1974: 66-98).

The mainstream Protestant denominations had formed the ecumenical Federal Council of Churches. In 1941, McIntire responded by founding the American Council of Christian Churches as a forum for separatist fundamentalist groups but his difficult personality alienated many who agreed with his theology. Instead of joining McIntire, a much larger body of evangelicals led by theologian Carl Henry and evangelist Billy Graham formed the National Association of Evangelicals. The NAE in turn helped form the National Religious Broadcasters (NRB) to oppose the near monopoly of radio broadcasting then enjoyed by the mainstream churches. Bob Jones Snr, the founder of the university that bears his name, was a founding director of NRB. In 1942 McIntire tried to take over the nascent NAE by suggesting it merge with his American Council but he was snubbed (Gasper 1963; Saunders 1968). Until 1958, McIntire addressed the nation largely through his newspaper the *Christian Beacon*. In that year he decided to enter large-scale radio broadcasting and, for the next decade, his combination of strident fundamentalism and a steady right-wing critique of progressive social policy made him one of the best known voices on the Christian right. In 1963, he was heard five times a week on 577 radio stations (Forster and Epstein 1964: 101).

Like Coughlin, McIntire saw all evil as the result of communist, communist-led, or communist-inspired conspiracy. Income tax

164

was communist. Trade unionism was communist. Racial integration was communist. And, above all else, the ecumenical movement was communist. Despite being based in Collingswood, New Jersey, McIntire's strongest following was in the south. Connecticut had only 2 radio outlets, Massachusetts 3, and New York state had only 4, of which 3 were in small towns. Texas had 27, Florida had 26, California had 23, Alabama had 20, Mississippi had 19, as did Georgia, and South Carolina had 17 radio outlets (much the same regional spread as modern televangelism). His period of prosperity was relatively short-lived. In one of its rare actions, the Federal Communications Commission rejected McIntire's application for the renewal of radio station WXUR (in aptly- named Media, Pennsylvania) on the grounds of persistent violation of the fairness doctrine. McIntire's appeal through the courts was firmly rejected. The United States Court of Appeals found:

> During the entire license period Brandywine (WXUR) wilfully chose to disregard commission mandate. With more brazen bravado than brains, Brandywine went on an independent frolic broadcasting what it chose, in any terms it chose, abusing those who dared differ from its viewpoints. The record is replete with example after example of one-sided presentation on issues of controversial importance to the public.
>
> (Quoted in Clabaugh 1974: 94)

McIntire threatened to broadcast from an off-shore pirate radio station but he was financially over-extended. His influence was further curtailed by his loss of status within the separatist fundamentalist circles he strove to dominate. In 1968, he fell out with the executive committee of his American Council of Christian Churches and the majority departed from him, accusing him of violating the separatist principle by becoming over-involved with non-believers in pursuit of political causes.

Billy James Hargis

One of McIntire's protégés was a young Disciples of Christ preacher from Tulsa, Oklahoma. Educated at the Ozark Bible College in Bentonville, Arkansas, Billy James Hargis was fired from his first charge in Ozark after accusing the local school principal of having an affair with one of his teachers and chiding his church elders for cinema-going. In 1948 he gave up the pastorate to found his Christian Crusade against Communism. Like McIntire, Billy James Hargis believed that the ecumenical National Council of Churches, the National Association for the Advancement of Coloured People and the American Civil Liberties Union were communist fronts.

He first came to public prominence in 1953 when he joined McIntire in protesting against the formation in Amsterdam of the World Council of Churches. McIntire countered by creating the International Council of Christian Churches and earned his organization considerable publicity by, with Billy James Hargis, floating bible texts and tracts into Warsaw Pact countries from the East German border.

From around 1956 to the early 1960s, Dr Hargis ran a growing and lucrative business which not only saw him increasing his number of radio outlets but also had him talking of starting a Christian college. However the more liberal climate of the post-Kennedy era found support falling away. There was something of a revival in the late 1960s but – a not uncommon problem for evangelists – there was a sex scandal. Hargis officiated at the wedding of two of his students. They reported that on their first night together, they decided to clear the air and confess their previous sexual misdemeanours; they found that both of them had had sex with Billy James (Bruce 1985).

Although McIntire and Hargis had, and indeed still have, enough support to make a living spreading the anti-communist message to the fundamentalist faithful, their organizations never grew beyond a few buildings, a couple of assistants, and a reasonable living for themselves. Compared to the operations of Humbard or Roberts, McIntire's Twentieth Century Reformation movement and Hargis's Christian Crusade were very small beer. McIntire was unwilling to, and Hargis incapable of, successfully making the transition to television and neither became genuinely nationally popular on radio. They were an important element in the network of the radical right but their audiences would rarely have gone beyond a million. They were very obviously less popular than preachers such as Billy Graham and Charles Fuller who eschewed overtly political preaching. Forster and Epstein, who as liberal Cassandras had an interest in making the *Danger on the Right* (the title of their book) as frightening as possible, estimate that Hargis's audience for the climax meeting of what they describe as a highly successful tour was 4,500 (1964: 83); impressive for an ordinary church service but thin for a major evangelist. The point is clear. The sirens of the radical right attracted enough of an audience to make a living from it but it was those evangelists such as Humbard, Schuller, and Roberts who stayed away from politics who built large and loyal followings.

THE NEW CHRISTIAN RIGHT

There is always something arbitrary about the cut-off dates which historians and journalists use to slice the history of gradual changes into neat units. There is also something contrived about the boundaries imposed on social movements by giving them names. The 'new' Christian right was really not all that new. Many of the values which informed the political activism of funda-mentalists in 1980 were the same as those which had motivated the generation of Hargis and McIntire. Many of the personnel were the same. But to recognize continuities is not to go as far as those who argue that there was nothing at all new about the period of activism from 1978 to 1988 (see, for example, Miller 1985). In the first place, there had been a lull in fundamentalist political involve-ment. Although it is not as neat as the business cycle, there is a regular pattern of involvement, disillusionment, retreat, and re-involvement. Conservatives gradually come to be concerned about the moral, political, and spiritual state of America. They get off their verandas and campaign. When the campaign fails, they go back to the verandas to concentrate on preserving their own purity while America continues to slide down the tubes. The 1960s had been the era of the liberal clergyman in politics. While Martin Luther King, fellow black clergy, and their white sympathizers campaigned for civil rights and later an end to the Vietnam war, fundamentalist ministers such as Jerry Falwell argued against ministers being diverted from their primary task of preaching the word to engage in things of the world.

The new Christian right differed from previous radical right Christian movements in that the main uniting point was not fear of communism (although most NCR people would be anti-

167

communist) but hostility towards 'secular humanism', a notion developed to draw together the complex of social and cultural changes which offended against the world-view of fundamentalist America. Fundamentalists did not like liberalism in sexual mores, increased use of abortion, changes in gender roles, the according of group rights to racial minorities or to women, or increased secularity in cosmopolitan culture. But more than that, they did not like the expansion of the power of the state or the increased centralization of cultural production which meant that the values and practices they found abhorrent were getting closer all the time and their ability to organize institutions which insulated them from these evils was under threat. The response was to campaign against both the specific values and practices they disliked and against the encroachments of the state.

The NCR also differed from previous incarnations in using the most advanced technology to bring together individuals and groups in the *appearance* of a mass social movement. Essentially it was constructed on (a) the audiences for the religious programmes of Jerry Falwell, James Robison, and to a much lesser extent Pat Robertson; (b) the names on their mailing lists; and (c) the informal and formal networks which linked fundamentalist Baptist ministers. This latter frame was especially important because it was local pastors who led voter registration drives and who tried to sensitize their congregations into a more active involvement in politics. Liebman (1983) is right to argue that we should not forget the informal contact networks of fundamentalist ministers in our attention on mass media.

Finally, the NCR was unique in the history of American Protestant politics in trying to build alliances with conservative Catholics, Jews, Mormons, and secular conservatives. Although supporters were mobilized by appealing to the threat to their religiously legitimated culture, once mobilized they were encouraged to work to save their 'shared Judeo-Christian' heritage rather than to preserve their Bible-believing Baptist fundamentalist world. In practice the alliance never gelled. It was asking too much of southern Baptists that on Sunday they hold the Pope to be the anti-Christ and on Monday they work amicably with Catholics. Even had fundamentalists been capable of such alternation, Catholics, Jews, and Mormons had good memories and found this new tolerant fundamentalism hard to believe, especially when one had Southern Baptist leaders such as Bailey Smith saying that 'God Almighty does not hear the prayer of a Jew' (in Bruce 1988: 128).

Hadden explained the growth of televangelism as being partly a product of a general shift to the right in culture and in politics:

> the electronic church's success reflects the cultural drift – some would say stampede – toward conservatism. . . . Culturally, large segments of our population are ready for change. Conservative political and economic views have much greater credibility than at any time since the Great Depression.
>
> (Hadden 1980: 611)

He also expected 'evangelicals to make a significant impact on the political scene in America' and to 'utilize the electronic church to gain a power base' (Hadden 1980: 612). His remarks seemed prescient when the NCR came to national prominence. One of its tactics in elections was to target liberals and accuse them of being anti-Christian, anti-family, anti-traditional values, and the like. Of 27 congressional liberals targeted in 1980, 23 – including well-known senators Birch Bayh, George McGovern, and Frank Church – lost their seats. The incautious and the interested hailed this as a great victory for the NCR but the swing against these liberals was the same or slightly less than the swing against Democrats in states where the NCR was not active (Lipset and Raab 1981). After the elections, Hadden wrote:

> The real importance of the Moral Majority and other New Christian Right organizations is not in what they accomplished during the 1980 elections, but in the *potential* they represent as a burgeoning social movement. . . . There is much restlessness and discontent in America today, and much of it is mobilizable in the name of Christian virtue.
>
> (Hadden and Swann 1981: 165)

That is as may be but beyond registering a large number of new voters (southern white fundamentalists are generally reluctant voters), the NCR seems to have had little impact on elections. None has been claimed for more than the occasional local contest since 1980. As for the claim that the NCR represents a general swing (or as Hadden put it 'stampede') to the right, there is no evidence for such a swing on socio-moral issues or on matters of personal demeanour and behaviour. This is an important point and some space will be given to a thorough discussion of it below (pp. 184–9).

The NCR's lack of success in elections not surprisingly, has, been accompanied by a lack of success elsewhere. Even with eight years of the most sympathetic president the NCR is liable to see, there have been few changes which the politically involved conservative Protestants could claim as victories. Not one piece of legislation promoted by the NCR was placed on the federal statute books. There were a number of successes at the level of state legislatures and more at the level of school board but significant decisions on fundamental constitutional issues get referred upwards by the centripetal legal system and come in the end to be judged by the higher courts and the Supreme Court. The NCR has tried to pass laws requiring that any time given to evolution in school biology classes or texts must be matched by equal time for 'creation science'; it has failed. The NCR has tried to have 'secular humanism' defined as a religion so that it can be expelled from classrooms and textbooks; it has failed. The NCR has tried to overturn the ruling that public prayer in schools is unconstitutional because it amounts to the state promoting a religion; it has failed.

PAT ROBERTSON FOR PRESIDENT

While the Reagan presidency, being high on rhetoric and low on action, must have been a disappointment to committed new Christian rightists, the close of that era brought them a unique opportunity to express their political faith. The candidacy of Pat Robertson for the Republican party's nomination for the presidential election of 1988 gives us a very clear indicator of the value of televangelism as a political base.

Robertson's relationship to the new Christian right had been ambiguous. He had co-chaired the Washington For Jesus rally with Bill Bright but, once Jerry Falwell's Moral Majority had started to make the running, Robertson withdrew from political activity. When I wrote to him in 1981 and asked if I could interview him in connection with my research interest in the new Christian right, he declined, saying that 'as I am not involved in politics', there was little point in seeing me. In a letter to the founding organizer, Ed McAteer, Robertson explained his resignation from Religious Roundtable, a new Christian right organization: 'I am vitally concerned with our country yet my personal leading from the Lord is to change society through spiritual rather than political means' (quoted in Hill 1986). However, he maintained quiet links with some grass roots socio-moral issue activists through his Freedom Council, an organization which provided funds and legal advice to fundamentalists fighting 'secular humanism' in the courts. In 1985 a whispering campaign was started, no doubt with encouragement from Robertson. *The Saturday Evening Post* ran a cover feature on him which mentioned him as a possible successor to Ronald Reagan. It what may be regarded as an own-goal, Paul Kirk, the Democratic party chairman, gave pride of place in a fund-raising letter to the spectre of Robertson running for the nomination. While Kirk's intention was to scare money out of faithful Democrats, the letter was immensely useful to Robertson. Secular newspapers picked up the story and began to run features on Robertson, who happily included copies of the Kirk letter in his press kit for most of the following year. With this head of the steam of publicity, Robertson went to the March 1986 meeting of nomination seekers at the Opryland Hotel in Nashville and impressed Republican party leaders.

Robertson became a serious candidate in May, showing the first signs of the strength of his grassroots support when he 'won' the Michigan delegate selection. This very early and organizationally arcane 'beauty competition' is usually ignored by commentators and hardly taken more seriously by candidates, but a rather nervous George Bush, hoping to get his campaign off to a good start, had given it some prominence as had the young congressman widely regarded as the best hope of the radical right or the 'movement' conservatives, Jack Kemp. Robertson made a third. Just what was at stake is not clear. As a *New York Times* columnist put it:

> What actually happened, though nothing may have, was possibly that some Republicans elected some delegates, some of whom may or may not have been pledged to one or more of the three candidates. These delegates in turn, though they might be pledged to somebody, don't have to stay pledged

171

even if bought; but that doesn't matter because they won't vote for any Presidential candidate anyway but only for some other delegates, who will in turn vote for still others.

(Quoted in Hadden and Shupe 1988: 187)

Whatever its real significance, Bush himself had made it important by entering and Robertson made it newsworthy by spoiling Bush's launch. Although there was considerable argument about details of numbers, the televangelist had registered as many delegates as Bush and more than Kemp.

In mid-September 1986 Robertson hired Constitution Hall in Washington and used his satelite network to beam the show to invited guests at 216 sites (*Time* 29 September 1986: 31). Oral Roberts, in one of his very few acts of support for the NCR, spoke warmly of Pat and of his fitness for the presidency. In an extremely astute move which allowed him to campaign without giving up hosting the *700 Club* (as he would have to do under electoral law once he declared himself a candidate), Robertson told the viewers:

If by September 17th, 1987, ... three million registered voters have signed petitions telling me that they will pray, that they will work, that they will give toward my election, then I will run as a candidate for the nomination of the Republican Party for the office of President of the United States of America.

Now the serious examination began. It was quickly discovered that Robertson had exaggerated his educational qualifications ('graduate study at the London School of Economics' was in fact an all-comers summer school), had married after impregnating his wife to be, and had radically inflated his war record. In early biographies, his heroic service in Korea was mentioned. In September 1986, Paul McCloskey, a Republican congressman wrote an open letter in which he challenged Robertson's version of his service record. McCloskey (who had won several medals including a Purple Heart) shared a troop ship with Robertson on the way to Korea and he recalls Robertson being left behind in Japan. Another lieutenant who was also held back for staff duties recalls Robertson saying he had talked to his father on the telephone. The clear implication of that report, and of McCloskey's letter, was that Robertson had been kept back from

172

combat duty because his father, a powerful senator from Virginia, used influence. Robertson vehemently denied this interpretation and filed a suit against McCloskey, but withdrew the action in 1988. He explained that he was abandoning the law suit because it would come to court at the climax of his campaign and be a distraction, rather than because he admitted the substance of McCloskey's charge.

It was not only in the detail that his curriculum vitae was contested. Robertson had skilfully altered his image so that he was now less of a televangelist and more of a businessman and a captain of industry (Bruce 1988: 129-30). To further that re-casting, Robertson had taken himself off the *700 Club* in late 1986 but People for the American Way worked hard to remind Americans of Robertson's previous persona. They put together a video of clips from his television shows. Particularly memorable was his claim to have diverted Hurricane Gloria from the Virginia coast.[1]

Fears of Armageddon

A considerable amount of hostile attention was given to the possible influence of Robertson's religion on his foreign policy. After all, James Robison had neatly articulated one element of fundamentalist thought when he said:

> If you believe that we are going to have peace on this earth before Jesus comes back, you are anti-scriptural, anti-spiritual, anti-God and anti-Christ. . . . Jesus has informed us that there will be wars and rumours of wars until the world's end. Not maybe. Not could be. There will be wars.
>
> (Quoted in Jenkins 1981: 23)

Serious attention focused on Robertson's 'pre-millennial dispensational eschatology',[2] although it was usually described in less formal terms as his 'apocalyptic vision'. There had already been some concern in the early days of the Reagan administration when it was reported that Reagan believed that the end of the world was nigh. What was especially troubling were the details of the eschatological scheme. In the pre-millennial dispensationalism popularized by the 18 million sold copies of Hal Lindsay's *Late Great Planet Earth* the world ends in the following fashion. An Arab-African confederacy headed by Egypt will invade Israel. Russia and her allies will also attack Israel before turning on the Arab-African forces and destroying them. The Russians will kill millions of Jews before God kills five-sixths of the Russians. With the Russians out of the way, the final all-out war between western civilization, captained by the anti-Christ, and the hordes of the orient, led by the Chinese, will begin. And thus the world ends on the plains of Armageddon.

But before the slaughter begins, the converted saints will be lifted out of this world (the technical term is 'raptured'). As Tim La Haye puts it:

> The Rapture will be an event of such startling proportions that the entire world will be conscious of our leaving. There will be airplane, bus and train wrecks throughout the world. Who can imagine the chaos on the freeways when auto-mobile drivers are sucked out of their cars?
> (Quoted in Dobson and Hindson 1986: 20)

Who indeed? The general fear was that, if he knew he would be spared the wars and plagues which will attend the end times, might the born again Christian not be slow to act to prevent wars? America, the Soviet Union, the NATO alliance, and the countries of the Middle East all have parts to play in the Lindsay vision of the unfolding conflict between Christ and anti-Christ. Dispensation-alists such as Robertson are fond of identifying this or that regional conflict as evidence of the end times. Would someone who saw the players and circumstances of geo-political tension as evidence of an event they welcomed be as committed to conflict resolution as someone who saw no merits in the apocalypse?

This was all sufficiently worrying when it was reported simply as a set of beliefs to which President Reagan assented. Most com-mentators supposed (quite rightly as later revelations about Nancy Reagan consulting an astrologer showed) that Reagan was not actually terribly committed to any body of religious doctrine. But Pat Robertson believed it!

There is actually little reason to suppose that those who believe that the end times are upon us will act very differently to the rest of us. Given the impossibility of knowing just when the Lord will return, one can only 'plan for a hundred years but live as if Jesus would return tomorrow', to use a common fundamentalist expres-sion. Falwell and Robertson carry insurance and make plans for the future. But that the fear was unnecessary did not prevent people being concerned about Robertson's eschatology and his opponents were quick to exploit that concern.

As if he did not have problems enough, the spring of 1987 brought the Bakker scandal (see Chapter Ten). Having worked so hard to reconstruct his biography as businessman rather than evangelist, he now found himself at every press conference being asked for his reaction to the slowly emerging details of Jim Bakker's sexual and financial misdemeanours. Pat Robertson was a candidate because 'born again' Christianity was becoming respectable and even influential and suddenly every worst caricature of the licentious and greedy preacher feeding his lusts on the credulity of his flock was confirmed. And it was confirmed by the man who had been given his start in the business by Pat Robertson.

A year of campaigning with his new biography while not yet openly running did little to change public responses. By September 1987 Robertson had his three million signed up supporters and he had $10 million to spend, but the thickness of his Jericho walls can be gauged from reponses to a *Time* poll published in that month. Respondents were asked nine questions about the six Republican candidates. On seven of the themes, Robertson was rated last. For example, when asked if the various candidates were someone they 'would be proud to have as President', Republican voters and 'leaners' chose in the following proportions:

	%
George Bush	69
Bob Dole	68
Jack Kemp	58
Pete Du Pont	49
Al Haig	46
Pat Robertson	26

When asked if they thought the candidates would be effective in dealing with the Soviet Union, the sample responded as follows:

	%
Al Haig	67
George Bush	58
Bob Dole	55
Jack Kemp	49
Pete Du Pont	42
Pat Robertson	19

Haig's elevation from his usual position of second last reflected his experience in the army, on the National Security Council, and as Secretary of State; the image of the tough no-nonsense soldier was accepted by the sample. The only question which might have given a similar advantage to Robertson was 'Is —— someone you can trust?'; the rank order is interesting enough but the distance between top and bottom is significant.

	%
George Bush	80
Bob Dole	73
Jack Kemp	69
Pete Du Pont	61
Al Haig	49
Pat Robertson	43

While Robertson could expect to score low on experience (only 10 per cent thought he had the experience to be President), to have had a chance of performing any better than badly, he would have had to have been appreciated for personal qualities of character. Yet he was regarded as less trustworthy than four professional politicians and a soldier!

Even among southerners, he had a problem. A poll by the Roper organization for the *Atlanta Constitution* showed that only 16 per cent of adults in twelve southern states said they would consider voting for Robertson. More importantly, 69 per cent said they felt negative towards Robertson's campaign. This was the strongest negative rating of twenty potential Democratic and Republican candidates (Taylor 1987).[3]

However, once the race got under way, Robertson's prospects appeared to improve. In the first contest – the Iowa caucuses – he managed to beat Vice-President George Bush to come second behind Bob Dole (with 25 per cent to Dole's 37 and Bush's 19). Commentators were quick to point out that this had little significance for the final result. Party nominees are chosen by delegates at a nominating convention and the delegates are chosen in a variety of ways. In most states, delegates are elected in full primary elections by registered party voters. In America one has to register in order to vote. In most states and counties one is asked to register as a Democrat or a Republican. Being a registered Republican does not actually mean that one has to vote Republican and it certainly does not mean that one has to be an active member of the party. But it entitles one to vote in primary elections and a large proportion of voters exercise this right. The states which choose delegates by primary election thus contribute to the nominating convention approximately in conformity with the popular views of Republican voters in that state.

But some states, predominantly small ones, chose delegates by some version of a caucus. Instead of voting for a delegate who represents a particular candidate (that is, a Robertson man or a Bush woman), interested registered voters have to turn up at a particular place at a particular time and stand around in a Robertson or a Bush group. The obvious weakness of the caucus system is that it weights the opinions of the most committed. It is thus ideal for a candidate such as Pat Robertson who polarizes opinion, who is extremely popular with a small proportion of the population but disliked intensely by the rest. Every ounce of his support is on view because all the people likely to vote for him are committed enough to turn up for the caucus; much of the dislike he arouses is hidden because many of the people who will stop by the voting booth on election day and register an anti-Robertson vote will not bother to declare their feelings in the caucus by turning out for Bush or Dole.

But for all that commentators explained why Robertson's second place in the Iowa caucuses told us more about the commitment than about the breadth of his support, the press found Robertson's performance a useful angle on what was otherwise a very dull competition. All logic had George Bush winning because he was more popular and had more money than any other candidate and he enjoyed the backing of a very popular President. One way to make the race newsworthy was to talk up Robertson.

Robertson thus moved to the New Hampshire primary – a much more realistic test of popularity – with considerable momentum. His supporters were buoyed up, the press was treating him as a serious candidate, and the other Republican candidates had decided to treat him (in public at least) as the representative of a body of legitimate opinion. All of this made little difference as voting began to fall into the expected patterns. George Bush took 38 per cent of the vote against Bob Dole's 28 per cent; a considerable margin in a five horse race. Jack Kemp was third with 13 per cent, Pete Du Pont had 10 per cent, and Robertson had 9 per cent.

In some of the smaller states which chose delegates between New Hampshire in February and the simultaneous primaries in fifteen states on 8 March, Robertson's campaign continued to record very small percentage votes but for his candidacy to be at all meaningful, he had to do well in the south, the heartland of conservative Protestantism. A *Time* poll in late February suggested that 'Super Tuesday' would bring Robertson little good news. Only 15 per cent of southerners who said they were likely to vote in the primaries supported him and his negative ratings were as high in the south as anywhere. Given that the general election in the south would see many conservative Democrats voting for the Republican, it is sensible to consider the answers for voters of both parties to the question who 'would you definitely not vote for'. With 72 per cent, Robertson was less popular overall than even the liberal Democratic candidates. But most worrying was his failure to unite conservative Protestants. Likely Republican voters who described themselves as evangelicals or fundamentalists divided 44 per cent for Bush, 30 per cent for Dole, and only 14 per cent for Robertson. Even the conservative Protestants, when asked if they were more or less likely to vote for him in view of his former status as a clergyman, answered 'less likely' by 42 to 25 per cent (Barrett 1988: 13).

In the event, the poll was remarkably accurate. In almost every state (including his home state of Virginia), Robertson came a poor third, being beaten by Bush in every demographic group including fundamentalists. Even conservative southern Republicans – the people who form a very large part of Robertson's audience for the *700 Club* – did not want him as president.

Chapter Nine

CONSERVATIVISM, POLITICS, AND TELEVANGELISM

In a review of the influence of evangelicals on the Reagan administration, a senior editor of *New Republic,* himself an evangelical, said:
'Very little has been achieved. I would say that there is less of an
evangelical presence now in Washington than when Reagan came
into office' (Aikman 1988: 22). Robertson's attempt to move
conservative Protestant politics up a gear, from congressional to
presidential elections was a failure; he was unable to translate his
television audience into a coherent political movement. If one
wanted to argue that, *contra* the obvious inference from the
Robertson campaign, televangelism is a potent political force,
there are two analytically separable routes which could be taken.
First, one could consider the religious television audience as the
basis for the mobilization of a political movement. Second, one
could claim that the popularity of televangelism is symbolic of a
wider swing to the right in public opinion.

Taking these possibilities in order, let us consider the extent to
which televangelists stimulate political concerns in their audience.
Although the direction of cause is not obvious, there is a clear link
between the popularity of a televangelist and his political involvement; those preachers who have been most active in politics are
those of the second and even third division. Although some of the
first division – Humbard, Schuller, the Bakkers, and James
Kennedy but not Jimmy Swaggart – were present at the Washington For Jesus rally, they did not become active in the NCR. The
Bakkers, for example, gave a useful platform to various NCR
activists as they had earlier given publicity to Anita Bryant in her
fight against homosexual rights campaigns. If Falwell's name came
up in conversation with a guest celebrity, Jim Bakker might make

some reference to him being a 'man of God' or offer some other anodyne endorsement but he did not commit his prestige, name, and resources to the cause. New Christian right leaders were treated in the same way as other guest celebrities. They were lauded and given a platform to 'puff' their product but the promotion of them always took second place to Bakker's self-promotion.

Oral Roberts stayed away from socio-moral campaigns until his endorsement of Pat Robertson at the Constitution Hall meeting and then did nothing, either because he was not ideologically committed to such activity or because his funding difficulties with his medical school were more pressing. Humbard stayed away from the NCR and Schuller publicly dissociated himself from the movement. Even James Robison, the figurehead for McAteer's Religious Roundtable and a member of the board of Tim La Haye's American Coalition for Traditional Values, soon seems to have lost enthusiasm. After making a couple of television specials on the moral degeneracy of America, he became more interested in healing and in spirits than in elections and apart from delivering a prayer at the Dallas Republican party nominating convention of 1984, he does not seem to have been terribly active.

The impression that the main televangelists do not commit the prestige of their programmes to promoting political concerns is supported by some statistical research (Abelman and Neuendorf 1985, 1987). The contents of three episodes of each of the 27 most popular religious television programmes were analysed in some detail. A count was done of how often certain topics were raised and how much time was spent on them.[1] With the exception of the few shows modelled on current affairs 'magazine' programmes, 'Political topics receive little discussion, and only two percent of all program content has an overriding political emphasis' (Abelman and Neuendorf 1985: 109). When they are political, they are conservative, but they are not political very often. Only 3.8 per cent of the time was taken with politics, while 'social' issues accounted for 23.3 per cent of the programmes, and 72.9 per cent of the time was spent on 'religious' topics (Abelman and Neuendorf 1987). Furthermore, in the sorting classification, 'political' is a broad concept that includes mention of such matters as prayer in public schools and religious freedom. Most of the social issues discussed (death and dying by a long way the most popular) did not imply a political agenda and were not presented in any especially partisan manner. Rather they figured in advertisements for the personal relevance of salvation or in fund-raising justifications for the usefulness of the programme.

It should be no surprise that televangelists spend the vast majority of their time on air promoting salvation and the place of their work in furthering that worthy goal. For someone like Falwell, who could benefit considerably from the publicity, leading the Moral Majority was a good idea. Whatever it did to promote conservative socio-moral legislation, it did far more to promote Liberty University. But for someone who is already established and who has a very large following, political advocacy has the drawback that it may well divide the television audience and detract from the main task of promoting salvation and the fortunes of the preacher, his organization, and his programmes.

The likely consequences for audience size of political advocacy depend on the homogeneity of the audience. We know that religious television watchers share some characteristics other than their liking for fundamentalist television (see pp. 107–13), but we also know that the characteristics in question are not terribly good predictors of attitudes on a wide range of issues and that they do not produce anything like uniformity, even in simple situations of only two choices. Tamney and Johnson's series of studies of religion and politics in Middletown (Johnson and Tamney 1985) show that supporters of the NCR tend to be a sub-section of watchers of religious television, but even amongst what one might suppose is a relatively homogeneous group there was not a strong relationship between their religion and voting for Ronald Reagan in 1984.

To what extent does the televangelism audience agree on socio-moral issues? Leaving aside for a moment economic, welfare state, or foreign policy questions, is it the case that the televangelism audience is united on such matters as abortion, school prayer, the teaching of creation science, sex education courses in schools, and the other issues which the NCR has tried to mobilize around? As is often the case, we do not have good data which directly answer that question but we do have poll data which is suggestive. In 1988 the evangelical magazine *Christianity Today* polled a random sample of its subscribers on a number of socio-moral issues and discovered a complex situation. There was considerable agreement but not unanimity on some issues. 74 per cent of subscribers wanted creationism taught alongside evolutionism in schools but the rest did not; 80 per cent wanted more religion in textbooks but again – and remember these are committed evangelicals – the rest did not; 82 per cent wanted public prayer to be possible in schools but only 32 per cent wanted institutional, that is, school-led, prayers; – just under half were opposed. On the question of mandatory sex education classes those polled divided evenly for and against. On abortion there was considerable agreement; three-quarters supported a constitutional amendment to ban abortion except to save the life of the mother and a similar proportion wanted to stop federal funding of abortion and abortion-related activities.

Once one moves away from the penumbra of issues which have traditionally been seen as 'religious', much more disgreement appears. 65 per cent opposed the ERA (the equal rights for women) amendment but the rest did not; while just under half opposed making big cuts in the defence budget, an only slightly smaller number favoured such cuts; 42 per cent favoured deploying the 'strategic defence initiative' or 'star wars' technology (a big favourite with Falwell and the new Christian right) but 27 per cent opposed it.

On the economy, almost everyone wanted a mandated federal balanced budget. Like sin, budget deficit was something which everyone was 'agin' but there was little agreement about how fiscal righteousness was to be attained. An exactly equal number wanted taxes raised and opposed tax rises; 38 per cent on each side. Similar proportions favoured and opposed cost-cutting reform of Medicare and social security. On the use of import controls to reduce the foreign trade imbalance and on the question of the government taking a strong role in controlling the stock market, the sample divided almost equally between for, against, and undecided.

Consider the responses to foreign policy questions: 47 per cent supported but 25 per cent opposed military aid to the Contras; 44 per cent did not want America to take a less interventionist line in policy, but the rest did; 54 per cent wanted the US to 'work harder at fighting communism around the world'. Considering the history of anti-communism among American evangelicals this is remarkable; only just over half of a sample of *Christianity Today* subscribers endorsed what twenty years before could have stood as a test of fellowship in most conservative Protestant circles. And this when Falwell, Robertson, and such movement organizations as Beverley La Haye's Concerned Women of America had been campaigning for political support and raising money for the Nicaraguan 'freedom fighters' (Lawton 1988: 50-1).

Not only are conservative Protestants divided in their stated attitudes to specific issues but, more importantly, they are divided about *the extent to which they should agree.* That is to say, there is no consensus about what part religion ought to play in their thinking about socio-moral and political issues. In theory most conservatives are like other people; they hold simultaneously that religious beliefs should inform all one's thinking and that there ought to be some distance between religion and politics. In abstract this is fine, but when it comes to specific cases, conservative Protestants cease to agree. A study of Moral Majority activists in Ohio (Wilcox 1988) suggested that, when divided theologically into evangelicals and fundamentalists, it was the evangelicals rather than the fundamentalists who were keener on political involvement. This, of course, is exactly what a historically informed perspective would lead us to expect. Fundamentalists have traditionally retreated from the world and the temptation to go back to their isolationist position of protecting their purity from worldly entanglements is so strong that their commitment to politics will always be fragile. While evangelicals are more disposed to involvement, they are less conservative than fundamentalists. Thus the two tendencies – the general affinity between conservatism in religion and politics and willingness to be politically active – look like cancelling out.

In another study, 552 Baptists and Methodists in a city in south eastern America, most of them theologically conservative, were questioned about their television watching, their attitudes to various sorts of political entanglements, and the weight that they gave to the political direction of various sources of opinion. The first interesting observation was that, although there was a high level of support in principle for churches taking political stands, there were no great differences between those who watched televangelism and those who did not (Mobley 1984). When asked to rank seven possible sources of political advice, all put televangelists last, below their own children! Gaddy similarly concluded: 'it does not appear that religious broadcasts are having any impact on the views of their audience on [the public role of religious organizations]' (1984: 296).

AN EXCURSION ON TECHNICAL PROBLEMS OF OPINION POLLING

The above data have been introduced to give some idea of the variety of opinion within what would be the core of any movement mobilized on the audience for religious television. However, there are a number of serious technical problems which must be considered if we are to avoid drawing rash conclusions from such material. In a short but incisive article in 1954, Herbert Blumer raised fundamental issues about the nature of public opinion which are to this day ignored by pollsters and those who make confident use of their results.

The relative proportions of *Christianity Today* subscribers holding this or that view were arrived at by asking individuals to answer questions or respond to opinions. Pollsters assume that respondents understand the questions in the same way as they do and in the same way as each other; it is taken for granted that all respondents are hearing the 'same' question. Furthermore, it is assumed that the answer represents the opinion of the respondent in more than the trivial sense. That is, it is supposed (a) that respondents have an opinion about the matter in hand before they are asked about it; (b) that they will continue to hold that opinion for some time to come; and (c) that they care. There are problems with these and related assumptions. There are, of course, relatively few difficulties in accepting at face value what individuals say about their intentions to act in some simple and predictable future circumstance, such as an election (and pollsters still get results wrong). The further removed the projected circum- stances and the more ambiguous the situation one has to imagine in order to answer the question, the less reliable the answers are as predictors of action.

But Blumer raises an even more profound difficulty about the nature of public opinion. Pollsters have no notion of what sort of thing this public opinion is other than their operational definition: public opinion is what they get when they ask a random sample of the supposedly relevant 'public' questions about their opinions.

Public opinion is thus the aggregate of expressions of opinion given by a random sample of individual members of some public.[2] But opinions are not things we all arrive at idiosyncratically: they are collective products. They are produced in the interactions of people in groups. And any competent layman knows that, within a group, not everyone's opinion counts for the same. Furthermore, the views of some groups count for a lot more than the views of others.

> The formation of public opinion occurs in large measure through the interaction of groups. I mean nothing esoteric by this last remark. I merely refer to the common occurrence of the leaders or officials of a functional group taking a stand with reference to an issue and voicing explicitly or implicitly this stand on behalf of the group. Much of the interaction through which public opinion is formed is through the clash of these group views and positions.
>
> (Blumer 1954: 73)

It may be that there are some sorts of actions which individuals perform on the basis of their opinions without consulting anyone else, or considering the expressed views of anyone else, or talking with anyone else about their actions, but I cannot think of any which are not trivial. In all other cases where we might be interested in knowing how people might behave, public opinion in the sense in which pollsters define it through their polling activities, is of little value. Opinion matters only when the base is *mobilized* and turned into pressure on decision-makers. For public opinion to matter, Supreme Court justices, elected politicians, and businessmen must respond to what they suppose is the public mind. And that is in the simplified model of political science textbooks. In reality, what matters to a politician is his active electorate, not the public, and a skilful politician can usually narrow down even further the 'swing vote' who really need to be courted. Businessmen worry about their customers, not the public. What justices and judges consider remains a mystery.[3]

Although the technical details may be a little tedious it is important to get an idea of just how murky these waters are. At the

same time, we can consider the evidence for the main theme of
Hadden and Shupe's study of televangelism: the claim that there
has been a major swing to the right in America. A crucial 'text' in
most recent discussions of public opinion on socio-moral contests
and the rise of the new Christian right is a paper by John Simpson
(1983) in which he attempted to measure general public support
for the platform of the Moral Majority, using opinion poll data.
Simpson concluded that the Moral Majority platform was accepted
in its entirety by 30 per cent of the American public and that a
further 42 per cent were ideological fellow travellers of the new
Christian right. These figures were arrived at by analysing
responses to four items in the NORC General Social Survey (GSS)
for 1977. The four concerned women's role in society, abortion,
homosexuality, and school prayer. Simpson labelled certain
responses to each item as consistent with the Moral Majority
platform.

> Some 30% of the 1977 GSS respondents said that women
> should take care of the home and family while men work
> outside the home, that women should not be able to obtain
> a legal abortion for any reason, that homosexuality is always
> wrong, and that mandatory religious exercises should be
> permitted in the public schools.
>
> (Sigelman and Presser 1988: 327)

Although Simpson's conclusions seem at first sight supported by
the data, Sigelman and Presser's re-analysis casts considerable
doubt on Simpson's findings. I will look closely at two such
difficulties. For two of the items – school prayer and abortion – the
questions allowed three responses: agree, disagree, and don't
know. Although we might argue with Simpson's decision to count
the 'don't knows' as being supporters of the Moral Majority
position, there are such small numbers in that category that
moving them into the disagreement box would not make a big
difference: the 30 per cent becomes 27 per cent. Here the placing
of the cut-off line does not make much difference. But the issue of
women's roles was raised in a question for which there were *five*
possible responses. The statement 'It is much better for everyone
involved if the man is the achiever outside the home and the
woman takes care of the home and family' was presented and
people responded in the following percentages:

Strongly agree	18.0
Agree	46.0
Disagree	27.7
Strongly disagree	6.0
Don't know	1.5

Now we have to decide which positions to take as representative of the NCR view and hence where to place the cut-off line. Simpson put it between the second and third positions. That is, he took both the 'strongly agreed' and the 'agreed' to be pro-NCR. This is contestable. After all the new Christian right is extremely conservative in its view of the family and one might reasonably expect committed Moral Majoritarians to 'strongly agree'. Furthermore, the question is worded in such a way as to allow many people who are not personally committed to separate gender roles but who nonetheless feel that it is easier to acquiesce than to fight against the status quo, to agree. If one puts the cut-off between the first and second items, and then goes back to count how many respondents agree entirely with the Moral Majority platform, instead of 27 per cent of the GSS respondents, one has only 9 per cent.

Sigelman and Presser offer another criticism of the Simpson conclusion; that he confuses attitudes with policy positions. We know from many other studies that there is often an important difference between the general attitudes people have towards some issue and their support for particular attempts to formulate a *policy* about that issue. As they note:

> Whether homosexuality is 'always wrong' is not a policy issue, though it is full of policy implications, such as whether homosexual activity between consenting adults should be illegal. By the same token, whether women should tend to the family while men work outside the home is not a policy issue but whether the Equal Rights Amendment should be adopted is.
>
> (Sigelman and Presser 1988: 333)

Sigelman and Presser then go through the same GSS items and look for *policy statements* which accord with the new Christian right platform. On the question of abortion, Simpson had used the item: 'Please tell me whether or not you think it should be possible for a pregnant woman to obtain a *legal* abortion if the woman wants it for any reason?'; that is, an item which asks for a view about abortion on demand. But there was another abortion question in the 1977 GSS: 'Do you think abortions should be legal under any circumstances, legal only under certain circumstances, or never legal under any circumstances?' On this item, the Moral Majority position would be 'never legal under any circumstances'. Sigelman and Presser take this second abortion question, the school prayer question which Simpson uses, and questions about sex education and the Equal Rights Amendment – both issues on which the Moral Majority has a very clear position. In answer to 'Would you be for or against sex education in the public schools?', the Moral Majority would be 'against'. In answer to 'Do you strongly favor, somewhat favor, somewhat oppose or strongly oppose [the Equal rights for women] amendment?', the new Christian rightist would answer 'strongly oppose'.

Taking these four questions as their surrogate for the Moral Majority platfom, Sigelman and Presser find that only six people – 0.4 per cent – shared the Moral Majority view. Even shifting the cut-off point between the middle answers to give as broad an interpretation as possible to the Moral Majority position produced only 5 per cent in favour!

We clearly have an enormous difference here. On the one hand we have Simpson claiming that the 1977 GSS shows 30 per cent of Americans completely agreeing with the Moral Majority and a further 42 per cent coming close. On the other hand, we have Sigelman and Presser using the same survey data plausibly to argue that this is a massive exaggeration. My tendency is to agree with Sigelman and Presser that the items they have selected from the survey are more narrowly focused on clear NCR policy positions and are thus a more useful test of likely support.

The debate strongly suggests that Blumer was right: it just does not make sense to search for *the* opinion of a public. To aggregate responses to a number of questions and suppose that one has tapped into the world-view or ethos of a large population is profoundly naive. Apparent inconsistencies abound. Just to stress the point, the following are the percentage responses to the GSS question 'Do you strongly favor, somewhat favor, somewhat oppose or strongly oppose the Equal Rights Amendment?':

Strongly favor	17.9
Somewhat favor	40.0
Somewhat oppose	13.3
Strongly oppose	7.8
Don't know	20.0

Its opposition to the ERA is probably the only success the new Christian right can claim and the Moral Majority position is well-known but it is shared by less than 10 per cent of those asked. Yet by aggregating responses to other questions in the same survey, Simpson can claim that a large majority of Americans are supporters or fellow travellers of the new Christian right. Other attempts to measure general support for NCR positions have failed to produce similar results (Mueller 1983).

To return to the general problem of Hadden's claim for a 'stampede' towards conservativism, a wide-ranging review of survey studies of opinion during the first five years of the Reagan presidency could find no evidence for a general movement to the right. Ferguson and Rogers (1986) concluded that there had been a rightward shift on economic and related fiscal and regulatory matters. But the trend was not to a blanket conservativism. Rather people combined being (a) Reagan conservatives on the economy and foreign policy, (b) moderate Democrats on the welfare state, and (c) libertarians in their personal lives. Furthermore, to return to the moral of Pat Robertson's election campaign (which unfortunately occurred after Hadden and Shupe had made their erroneous assessment), even amongst those people who see themselves as socio-moral conservatives, there is considerable reluctance to support a movement such as the NCR.

CONSCIOUSNESS RAISING?

What implications do the above considerations have for the likelihood of the televangelism audience becoming a powerful social or political movement? Given that it does not seem to be a harbinger of a wider conservative swing, such power as televangelists will acquire must come from the mobilization of some or all of their own audiences. We have already seen that such audiences contain a wide variety of opinion on socio-moral and political concerns and are divided even on the extent to which religion should influence politics. It follows that televangelists can only

189

become politically powerful in so far as they can reduce internal disagreement as they 'raise the consciousness' of their audiences (supposing for a moment that they wanted to do such a thing). An obvious point which seems to have eluded Hadden and Shupe is that internal disagreement might be reduced but at the cost of the televangelist *alienating* that part of his audience which disagrees with the political lead he offers and thus reducing his reach. There is good reason to suppose that increased politicization will be accompanied by decreased market share for those evangelists who try it.

There is some evidence for this. The Sigelman and Presser re-analysis of Simpson's opinion poll data points out that they are more than a decade old and that, even if taken as an index of 'public opinion', represent something which may well have changed. The four items of the 1977 survey which Simpson uses as a surrogate for the Moral Majority platform also appear in the 1985 GSS. On abortion the response was almost exactly the same and agreement that homosexuality was always wrong had increased slightly (probably a response to AIDS). But there were substantial shifts away from the Moral Majority positions on the role of women and on school prayer. The following are the responses to the question: 'The United States Supreme Court has ruled that no state or local government may *require* the reading of the Lord's Prayer or Bible verses in public schools. What are your views on this – do you approve or disapprove of the court ruling?

	1977	1985
Approve	33.5	43.1
Disapprove	64.2	53.9
No opinion	2.3	3.1

In the intervening period, the NCR had had considerable success in making school prayer an issue. Bills had been tabled in Congress. Senators had proposed constitutional amendments to return the matter to the states. The President had declared himself in favour of school prayer and there had been a stream of well-publicized court cases. And televangelists had given air-time to the issue. Yet far from opinion moving in its direction, the NCR had lost ground; fewer people in 1985 disagreed with the Court decision. There are two possible interpretations of this, either of which deflates the potential for a successful new Christian right movement. It could be that the televangelism audience has become *more* committed to school prayer while the rest of the public has swung against it. This is certainly a possibility given other findings that organizations such as the Moral Majority are so unpopular that the support they raise is outnumbered by the detractors they stimulate into acting against them (see Johnson and Tamney 1985). Or it could be that the targets of consciousness raising activity thought more about the issues and decided that the NCR was wrong.

It has to remain likely that politicization, especially when it will be accompanied by a liberal counter-campaign, will backfire as supporters of conservative positions realize that there are actually some good reasons, apart from the Supreme Court being an agent of communism or secular humanism, for decisions they previously derided.

The GSS data is interesting but the most impressive evidence for the claim that a higher political profile for televangelists will be self-defeating has already been presented: the fate of Pat Robertson's campaign. The religious television audience, and the American public at large, were offered a close look at an advocate of 'traditional family values' who had a strong core of committed supporters and a very large war chest, and they turned him down.

SUMMARY: GROSS AND SUBTLE EFFECTS

Hadden and Shupe (1988) go from arguing that a lot of Americans do not like the idea of abortion, favour school prayer, and like the traditional family to supposing that there is in the country at large (but especially in the televangelism audience) a sleeping political giant just waiting to be woken. But, as Sigelman and Presser correctly observed, there is all the difference in the world between assenting to a poll question about some value and agreeing to support any particular policy instrument which is claimed to be supportive of that value. Apart from anything else, poll answers come from choices between hypothetical positions. Actions in the real world stem from choices between competing alternatives. The experience of the Reagan era with its various attempts to create a viable religio-political movement suggests that, while a sizeable minority of Americans support socio-moral positions which are more conservative than those presently enshrined in policy decisions, they are not sufficiently disturbed about these to be willing to put such concerns ahead of more secular considerations. There are good grounds for rejecting the Hadden and Shupe claim that their command of large amounts of television time gives televangelists a good base for a powerful political movement.

But it might still be argued that televangelism does have political impact. If it is the case that overt political advocacy is self-defeating, might it not be argued that the least obviously political evangelists are having the greatest long-term impact? Viewers can mentally insulate themselves from the overtly political. We know that viewers are quite capable of liking some parts of a programme and disliking others, of agreeing with some sentiments but rejecting others. In one community we find conservative pente-costalists who reject the wearing of cosmetics and fancy clothes enjoying some parts of the Bakkers' *PTL Club*, and hosts hardly come more made-up or flashy than Tammy Faye Bakker (Bourgault 1985). It may be that viewers who are not impressed by Falwell's Moral Majority activities still like his church services. It might follow that it is precisely when they are not doing politics but are offering apparently religious or ethical guidance that televan-gelists are being most effective in creating a general receptivity to conservative politics in their audience. This would be a two-phase model of political impact. Televangelism plays the part of generally preparing the audience for conservatism (by, for example, promoting individualism and self-reliance and associating wealth with godliness). In the second phase, secular conservatives, unhampered by controversial church and state entanglement baggage, reap the benefits.

This is an extremely plausible model but it does nothing to sustain the Hadden and Shupe view of the power of televangelism. It would only be relevant if a large part of the audience were in the middle or to the left of centre of American politics. But we know that the vast majority of supporters of religious television are already believers and already possess all those characteristics loosely related to conservativism. While televangelists may be having an effect in sustaining the conservativism of their viewers (always supposing that there were reasons why, without such sustenance, they might be changing) they can hardly be influential when they primarily attract people who already agree with them (Gaddy 1984).

192

THE FALLACY OF SOCIAL NEEDS

The above seems so much the obvious conclusion that the failure of Hadden and Shupe to come to it itself calls for explanation. The style of their book makes it a little difficult to separate the various grounds for their assessment but it seems that they are persuaded, not only by a reading of survey data at odds with my own, but also by contestable assumptions about a society's need for a shared value system. The key text is their discussion of Robert Bellah *et al.*'s *Habits of the Heart* (1985). In 1975, Bellah had published *The Broken Covenant* in which he argued that America's self-image had always had a religious core, a notion of a covenant between a chosen people and God. Since the foundation of the Republic, the 'civil religion', which bound the American people together despite their being divided in competing denominations, had faded. Idealism and commitment to shared liberal values had waned. In 1985, Bellah and his associates returned to the topic and pessimistically concluded that modern America had very little sense of commitment to *community*.[4] There was only cancerous individualism.

Hadden and Shupe follow mention of Bellah's work with an account of Pat Robertson's offer of a new vision to replace the old covenant and suggest that Robertson may succeed (or, if not him, then some other evangelical leader) because he has a social vision.

This is a *functionalist* argument. It supposes that societies can only remain stable if they are grounded in some decent shared values, a vision or a covenant. Conservative political thinkers such as Richard Neuhaus (who believes that modern America is unstable because religion has been removed from its centre to leave a 'naked public square') wish to provide a shared value system. Functionalist sociologists may not have one to offer but expect that one will appear. Just as in children's heroic history books where the hour provides the man, society's needs will be answered. Although they are not explicit, their juxtaposition of Bellah and Pat Robertson suggests that Hadden and Shupe believe: (a) that societies require shared visions; (b) that in modern America there is an absence of convincing secular or liberal Protestant versions; and thus, (c) that the conservative evangelicalism offered by the televangelists will become very popular. Robertson and Falwell (or their heirs) will succeed because society needs a shared world-view and theirs is one of very few on offer. And more than that, it is a world-view promoted with skill and resources on what Hadden and Shupe take to be a powerful and persuasive medium of communication.

There are a number of serious problems with this argument. The first has both an empirical and a theoretical element. Is it historically the case that societies have had shared visions? It is certainly possible to answer in the negative. Outside either very small undifferentiated societies or brief (often emergency) periods in the history of large societies, it is hard to find consensually shared ideologies. Abercrombie, Hill, and Turner (1980) demonstrate with admirable clarity that a number of societies which are known for their supposed possession of some integrating 'dominant ideology' were very far from being so integrated. Bellah's own work on civil religion is unpersuasive. While one can demonstrate that some Americans have been fond of invoking God as the source of their desires and schemes, one cannot show that the lives of most Americans have been informed by common beliefs and values. To take just what is usually offered as the first instance of 'civil religion' in America – the puritanism of the New England settlers – it is poor history to forget that half the settlers were not believers driven to escape religious persecution but adventurers seeking economic opportunities.

It is as plausible to see communities held together by economic necessity and mutual dependence as it is to see them being integrated by shared beliefs. Obviously, common material interest and circumstances, supported by frequent interaction, will tend to produce some shared understandings and culture but this is a long way from supposing that the community requires a shared ideology or social vision.

But even if the claims about the binding effects of shared religion in the past were correct, this would tell us nothing about the future, unless it were the case that the shared religiosity of the past were explained by society's *need* for such a thing. This sort of argument has been thoroughly discredited, for reasons which can briefly be demonstrated. It might be the case that a common religion causes social integration but this does not mean that we can explain the existence of the common religion by 'social integration'; an effect or consequence follows an action and cannot be the explanation of it. Only the desire for a consequence can be the cause of the action and that version requires a mistakenly anthropomorphic view of 'society' as an entity with conscious desires.

Functionalist explanations work well for understanding closed systems with feedback mechanisms. If we leave aside its minimal power of reasoning, my cat will do as a model of such a system. It has the 'need' to eat and knows this because not eating makes it weak (and eventually kills it). Hence we can treat eating as being caused by the part it plays in meeting a system need. Efforts to portray societies as such closed systems have failed miserably because there is no equivalent of a society weakening or 'dying'. Societies change all the time. At what point in a pattern of constant flux do we send the body to the morgue?

There is no America which feels that it could do with some more social integration and which thinks that a shared religion would be the best way of attaining this goal. It follows that, if we are to assert that the need for integration will produce a religious revival, the account must involve the conscious motivation of Americans. Let us suppose that many of them, even most, read Neuhaus or Bellah (they don't!) and conclude that America needs some social cohesion and that an excellent way of attaining that goal is the adoption of a shared supernatural belief system. What follows? That one wishes some of the consequences of a belief does not mean that one can believe. Even for any one individual, it is quite possible to mourn the passing of some state of affairs and yet be unable to recreate it.

For more than one individual, impotent nostalgia is an even more likely fate. Take the example of the decline of the rural village and small town community. It is very difficult to find anyone who thinks that the decline of a sense of community is a good thing and yet all the will in the world has not recreated it, for the obvious reason that the structural conditions for community – a degree of residential stability and sufficient commonality in the material position of people so that many of them stand or fall together – are usually not present in modern urban and suburban areas.

Thus even were it the case (a) that America fifty years ago was glued together by some shared moral consensus and a common vision; and (b) that many people are unhappy with the present absence of such a shared world-view, this would tell us nothing at all about the likelihood of conservative Protestantism forming the basis for a new popular consensual vision.

THE PLURALISM OF MODERN SOCIETIES

In *The Rise and Fall of the new Christian Right* (Bruce 1988) I argued that movements such as the new Christian right were severely handicapped by a fundamental condition of a democratic industrial society: the privatization of strong religious and cultural preferences. Our societies deal with the heterogeneity of the subjects of any nation state by removing as many matters as possible from the public arena. A society of fundamentalists, liberal Protestants, Catholics, Jews, Mormons, Muslims, and atheists reduces conflict by allowing enormous variety of religious expression in private and permitting only the blandest religion in the public arena. There are other reasons, of course, why conservative Protestants have been politically unsuccessful and many of these have been mentioned but in the end movements like the Moral Majority are defeated by the pluralism of the modern industrial society. Conservative Protestants are sufficiently numerous to be taken seriously in some *fora*. That section of the televangelism audience which does come to desire the same goal with similar intensity is large enough to place its desires on the public agenda. In ways I have described elsewhere, the structure of American polity, public administration, and broadcasting all encourage interest groups to pursue their agendas but it does not permit such groups to impose their views on the centre (Bruce 1988).

I have talked about conservative Protestant politics as if only the checks and counter-balances of a pluralist tolerant democracy keep zealot fundamentalists from establishing a religious *imperium*. There is a certain economy in telling the story that way but it does not do justice either to the complexity of views about democracy within conservative Protestantism or to the depth of genuine commitment to pluralism. Many fundamentalists and evangelicals did not support the Moral Majority and did not vote for Pat Robertson and some of these abstainers were motivated by a sincere commitment to the separation of church and state.[5]

Approximately one in twenty viewers of religious broadcasting

196

make a donation. Taking the best guess of audience size, perhaps 2 per cent of American households support televangelist organizations. Even if a socio-political campaign could attract the same number again from those currently watching the programmes but not feeling sufficiently moved to send in their dollars, that is 4 per cent of households. Even if they all voted for Robertson, they would not win anything. But even that proportion did not vote for him. In the end there were many evangelicals like the Episcopalian who agreed that Robertson had 'remarkable political skills' and still opposed his candidacy:

> We don't have religious political parties in America and Robertson's candidacy would amount to that. It would tend to isolate Christians and make them subject to ridicule. It would also suggest that Christians have a hidden agenda of politically taking over America. . . . The Lord instructed us to be involved in the world. But we do not need religious political candidates, which Robertson would be. . . . Another problem is that a Robertson candidacy would convey the wrong impression about what a Christian should believe on any political issue. On most issues – such as Gramm-Rudman, sanctions against Southern Africa, NATO and SALT II – there isn't a Christian position.
>
> (Barnes quoted in Aikman 1988: 22)

Chapter Ten

SCANDAL

Opinion polls taken during Pat Robertson's campaign for the Republican party nomination for the presidency showed clearly that Americans are radically divided in their attitudes to television evangelists. The ability of even the most obviously fraudulent evangelists to raise money shows that many Americans have a strong tendency to trust those who claim to be servants of God. The very low ratings which Robertson scored on the question of trustworthiness show that a sizeable part of the American people is intensely suspicious of 'holy rollers'. Reasonable assessments of the impact of Falwell's Moral Majority and other new Christian right organizations suggest that, although they have failed to win any major victories on their agenda, they have helped to make fundamentalism and its associated socio-moral positions (and hence the people who promoted them) legitimate. Robertson's election campaign can be seen in this light: evidence of the increasing respectability of conservative Protestantism. This chapter discusses two scandals which together were a major setback to that improvement of televangelism's image.

JESSICA HAHN AND PTL

After leaving Pat Robertson's CBN in 1972, Jim Bakker went to head the Crouches' Trinity network before leaving them a year later to create his own PTL. In 1978 PTL Satellite Network became the first to broadcast Christian programming 24 hours a day to all of North America (Barnhart 1988: 39). Nine years after the successful move into satellite, on the 19 March 1987, Jim Bakker announced that he was turning over control to Jerry Falwell. He confessed that in December 1980, he had had a sexual encounter in a Florida hotel room with Jessica Hahn, a church secretary from Massapequa, New York state. Richard Dortch, Bakker's chief deputy, became PTL president and took over hosting the show. Falwell became chief executive. Unaware of the extent of the scandal, Falwell publicly called Bakker a good man who had erred and confessed his sin. Elliptically at first and then explicitly, Bakker explained that he was inviting a Baptist fundamentalist to shepherd the network because he believed he was the victim of a hostile take-over from another pentecostalist and fellow minister in the Assemblies of God, Jimmy Swaggart.

Bakker had resigned because he could no longer stifle rumours of the Hahn affair, which an increasing number of Assemblies ministers knew about and which had recently been the subject of an internal Assemblies leadership meeting. Curiously, given the history of feud with the paper, Bakker had himself given the story to the *Charlotte Observer*. Once the news broke, ten year's worth of *Observer* investigations, which many had regarded as vindictive, were reappraised and many former PTL employees came forward with further details of corruption, deceit, and fraud on a grand scale.

Hahn's story, given under oath, was that she had been the victim of what could reasonably be called a double rape and that she had subsequently been paid for her silence.[1]

One of the appeals of the Bakkers' ministry had always been their willingness to let their audience be party to difficulties in their personal lives. Many commentators have described Bakker as the 'manic depressive' of televangelism, alternately buoyant and irrepressible, and lachrymose and inconsolable. At times when they were having trouble with their marriage, one or other would absent themselves from the show. In 1980 the Bakkers had been going through one of these difficult periods. John Wesley Fletcher, a pentecostal evangelist who had worked with Jim Bakker, who knew Hahn, and knew her to be a fan of the PTL Club, invited her to Florida to meet Bakker and to see a show being recorded.

She was elated about meeting the Reverend Bakker, whom she had seen on TV and admired. She admired Tammy also. Jessica was glad she had been invited, but says she became confused when, en route to the hotel, Fletcher informed her that Jim was having a hard time with his wife. More disturbing was the news that the Bakkers were going through a separation, Tammy having left for California.... Jessica listened to Fletcher reveal details about the Bakkers that made her uncomfortable, details that she felt she had no right to know.

(Barnhart 1988: 156-7)

After the event, she explained that she thought Fletcher was telling her these things to impress her with the intimacy of his relationship with the Bakkers. At the hotel, Fletcher took her to her room and gave her a glass of wine which she later believed to have been drugged. Jim Bakker came in from the hotel swimming pool, wearing nothing but a brief pair of swimming trunks. Hahn described him as being 'hyper' and said he talked about not knowing how he was going to make it, how he was going to handle his problems with Tammy. He talked in embarrassing detail about the difficulties he and Tammy had in sexually satisfying each other. Fletcher left only to return with a bottle of Vaseline Intensive Care. He said that Jim liked back rubs.

Jim Bakker's and Jessica Hahn's accounts diverge at this point. He insists that she was an accomplished and experienced lover who seduced him. She insists that she was a virgin who was forced into sexual intercourse by Bakker.

He started almost from the top of my head and didn't stop for what seemed like an hour and a half. He did just everything he could do to a woman . . . and he wouldn't stop. I told him I didn't want to be pregnant. He said 'Oh, I've had an operation'. Once wasn't enough. He had to keep finding new things to do. I just couldn't stand him. I just wanted to pull his hair.

(Quoted in Barnhart 1988: 162)

In the circumstances it might seem like a minor detail but it does infringe an important fundamentalist taboo: according to Hahn, Bakker forced her to perform oral sex with him. After Bakker had left, Fletcher returned and forced her to repeat her experiences with him.

Later that day, because, she said, she wanted to make sure that

Bakker and Fletcher had left the hotel, she turned on the television to see the two evangelists on the *PTL Club*:

> I heard John say to Jim Bakker, 'You had a good rest today.' And Jim answered, 'Yeah, I need more rest like that.' John then added 'The Lord really ministered to us today. We need more ministry like that'. I felt they were making fun of me right on television.

(Quoted in Barnhart 1988: 163)

Hahn flew back to New York state and initially did nothing but, after receiving what she regarded as a threatening phone call from PTL, she confided in her pastor who in turn told Paul Roper, a Californian business consultant. Roper contacted PTL and after much negotiation, conducted primarily through Richard Dortch, arranged for Hahn to be paid $265,000 over a number of years for her silence. In the event she saw almost none of this money.[2]

With obviously little sense of the extent of his scandal, Bakker expected his absence from PTL to be brief. After an appropriate period of penance, he would return to his kingdom. It was probably this that explains why he asked Jerry Falwell to act as caretaker. Bakker is an Assemblies of God pentecostalist who believes in such gifts of the spirit as 'speaking in tongues'. Falwell is a fundamentalist Baptist who has said that anyone who speaks in tongues has had 'too much pizza the night before'. Another pentecostalist such as Swaggart would have been a more ideologically consonant choice but such a person might have been more likely to take root.

The Falwell invitation provoked a lot of hostile mail from regular PTL supporters who appreciated the extent of the denominational differences and feared that the specifically pentecostal aspects of the ministry would be played down. Such fears seemed confirmed by Falwell's board appointments. Although he moved quickly to establish a patina of respectability by inviting onto the board retired evangelist Rex Humbard, Bailey Smith (former president of the Southern Baptist Convention), and James Watt, a well known conservative Baptist who had been Secretary for the Environment in Reagan's first cabinet, it was noticeable that fundamentalists outnumbered pentecostals on the new board.

Three months after handing over PTL to Falwell, Jim Bakker

went on the record to demand his network back and insisted that Falwell had usurped his organization. When Bakker talked of returning to the ministry, Falwell called a press conference to declare that Bakker 'either has a terrible memory, or is very dishonest, or he is emotionally ill' (*Time* 8 June 1987: 44).

There were a number of reasons why Falwell's attitude had hardened. First there were the details of financial impropriety which became evident to the accountants brought in to stabilize the corporation. The *Charlotte Observer* had not even scratched the surface of the Bakkers' fraud. PTL had vastly over-sold the 'partnerships' which guaranteed free accommodation at the Heritage USA theme park. While only $12 million had been spent on the Towers Hotel project, some $70 million had been raised in partnerships. Jim Bakker's response to the running deficit in PTL had been to sell even more partnerships, which brought in needed money but at the cost of amplifying the problem. 9,700 partners had been sold the right to stay regularly in what turned out to be a bunkhouse with 48 beds.

It was also obvious that the Bakkers had displayed considerable contempt for their viewers and had often lied in their fund-raising. In one memorable instance Tammy had cried on TV that they had given all their savings to PTL to avert yet another crisis; three days later Jim Bakker had paid a $60,000 deposit on a 58 foot houseboat. Even by televangelist standards the Bakkers had lived high on the hog at the expense of their 'partners'. There were the houses. The 'parsonage' was valued in 1985 at $1.3 million. There was a condominium in Florida which cost $375,000 to buy and another $202,566 for fixtures and furnishings. In 1984 when PTL was laying off 99 employees as a cost saving measure, the Bakkers were buying a $450,000 chalet in California. This was soon sold and replaced by a house in Gatlinburg, Tennessee, on the edge of the national park. It cost only $148,000 but $275,000 was spent on improvements. And there was Jim's office jacuzzi and the 14 carat gold plated taps in the shape of swans in the presidential suite of the Grand Hotel at Heritage USA; and the two Rolls Royce cars, the vintage sports cars, and the houseboat. Although not quite in the Imelda Marcos league, both Jim and Tammy were compulsive shoppers who indulged themselves and family and friends. For her sixteenth birthday daughter Tammy Sue was given a full-length fur coat by Tammy Faye.

Few televangelists are known for their frugality and the Bakkers' own extravagance might have been forgiven but there was something sinister about the profligacy allowed to the Taggart brothers, who seemed to have no obvious role in PTL and yet were permitted by Jim Bakker to run up vast bills. David Taggart was Jim's personal aide, although what services he provided were never itemized or explained. His elder brother James worked for PTL as an 'interior designer'. Although they worked at PTL headquarters in South Carolina, they paid $660,000 for unfurnished space in a New York condominium. David Taggart was free with the company credit card; before his 1986 holiday, he took a $45,000 cash advance. In that year he charged $263,000 to the credit card, most of it unaccounted for. Although James was paid $120,000 a year, David signed a PTL cheque paying him $100,000 for 'consulting services'. A few years after joining PTL, David Taggart bought Tammy Faye a $25,000 pair of earrings and his mother a $12,000 pearl and ruby necklace (Barnhart 1988: 68-9).

In addition to the first evidences of this scale of spending by senior PTL employees, Falwell at his press conference had to hand a number of sworn statements from people who claimed that Bakker had engaged in 'homosexual behaviour'. This information came from Tennessee-based evangelist John Ankerberg.

Ankerberg had played a reluctant part in the exposure of the scandal. He had heard rumours about Hahn at, of all places, the annual meeting of the National Religious Broadcasters, and he had made contact with Paul Roper who showed him the documentation of the deal which he had arranged for Hahn with PTL. Ankerberg had wanted to deal with the whole matter in private 'according to principles set forth in scripture' but knowing that the story would leak out of the Assemblies of God, Bakker had told the *Charlotte Observer*. When Ankerberg had gone public to defend his friend Swaggart from the hostile take-over accusations, people rang him with further allegations. Having collected statements, Ankerberg passed these to the Assemblies of God leadership and, he says, would have kept quiet had Tammy Bakker not publicly demanded that he produce his evidence. He passed the statements to Falwell to block Jim Bakker's planned return to PTL.

Although in the context of the overall scandal, it was minor, Falwell seems to have been particularly irked by one small piece of evidence which he produced for the press: a note hand written by

Tammy Faye on her own stationery setting out for her negotiator her terms for retiring gracefully. She wanted $300,000 for Jim and $100,000 a year and a maid for herself, all royalties from PTL records and books, the mansion, two cars, security staff, and the fees for the lawyers and accountants they would need to protect themselves from the Internal Revenue Service. Even Falwell, who pays himself $400,000 a year, found it difficult to hide his distaste for the arrogance and greed displayed in such a demand and he coined the memorable phrase 'fiscal sin'.

As more journalists investigated, more details emerged. In particular, it appeared that Bakker had seen trouble coming and, rather than work to straighten out the mess, had increased his peculation. On 30 July 1986, a year before the story broke, Jimmy Swaggart had tabled details of the Hahn accusation before officials of the Assemblies of God denomination. In that last year, the Bakkers awarded themselves $1.9 million in special bonuses. David Taggart was rewarded when $110,000 in cash advances and loans were turned into a 1986 bonus. Bakker's personal secretary, Shirley Fulbright, received a bonus of $80,000 (Barnhart 1988: 9). In total, between January 1984 and March 1987, the Bakkers were paid $4.8 million by PTL. Although PTL had a board, members were later to insist that they were never provided with detailed or accurate financial statements. Importantly, they did not know the basic salaries of the Bakkers and other senior people; their willingness to rubber stamp large bonuses was partly caused by their supposition that the Bakkers were poorly paid. According to *Time* (3 August 1987), the Bakkers at one time had forty-seven bank accounts and seventeen vice-presidents, with financial control divided in four separate departments. Hardly consistent with Frankl's view of televangelism as an enterprise which differs from its mass evangelism progenitor in terms of its bureaucratic structure, PTL was such a mess that only Bakker and his closest personal aides had any idea of the overall picture.

To what extent Jimmy Swaggart was motivated by a desire to take over PTL is not clear. Despite his own later fall from grace, it seems more likely that he was driven by a dislike for what he saw as Bakker's frivolity. Although ministers in the same denomination, Swaggart and Bakker were worlds apart. Swaggart was offended by Bakker's 'easy believism' and prosperity theology. Jim's fancy braces and casual clothes and Tammy's wigs and make-up offended his more conservative values. The Bakkers built a Christian holiday park. Swaggart spent his money on air-time, foreign missions, and his college; the more usual tools of evangelism. If they were the ultra-modern pentecostalism of a new prosperous and confident south and south west, Swaggart in his Louisiana base was much closer to the old traditions generated in a climate of eschatological fervour, a sectarian pentecostalism untouched by the charismatic movement of the 1970s. As he said in a televised sermon:

> What made people give hundreds of millions of dollars to PTL when you could turn on the TV set and it was as obvious as a bull elephant charging down the road as to what it was? And yet they supported it and would get angry with you if you said one word about it. Why?

> (Quoted in Barnhart 1988: 50)

For Swaggart, Jim Bakker and Oral Roberts were evil in making outlandish and deceitful promises in the name of Jesus.

> There is something in [Roberts and Bakker] that makes people follow them. And it's spirits. And it's not the Holy Spirit . . . . Lying spirits, homosexual spirits that are in these men – and that's what these people follow. They don't recognize the true spirits, and [therefore] evil spirits come. . . . Brother, it's a power, I want you to know; and that's why people follow [them].

> (Quoted in Barnhart 1988: 48)

More prosaically, Swaggart was offended that he had been deceived. When he had first heard about the Hahn affair from John Wesley Fletcher, he had refrained from public criticism and instead taken the matter privately to PTL leaders. Dortch had denied the charges. Six months later, John Ankerberg, who had found the connection in Paul Roper, was able to tell Swaggart that he had been lied to.[3]

Rendering unto Caesar

Falwell's first priority had been to raise enough cash to keep PTL afloat. In May 1987 he launched a dramatic appeal for funds and the 'May Miracle' brought in $8.5 million. But with a monthly deficit of over $1 million, this made little difference and a more mundane form of salvation was sought in the bankruptcy courts. Although apparently committed to saving PTL and earning considerable kudos as an 'elder statesman' of televangelism, Falwell resigned in October 1987 after the bankruptcy court ruled that PTL creditors could submit their own reorganization plan as an alternative to his model. David Clark, a senior officer at CBN (and co-author of the audience size research cited in Chapter Five) was selected by the court to act as trustee for PTL. Although thirty television stations had dropped the daily *PTL* show and about 1.5 million fewer homes were able to get it on cable, there was still a considerable audience. More importantly with the network and the theme park, there was between $175 million and $200 million worth of assets, against which had to be set something like $65 million worth of claims.

In October 1988, an Orthodox Jew, who had trained as a rabbi but preferred real estate to leading a synagogue, bought PTL (whose television network had been re-named Inspirational Network) for $115 million.

In December 1988, after considering evidence for sixteen months, a federal grand jury indicted Jim Bakker, Richard Dortch, and David and James Taggart on twenty-four charges of fraud and conspiracy.

THE PROSTITUTE AND JIMMY LEE SWAGGART

Social science is accustomed to seeing the world as irony; people in groups often achieve something close to the opposite of what they intended. But the next twist in the tale was so like the device of a Victorian novelist that it could almost form the basis for a new argument from design for the existence of God. Jimmy Swaggart had established himself as the scourge of sinners. He had played a major part in the defrocking and bankrupting of another Assemblies of God evangelist with a TV ministry, Marvin Gorman, for sexual affairs. With John Ankerberg, he had been instrumental in bringing Bakker and Dortch to the court of the church. In February 1988, Swaggart was himself summoned to the Assemblies of God to answer charges of consorting with a prostitute. In a day-long meeting, he broke down and confessed his liaison with the prostitute and a long-standing obsession with pornography. He denied that he had had intercourse with the woman: he had paid her to remove her clothes and masturbate in front of him.

He returned to face his own congregation and his millions of television viewers. In a grandstand performance, he asked for forgiveness from his wife Frances and from his son Donnie, from the pastors and missionaries of his denomination, and from his followers around the world. Finally he addressed God:

> I have sinned against you, my lord, and I would ask that your precious blood would wash and cleanse every stain until it is in the seas of God's forgetfulness, never to be remembered against me anymore.

He then read Psalm 51.

> Have mercy upon me, O God, according to thy loving kindness: according unto the multitude of thy tender mercies blot out my transgressions.
>
> Wash me thoroughly from mine iniquity, and cleanse me from my sin.
>
> For I acknowledge my transgressions and my sin is ever before me....
>
> Cast me not away from thy presence; and take not thy holy spirit away.
>
> Restore unto me the joy of thy salvation; and uphold me with thy free spirit.
>
> Then will I teach transgressors thy ways; and sinners shall be converted unto thee.

Faced with this third scandal within two years, the Assemblies behaved commendably. The Louisiana district elders had fixed for Swaggart what many thought was too lenient a punishment, a sentence determined by his status rather than by the seriousness of his offence: he was to relinquish the pastorship of his church for three months and refrain from preaching for that time. In addition he was to place himself under the supervision of fellow clergy for two years. The contrast between this and the defrocking of Gorman, Bakker, and Dortch struck many as too great and raised speculation that Swaggart could not be disciplined as other ministers because the income from his ministries formed a major part of the funds of the Assemblies (about a sixth of the foreign missions budget). The full meeting of 250 national elders voted to support the more severe punishment recommended by the executive committee: a year's ban from preaching. In repudiation of his initial willingness to accept the church's discipline, Swaggart refused to submit and was dismissed from the denomination. At the 1989 annual meeting of the National Religious Broadcasters, Swaggart was expelled from his professional association.

It would be easy to respond to the Bakker and Swaggart scandals (and the many others; see Bruce 1985) by seeing them as evidence of hypocrisy. We clearly lack the information required for a detailed socio-psychological profile but I would suggest an alternative to the easy judgement that these (and by extension other) evangelists are reprobates whose true natures have finally been exposed. It seems more likely that Swaggart's constant almost obsessive preaching against sexual licence reflects a genuine fight with his own desires and his own human nature. Some insight can be gained from considering the case of Jimmy Lee's cousin, Jerry Lee Lewis. The two grew up in a culture which produced both the sexual freedom of New Orleans' Bourbon Street and the repression of rural Louisiana pentecostalism. Jerry Lee wanted to be a minister but was rejected and at times since has believed his success as a rock and roll performer to be the result of a pact with the devil. From the same family and same background one cousin had tried to serve God and then devoted himself to rock and roll, drink, drugs, and sex with very young girls, while the other had taken the same musical talents and harnessed them to denouncing that life. Joe Barnhart (1988), in a discussion considerably more sensitive than most, draws on the struggle for control over sexuality admitted by Texas evangelist James Robison. Both in his sermons and in interviews, Robison has shown an unusual frankness and insight into the sexuality latent in the role of evangelist. He admits that he is attractive to many of the women in his audience, that he has been sexually attracted to them, and that a number of times he has come close to giving way to temptation. Unlike most conservative evangelicals, Robison was willing to seek professional counselling help. None the less, even Robison has been unable to break from the prevailing evangelical orthodoxy that such urges, rather than being the product of human biology, are the work of the devil. Swaggart, perhaps because he was raised in an even more thoroughly repressed pentecostal culture, was unable to seek help in dealing with his desires. Seeing them as the work of the devil, he responded to them by attacking, with ever more ferocity, sexual licence. His way of handling his own obsession with pornography was to preach against it and to call for severe punishment of pornographers.

It is of no great consequence but it is interesting to compare the ways in which Swaggart and Bakker responded to public humiliation and to see the differing extent to which the two men had moved from the rural pentecostal culture of their childhoods. Bakker, although not denying his affair with Jessica Hahn, has refused to take responsibility for it and prefers to blame his troubles on the media, secular humanism, enemies of the gospel, envious evangelists, and the devil. In a wonderfully perverse piece of reasoning he explains that Satan struck him down because he was doing too much good and saving too many souls. In contrast, Swaggart, although he rejected the discipline imposed on him by the Assemblies of God, has been more willing to take responsibility for his fall. He tearfully confesses his sin and describes it by saying: 'I do not plan in any way to whitewash my sin. I do not call it a mistake, a mendacity. I call it sin' (*Christianity Today* 18 March 1989: 48). Both deny that their scandal invalidates their message and both try to turn it to their advantage but they do so in different ways. Bakker claims the devil's arrangement of his demise as proof that he is good at what he does and that hence he deserves further support. The devil would not bother to disgrace a poor evangelist; Jim Bakker is disgraced; therefore Jim Bakker is a good evangelist. Swaggart's method is closer to the conservative Protestant mainstream. He argues, not that his disgrace establishes his worth, but that his example shows that we are all in sin since the Fall, that the flesh is weak, and that we need more gospel preaching to keep us on the straight and narrow. Swaggart's fall proves that we all need the saving message of Christ's blood. His own transgressions qualify him to preach to all of us because that 'all of us' now includes him.

FUTURE IMPACT

Bearing in mind my earlier observations about the difficulty of gauging public opinion, these comments on the impact of the two scandals can only be supposition but two things seem clear. The first is that no lasting damage has been done to the standing of conservative Protestantism and televangelism in the eyes of the core constituencies. Most evangelicals and fundamentalists appreciate the preaching of this or that evangelist but their primary loyalty is to a cluster of beliefs and practices and to local churches and associations as the arenas for acting out their faith. After all, on their first exploration of the possibility of full-time Christian work, Jim and Tammy Faye Bakker were taken for a ride by a travelling evangelist who enlisted them in his dream of raising money to evangelize along the Amazon in a yacht once owned by Errol Flynn. He was a fraud who kept all the money he raised at solicitation meetings. There was no yacht and no serious intention of evangelizing in Latin America. But the Bakkers did not generalize their discovery that their hero was corrupt into a general revaluation of their faith. Evangelists have come and gone before. Some of the 'faith partners' who have been large contributors certainly feel cheated and they may cease to make gifts to such ministries in future but there are many more televangelists whose reputations are still intact.

Moreover, there is in fundamentalism an imperative to *forgive*. A central part of the emotional appeal of televangelism is that sins can be forgiven. Indeed, the sinner who repents is a better catch than someone who has lived a blameless life. Richard Dortch's career was only temporarily stopped by the Assemblies revoking his ordination. He now runs 'Life Challenge', a non-profit-making ministry to help high-profile people who have undergone major life crises (*Christianity Today* 18 March 1989). John Wesley Fletcher, who also had his ordination revoked, has been ordained by Victory Way Ministries of Union City, Tennessee, and maintains a full schedule of preaching engagements. One of Swaggart's regular viewers, an old lady said: 'Brother Swaggart is an imperfect human being but the Bible says those who love the Lord and seek the truth shall have their sins forgiven if they repent' (Ostling 1988: 30). The more there is to repent of, the more interesting the preacher. The most popular speakers on the 'born again' circuit are those who have the most to tell about their previous evil lives. Charles 'Chuck' Colson, notorious as the amoral 'fixer' of Richard Nixon's Watergate scandal White House is now a major figure in the evangelical world. Until a recent theft charge suggested he had returned to a life of crime, the notorious Black Panther leader Eldridge Cleaver was, in his 'born again' persona, a popular preacher and evangelical chat show guest. There is a very popular paperback literature of conversion stories by people who have led depraved and perverted lives before they found Jesus. It is not too cynical to suggest that the longer and more excessive the life of pre-conversion sin, the more appealing the testimony. Whether those who have reversed the normal career and appeared to be holy for many years before falling from grace can also benefit from this tendency remains to be seen but it would be a mistake to suppose that the careers of Bakker and Swaggart have been irretrievably damaged.

If we move from these two individuals to televangelism generally, we find that far from eroding the faith of the core audience, the scandals have produced an increase in commitment as the faithful rally round. Audience has declined. Recent figures (which have all the weaknesses discussed in Chapter Five) suggest Swaggart's broadcast audience down from over 2 million to well under 1 million. Pat Robertson's audience has been halved (but at least some of this must be a switch to cable), as has Robert Schuller's.[4] But donations are up. Jerry Falwell not only managed to produce $8.5 million for PTL in his 'May Miracle' but by presenting the audience with the fear that televangelism in general was threatened by Bakker's disgrace and the renewed efforts of rampant secular humanists, he was able – by bringing in $5 million – to break all records for fund-raising for *The Old Time Gospel Hour*. Schuller, who also experienced a temporary sharp drop in donations, was able to persuade his contributors to reach deeper into their pockets and his income post-scandal was higher than it had been before.

Where the impact does seem likely to be negative and considerable is in confirming the hostility of that part of the public that was never sympathetic to religious television. Those who always suspected it was a swindle now know they were right. Falwell, Robertson, Robison, and others had spent years trying to make Americans outside the cultural *laager* of conservative Protestantism take them seriously. They had cultivated Ronald Reagan and other leading conservatives and had shifted their public image a long way from the snake-handling 'heal, heal' demagoguery of the sawdust trail. And now even conservative commentators were making fun of them and every comedian worth anything had Bakker and Swaggart jokes in his repertoire.

Other televangelists would be best served by Bakker and Swaggart withdrawing from the limelight but Swaggart's shows are still on the air and still popular. More surprisingly, Jim and Tammy Bakker went back on the air in January 1989 with a one hour programme recorded in their front room. Although there were a number of references to struggles with the devil and the trials of the previous two years, no specific reference was made to Jim's offences. The show was distributed by Video Programme Network, which broadcasts some 18 hours of religious and family programming through a number of small cable networks. On the second show, they began their fund-raising, offering Tammy Faye's new album *Peace in the Midst of Storm* as the inducement for the remnant faithful to send in their donations. With the Bakkers trying to rebuild their audience and Jim's fraud trial liable to be lengthy, the erring evangelists will be kept in the public eye.

In Chapter Five, I made the point that no religious television performer since Bishop Fulton Sheen has been genuinely *popular*. Even with their new formats, televangelism shows have not taken the gospel to the American people at large but have served mainly to present the faith to the faithful in a new medium. Even without the Bakker and Swaggart scandals, this was unlikely to change. With them, the existing polarization of the American public will be deepened.

Chapter Eleven

NEW, THIRD, AND OLD WORLDS

Given a choice of labels, many conservative Protestants will call themselves 'evangelicals', a sign that a vital part of their self-image is the engagement in evangelism. Enlistment in active support of the great commission – the spreading of the Word – is regarded as an inevitable corollary of being born again. It is not enough to luxuriate in the satisfaction of knowing that one's own eternal salvation is assured; the message must also be carried to those less fortunate than oneself. Evangelism is also vital to religious broadcasting. It is not just that most broadcasters see their own work as a form of evangelism, although they do. There is also the point raised in the discussion of fund-raising: it is difficult to raise money to pay for the routine expenses of broadcasting. Even committed supporters of religious broadcasters want to see more for their money than more of the same. Bricks and mortar projects attract funds because they offer 'concrete' evidence of the forward march of the gospel. Foreign missionary work is the other great draw.

There is also a need for continuing growth. Like any other business, television evangelism needs to be constantly expanding. To stand still is to fall behind. But the domestic American market appears to be saturated (Hoover 1987). The need for continuing growth combines with the desire to save the heathen to create an obvious opportunity in exporting the televangelism product overseas. This chapter will consider the present impact of American televangelism on the Third World and the plans to expand into Europe.

THE THIRD WORLD

My interests in this chapter are limited. I do not plan to review the spread of Protestantism in every part of the Third World. A few examples will be discussed to give some idea of the phenomenon and to raise the questions which pertain most closely to the impact of televangelism. Much of what follows comes from an excellent study by David Martin (forthcoming)[1].

As some data presented below show, the spread of Protestantism is impressive. In Latin America, for example, about one eighth of the population now belong to fundamentalist, pentecostal, or evangelical churches (Lernoux 1988). There is no doubt that the weakness of the Roman Catholic Church has been a major contributing factor. Although Latin America may seem thoroughly Roman Catholic, strong ties at the level of the state and official culture are often accompanied by organizational weakness on the ground. In many countries there has always been an acute shortage of priests.

> Dominated for three centuries by the Crowns of Spain and Portugal, and then subjected to the ideological hostility of liberal secularism in the years following Independence, the Church has been institutionally inadequate for most of its existence.
>
> (Norman 1981: 69)

Catholic bishops oriented themselves to the state and the ruling classes with very little reference to other lower church officers. Although the religious orders had considerable wealth, they worked independently of the Church hierarchy and institutional weakness was further compounded by the fact that most rural priests owed their first allegiance to their employers – the owners of the haciendas which dominated rural areas – and not the Church.

In so far as one can find a simple principle which explains why evangelical Protestantism has spread more rapidly in some countries of Latin America than in others, Martin suggests that it does best where the Catholic Church has been institutionally weakened but where the culture remains religious.[2] In Argentina, Paraguay, Uruguay, and Mexico, Protestants make up only about 2 per cent of the population (Norman 1981: 69). In Chile, they are between 10 and 15 per cent. Then one has the highs of Guatemala (20-30 per cent), Nicaragua (20 per cent), and Costa Rica (16 per cent). In Brazil 20 per cent of the population are Protestant. In considering these statistics it is worth remembering that generally only members and regular attenders are being counted on the Protestant side while the remainder, irrespective of regularity of attendance, are being taken to be Catholic. That such membership statistics under-estimate Protestant strength is made clear by data on clergy. To take the example of Brazil, in 1985 it had 13,176 Catholic priests and about 15,000 Protestant ministers.

Much of this Protestant strength is relatively recent and it is clear that it is not the Protestant denominations which began missionary work in the last century – the Lutherans, Presbyterians, and Methodists – which have been growing most rapidly. It is the Assemblies of God, the Christian and Missionary Alliance, the Seventh Day Adventists, and other pentecostalist sects (or local variants of these bodies) which have been recruiting most rapidly. This is true not only of Latin America but of most parts of the Third World. While East Asia had less than 2 million Christians in 1900, it now has 80 million and of these perhaps 80 per cent are pentecostal or charismatic (Barrett 1989: 20). In the Philippines, Protestants are still a small part of the population (perhaps about 12 per cent) but since the 1950s the mainstream churches associated in the National Council have either remained static or declined while the pentecostal bodies have grown (Elwood 1968). In Jamaica, only 4 per cent of the 1943 population were pentecostal. By 1960 the proportion had grown to 13 per cent, in 1970 it was 20 per cent, and the growth has continued.

As is often the case, the market for a new religion has been prepared by the dislocation of rapid social change. At the most abstract level, the spread of Protestantism in Latin America has been contingent on the break up of the organic unity between nation and Church. All over the Third World, the stable communities which sustained the previous culture and religious identity have been destroyed by the growth of cities and by the economic developments of large-scale capitalist agribusiness in the interior. Mexico City is the largest conurbation in the world with a population of at least 15 million, Buenos Aires has 10 million inhabitants, Sao Paulo has 9 million. As old social relationships have been called into question or utterly eradicated, so there is a demand for new forms of association and new values and attitudes. Although the parallels will not be pursued here (they are the subject of Martin's richly detailed study), conservative forms of Protestantism, especially pentecostalism, are being used by the newly displaced peoples of the Third World to adapt to modernization in much the same way that Methodism served the new citizens of England during the industrial revolution. The bleakest circumstances which create a demand for a new religious world-view are described in a report by the Belgian-based Roman Catholic Mundi Vita: 'Many peasants and slum inhabitants need religion as a refuge in a society in permanent and progressive disintegration in order to deal with fear, threats, repression, hunger and death' (quoted in Lernoux 1988: 52). Most likely to convert are displaced peasants, the small disaffected tribes and larger ethnic subordinate groups on national peripheries (like the Maya and the Quechua), and those dislocated from haciendas to the mega-city.

However, another type of convert suggests a more positive appeal of the new religion. Just as the dissenting denominations of the Secession in Scotland and Methodism in England did in the eighteenth century, pentecostalism recruits from the small people with a degree of independence, the craftsmen and journeymen who are, as Martin puts it, outside the downward thrust of elite power and free from the lateral ties of the organic community. For these people the new church offers a new character of peaceful self-control in place of *machismo*, of purpose in place of fatalism, and of self-worth to be found through a spiritual critique of socio-economic superiors.

That the new religion is largely promoted by north Americans may carry negative associations for new countries engaged in defining an identity against 'western imperialism' but there are also very powerful positive connotations in that the new world-view is made more attractive by its association with affluence and power.

Ideological interventions

In using the spread of Methodism to explain why there was no revolution in industrial England, French historian Elie Halevy (1937) avoided suggesting a ruling-class conspiracy. Although there were evangelicals like William Wilberforce or Hannah More who advertised the virtues of an evangelical revival to their wealthy friends in terms of civilizing the urban masses and diverting incipient revolutionary pressures, much of the very real popularity of Methodism came from its ability to provide new forms of motivation, a new personality, which was well-suited to both the disciplines and the opportunities of the new industrial world. Similarly, although some north American Protestant missions have been encouraged by governments, the phenomenon is simply too large to be explained by ruling-class manipulation.

This is not to say that US missionaries have not also promoted American geo-political interests. To give one recent example, Pat Robertson's CBN has been active in supplying the Nicaraguan *Contras* based in Honduras. When the US Congress hesitated in providing more aid in 1985, Robertson used his television programme to denounce 'the craven submission of our leaders and Congress to the demands of communism [which] makes you sick to the stomach'. During a visit to *Contra* troops, he said: 'I think God is in favor of liberty and justice and He is against oppression. . . . If we can do something to help these men fight for freedom, I think it is perfectly in God's plan' (quoted in Lernoux 1988: 53).

There is also no doubt that in the recent pentecostal growth some missionary organizations have been encouraged by governments keen to deploy them in their own internal struggles, just as the older Protestant churches were sometimes encouraged in the last century by liberal nationalists keen to undermine the bond between monarchy and Catholic church. In the 1970s and early 1980s the Catholic church in Guatemala was severely persecuted by successive governments for its defence of human rights against unsavoury military regimes. Under evangelical General Rios Montt, many Catholic priests and church workers were murdered while US-based fundamentalist churches were encouraged. Some estimates suggest that by the end of the century more than half of the Guatemalan people will belong to such churches (Lernoux 1988: 51).

In Chile, fundamentalists and pentecostalists are sometimes called the 'Reagan cults' because of their supposed close association with right-wing American interests in central and Latin America. General Pinochet undoubtedly finds conservative Protestantism much more congenial than the socially activist Catholicism promoted by liberation theology.

But while identifying political or ideological agendas may explain part of the enthusiasm of US missionaries (and it does explain no more than part) or of 'receiving' governments for such activity, it does not explain why people convert to pentecostalism. For that we must go back to the general account of the changes which destroyed the old social relationships and the old religion they supported and the needs which such dislocation creates. In so far as pentecostalists have a political posture, most are quietists in that, along with their new faith, they have adopted the separation of church and state inherent in the European Protestant model of a free church in a free state. Most also tend to regard governments as a part of God's work that one simply accepts. On Pauline principles, many congregations will be critical of involvement in the political world beyond voting. What is wonderfully clear from Martin's detailed analysis is that the easy application of terms such as 'right' and 'left' to many Third World settings is misleading. Is the desire for a separation of church and state radical or conservative? In the context of Iberian culture it is radical and was a key element of the agenda of nineteenth-century liberal nationalist reformers. Yet its consequence in avoiding entanglements with the world may well be inadvertently to lend support to military dictatorships. Some missionary organizations and local churches have been helpful to their governments and capitalist agribusiness by converting and assisting in the destruction of the way of life of indigenous Indian peoples.[3] But is this right or left?

Clearly their religion makes pentecostalists anti-Catholic and anti-communist. However, local political concerns can produce strange bed fellows. Despite his support for the *Contras*, Nicaraguan *Sistema Sandinista* television has just signed a contract with Pat Robertson to air his programmes. The government needs the dollars and sees some value in undermining the Catholic church, some elements of which have become increasing critical of the regime.

Syncretism

In his discussion of recent Protestant growth in the southern hemisphere, Edward Norman reminds us that the label 'pentecostal' is not a particularly helpful one because it leads us to expect continuity with the European experience of religious revivalism and

218

'does not accurately describe the peculiar mixture typical in the Latin-American churches' (Norman 1981: 67). The same could be said of the spread of pentecostalism in parts of Africa and Asia. I have suggested that some of the appeal of varieties of enthusiastic conservative Protestantism is their connection with what for the sake of brevity I have called 'modernization'. Pentecostalism also appeals because it is highly supernaturalistic. It takes spirits seriously and thus has considerable resonance with the pre-Iberian Catholic religious culture of Latin America and with the native cultures of Africa and the east. In reviewing recent trends in church growth, Barrett says:

> Another aspect is the rediscovery of what are being termed power evangelism, power healing and power encounters. These means of spreading the faith are activities accompanied by signs, wonders, miracles, healings and other evidences of the supernatural.
>
> (Barrett 1989: 20)

Speaking of Jamaica, Martin explains:

> The basic reason for the expansion of Pentecostalism quite apart from any aura of modernity or any external financial help, is its capacity to combine a 'New Man' with an ancient strain of spirit possession and healing. It is at once the most recent expression of Christianity, and in touch with the therapeutic cults embedded in a world-wide 'archaic' religiosity.
>
> (Martin, forthcoming)

The possibility of syncretic expansion is exaggerated by the Protestant tendency to local congregational independence. In Reformed theology there is little legitimation for a strong centralized form of control. Although many Protestant associations have developed hierarchical organizations (such as the Presbyterian structure of kirk session, presbytery, synod, and general assembly) these are really matters of human convenience. There is no suggestion that salvation requires obedience to such structures. The relative freedom from constraint undoubtedly plays a major part in the spread of Protestantism. Unhindered by a 'head office', Protestant leaders can tailor their message to suit the interests of their potential members. The possibility of such

219

local adaptations makes adoption more likely but at the price of allowing the new local members to determine what it is that counts as the saving faith. Of all varieties of Protestantism, pentecostalism is the most vulnerable to considerable alteration in transmission because it places feelings and spiritual experiences so far above knowledge in its hierarchy of values. The point about ecclesiastical independence and growth is important in thinking about the spread of pentecostalism through the Third World. It is easy to be impressed by the scale of the phenomenon and forget that we are not viewing the conversion of millions of people from a very large number of quite different cultures to the one unitary new religion, an occurrence which would be sociologically implausible. What we are seeing is the adoption by millions of a large number of importantly *different* re-workings of a common religious core into a lot of different religions, each of which makes sense in terms of that particular culture and language of expression. To give two examples which fit one inside the other like Russian dolls, the Chinese 'Three Self' Christian Church (so-called because the communist government insisted that it be self-governing, self-supporting, and self-propagating) has been largely isolated from western influences since 1949 and is already importantly different from the traditions which evangelized China. Now its leaders are concerned to absorb China's growing underground pentecostal house churches into Three Self so that they can eliminate 'the magical and superstitious elements which often take root in secret religious societies deprived of an educated leadership' (Browning 1987: 220).

American missionaries may fail to appreciate the extent of distortion but the words they speak and the words heard by their converts are often very different. This is, of course, a variable matter. The Seventh Day Adventists are tightly organized and doctrinaire. So too are the Jehovah's Witnesses (if they may be allowed into the discussion). The mission churches of these organizations tend to be more faithful to the American originals than are the products of Elim and Assemblies of God proselytizing. Bryan Wilson has drawn my attention to the possibly temporary nature of much apparent conversion to pentecostalism in the Third World.[4] When the faith adopted is sufficiently altered so that it can be seen as just a new expression of the traditional beliefs, and when there is such a strong tendency to fragmentation and autonomous congregational development, it seems very likely that some people who now call themselves pentecostalists will move on to some new spirit-possessed ecstatic religion, some new provider of signs and wonders.

The point about the vulnerability of pentecostalism to syncretic re-writing is important not just for the Third World but also for understanding its popularity in the old world. When one is thinking about the audience for televangelism or the vast readership for the publications of such 'health and wealth' gospel preachers as Kenneth Hagin, one needs to bear in mind the wide variety of ways in which people integrate such ideas with their other beliefs and concerns.

Broadcasting to the Third World

Those commentators who stress the imperialist aspects of western missionary activity in the Third World often forget the extent to which such activity is restricted. After the proclamation of the People's Republic of China in Peking in 1949, Christian missionaries were forced to leave the country and only in the last decade have contacts been re-established (Neill 1975: 465-9). Most Islamic countries either prohibit or heavily restrict Christian missionary work. Barrett (1982) estimates that half the world's population lives in countries where religious practice is restricted and an even larger part lives in areas where Christianity is permitted only so long as it is locally funded and organized. By happy coincidence the spread of wireless receivers in the Third World matched the closing of large parts of it to western missionaries. Even where political borders are no obstacle to evangelism, there are often physical barriers. Powerful short- and medium-wave radio transmitters have proved the answer to both sorts of problem. Short-wave radio waves are reflected off the ionosphere; as they return to earth, they spread out and cover a broad area. A 250,000-watt transmitter on the west coast of the United States can circle the globe and blanket the Soviet Union and eastern Europe. Medium-wave signals travel along the ground and provide a stronger clearer signal over a much narrower area. But as young Britons of the early 1960s who listened to Radio Luxemburg under the bed clothes will recall, at night, when there is less atmospheric disturbance, medium-wave radio is a powerful medium.

The first missionary radio stations used weak transmitters. HCJB began broadcasting in Quito, Ecuador with a 250-watt transmitter which could barely reach across the city. It now broadcasts 24 hours a day from 12 transmitters and 28 antennas. Together they provide more than one million watts of short-wave power to reach the Soviet Union, eastern Europe, the United States and Canada, South America and Japan with programmes in 13 languages.

The most powerful transmitters belong to TransWorld Radio (or TWR) which began in 1954 with a 2,500-watt station in Tangiers and now operates a 500,000-watt medium-wave transmitter in Bonaire in the Antilles and a 1.2 million-watt medium-wave transmitter in Monte Carlo. With four smaller transmitters TWR covers almost the entire globe and broadcasts in 75 languages. Leading American religious broadcasters were involved in these developments from the first. Paul Freed raised much of the money to start TWR by persuading the producers of such established radio programmes as *Hour of Decision*, *The Old Fashioned Revival Hour*, and *Back to the Bible* to make lump sum advances on the fees they would be charged for air-time (Freed 1979).

Given the sorts of difficulties in measuring audience size discussed in Chapter Five, it should be no surprise that we have no idea what proportion of the people who could receive the signals from TWR and other stations actually listen to their religious broadcasts. Missionary broadcasters can point to their often considerable mail from listeners in far-flung parts of the world but there is, of course, no formula to tell us what percentage of an audience ever write in for the free literature offered or to report conversions which followed a broadcast. It is worth noting however that much of the popularity of the programmes aired on these powerful transmitters stems from the lack of competition in the countries where they are heard. Either there is little local broadcasting or such broadcasting is stifled by the heavy hand of government propaganda. While some missionary broadcasting may be attractive because of its associations with the power and prosperity of the capitalist west, most evangelistic programmes show considerable cultural sensitivity and use native speakers wherever possible. Most broadcasters go out of their way to avoid the promotion of political views, not because they feel stung by the criticism of promoting 'Coca-Cola Christianity' but because they appreciate that a good part of their audience gets quite enough of that from their own governments and are seeking alternatives (Mumper 1986a: 25).

Televangelism and the Third World

Given that much of the Protestant growth in the Third World has been of pentecostalist varieties, we should not be surprised to learn that American pentecostalist broadcasters such as Jimmy Swaggart and Oral Roberts are popular. Shortly before his fall from grace, Swaggart was addressing meetings of tens of thousands in the Ivory Coast. Pat Robertson's recent deal with the state-run Nicaraguan television system has already been mentioned. Critics of American foreign policy are only too ready to believe the claims made by televangelists for their influence in the Third World. It is true that the promotion of Protestantism (in which the lead, in this as in everything else, passed from Britain to America between the wars) is the promotion of a polity and an economy as well as the dissemination of a religion. Indeed Martin begins his study of pentecostalism in Latin America by noting that this is just the latest stage in the continuing conflict between the Anglo-Saxon Protestant imperium, and the Hispanic Catholic imperium in which the Latin American heirs of the Iberian empires have continued to suffer defeat at the hands of the American heirs of the British empire. But when one moves from such abstract historical models to the actual mechanics of religious conversion there is only the loosest connection between the airing of prime-time televangelism specials and the spread of pentecostalism. As Martin notes for Jamaica: 'For every major crusade there are many minor crusades run locally in small towns and villages; and there is a level of fissiparous expansion well away from direct American influence' (Martin, forthcoming). To suppose that the purchase of air-time or even the sending of large numbers of missionary personnel into a Latin American country (even when the exported religion has all the cachet of American capitalism) is enough to convert people who watch or listen from their previous religion to pentecostalism is to fly in the face of everything we know about religious conversion. It is usually an unconsciously arrogant ethnocentrism: we know that we are not persuaded to change our beliefs just by watching a few television programmes but we are quite happy to believe that some Third World types are that easily swayed.

If one approaches the question from a consideration of American religious broadcasters, one tends to suppose that they are powerful and influential, but then one would expect them to exaggerate the importance of their work. And as was noted in the discussion of 'bait and switch' fund-raising in Chapter Seven, much of their Third World spending actually goes on the overheads of their college and production plant in the United States. If one approaches the subject from the other end, from studies of the spread of Christianity in the Third World, one gets quite a different picture. Possibly because they are now a little dated such standard histories of Christian missions as Neill (1975) make no mention of mass media. In a wide ranging review of church growth in Africa, Thomas makes no mention of mass media. The efficacy of even personal work by foreigners is challenged by a Gambian scholar, Lamin Sanneh, who notes: 'If we assess the effectiveness of Western missions by statistical standards of horizontal spread, they would fail abysmally. The most spectacular gains by Christianity occurred by other hands or after the formal withdrawal of missionaries' (quoted in Thomas 1987: 168). Almost all the case studies referred to by Thomas show that the key to successful evangelism has been the presence of indigenous leadership.

A spokesman for the Slavic Gospel Association has claimed that '80% of newly baptized Russian believers say their first serious thoughts about God occurred while they were listening to a gospel broadcast'. Leaving aside the specificity of the percentage, this may well be true, although 'first serious thoughts' could cover a very wide variety of responses. But the author of the article in which this claim is made inadvertently puts it in the correct context by starting the piece with an anecdote of a young Russian woman who listened faithfully to the SGA broadcasts and made copies of the broadcasts which she gave to her friends and relatives whom she encouraged to listen to the broadcasts (Mumper 1986a). To return to the argument made in Chapter Six, the mass media are generally most influential when their messages are reinforced by personal influence and personal contact. Moreover, as I have already noted, the religious broadcasts which are most likely to have been influential are those written and produced by natives of the country to which the programmes are directed. It is not the

Billy Graham and Jimmy Swaggart broadcasts which are most apparently successful.

To summarize, I do not wish to deny that mass media evangelists have played some part in the recent spread of Christianity. However, detailed studies of conversion and church growth make it clear that the dynamics of these processes are much the same in the Third World as in the first; personal relationships and contacts remain the main vehicle for the successful transmission of the new faith.

SAVING THE OLD WORLD

A major problem for evangelicals is that increasing penetration of the Third World coincides with loss of penetration in Europe. The secularization of the old world has created a vast new population of the heathen. To some extent this need not be taken as a setback to the 'great commission' of preaching the Word to all the peoples of the earth because one can suppose that a lot of Europeans have heard the Word and have deliberately chosen not to follow it. They have had their chance and do not need to be told again. But clearly there are many people – the children of atheists, for example – for whom such a judgement would be inappropriate. Thus Europe, once the exporter of Christianity becomes, for evangelicals, a suitable case for evangelization. Church growth specialists are fond of statistics of dubious validity but there is poetic truth in the claim made by missionary organization World Evangelization Crusade that 400 million of Europe's 700 million people have never opened a Bible.

Until very recently mass media evangelism was barely possible in Europe where most countries follow the British model of public service (and often state-controlled) broadcasting. In attempts to penetrate the gloom of British godlessness, some evangelists have used 'off-shore' commercial radio to beam to mainland Britain in 'deep fringe' time. Since the 1950s Herbert W. Armstrong's Worldwide Church of God has bought time on Radio Luxembourg, one of the very few powerful commercial stations in Europe. Popular (in so far as any are) British evangelist Dick Saunders rents time on Radio Monte Carlo. United Christian Broadcasting (based in Stoke) puts out religious programmes between 10 pm and 2 am on Manx Radio from the Isle of Man. In terms of either the size of the audience or of popularity compared to the mainstream religious broadcasting on public service broadcasting, these efforts are insignificant.

Potentially more important are the changes which many European governments have made to the control of their broadcasting systems in the last decade. Although the details differ for each country, the general direction of change is toward emulating the American system of less state control, a greater number of producers, and a more market-oriented philosophy. The British government recently instructed the BBC to buy a proportion of its programmes from independent producers and a number of small Christian firms saw this as an opportunity to break the mainstream ecumenical churches' control of religious broadcasting. One firm made a pilot of a thirty-minute light entertainment gospel programme and sent it to the BBC, several ITV companies, and Channel 4; all rejected it. Starcom, British agents for *The Jimmy Swaggart Show*, had short-lived success with TF1 (the French equivalent of BBC 1) but the sex scandal offered the BBC's head of television religious broadcasting *post facto* justification for his rejection of Starcom's approach. For the last decade, American religious broadcasters have prepared plans to air their programmes in Europe but as yet the willingness of governments to deregulate broadcasting generally have not been evidenced in any willingness of broadcasters to sell air-time to American-style (or American) televangelism.

Televangelists hope that development of satellite broadcasting will open up the market. Pastor Hans Bratterud, graduate of Oral Roberts University and leader of a charismatic congregation in Oslo, manages European Broadcasting Network which transmits the programmes of Swaggart, Schuller, and Copeland on New World Channel. EBN also transmits a thirty-minute programme called *Word for the World* which is produced by Bryn Jones and his Harvestime 'house church' movement based in Bradford.[5] Time is paid for by donations of the members and by the advertising of a Bradford firm. But almost no-one watches New World Channel.

The future for televangelism in Europe will depend on the number of people who acquire the new technologies. The problem will be discussed for Britain but the circumstances in other western European countries are similar. One technology of increased choice is cable television but cable has already fallen flat, defeated by the fact that most areas of Britain get very good signals from broadcast television and hence do not need one of the main advantages of cable – the clearer signal for broadcast stations. Another supposed advantage of cable is increased programme choice. In particular, it should provide earlier runs of new films which do not have to be cut to conform to the standards of broadcast television. But anyone who wants to see more films and even pornographic films can already do so by using a video machine. In America in 1980, only 1 per cent of households had a video but 20 per cent were already cabled. Those with videos increased by 1988 to 58 per cent while the number on cable was up to 51 per cent. About half the households in Britain now have a video machine and have ready access to low rental movies; well below 1 per cent have cable and there is no obvious demand for it.

With so little cable penetration, British satellite broadcasting channels have to be beamed direct to individual dishes attached to each receiving household. There are two British satellite broadcasters – Rupert Murdoch's Sky and BSB – and they have not agreed on a common receiving technology so any household which wants both will have to attach not one but two ugly dishes (one round and one square) to the outside of their dwelling. Sky became available first, in early 1989, but sales of its dishes were far slower than predicted. Three months after the launch (and despite massive advertising and promotion by Murdoch's extensive newspaper interests) only some 40,000 homes had dishes. By the end of the first year this is unlikely to have increased beyond 100,000 which is some way short of the 2.5 million viewers first predicted for the new medium. One of the main draws of Sky was to have been its Disney channel (which would also have produced additional income because it was to have been a subscription channel requiring a special decoder). Business has been so slow that Disney pulled out and Sky replaced it with a 'classic movie' (i.e. old films) channel.

The pan-European Super Channel is in receivership. Murdoch has shut down his European Sky channel (after losing $45 million in four years) to concentrate resources on the British-only version. These ventures may have failed because of the vagaries of national tastes made a shared Euro-product unattractive. However, the wide availability of video, the cost and ugliness of the receiving dishes, and widespread doubts about the desirability of the output, all

227

make it unlikely that satellite broadcasting will acquire a large audience in Britain.

Televangelists on satellite

At the moment Rupert Murdoch's Sky Channel is airing Robert Schuller's *Hour of Power* show free because there is as yet so little demand for satellite television that the time cannot be sold. With very small audiences, American television evangelists will be able to afford time but they will attract a miniscule audience. As the audience grows, the price will go up. European broadcasting is in considerable flux but one principle of future development is clear: the customers will get what they are prepared to pay for. In one way or another – pay-as-you-watch television or expensive satellite dishes with channel subcriptions – broadcasting will be ever more demand-led. Assuming for a moment that satellite television becomes well enough established for it to have a large popular audience which creates a system somewhat similar to American commercial television, then the amount of televangelism aired will depend on the popular response to it. The data presented in previous chapters make it clear that American religious broadcasting appeals very largely to those people who are already religious. Being part of the televangelism audience is an expression of faith, not a cause of it.

Although the figure has declined slightly since a high point in the 1940s, about 68 per cent in Americans claim church affiliation. About 40 per cent attended church or synagogue in a typical week (Gallup 1985). Only 15 per cent in the United Kingdom are church members. Only 11 per cent attend church in a typical week. No more than a quarter of these – about a million people – are conservative Protestants.[6] Consider the statistics for financial support of televangelism in America. Of regular viewers, 6 per cent give frequently, 13 per cent give 'once in a while' and a further 5 per cent give on special occasions (Fore 1984: 712). Although the people who make up the financial base are generous – the mean annual support is nearly $100 – the base is small: at most 24 per cent of viewers. Although some American viewers are not born again, it seems reasonable to suppose that there is some regular relationship between the size of the conservative Protestant population and the potential audience for televangelism. Evangelistic religious broadcasters trying to attract a British audience would be working in a market whose relative size was only a quarter of that of the American market. And this is putting the equation at its most hopeful. I am leaving aside the very likely consideration that British conservative Protestants – because the fundamentalist and pentecostal elements are weaker here than in the United States – will be less attracted to televangelism than their American counterparts. Although there is little data on this issue, a recent survey of British attitudes to religion on television replicated a 1968 study in which people were asked to rank ten possible purposes of religious programmes. Providing church services for the housebound was placed first and 'to make people stop and think' second in both surveys. 'To make people more religious' was placed seventh in 1968 and ninth equal in 1988. This last place in the 1988 survey was shared with 'to make people better Christians' which was also last in the list two decades earlier (Svennevig *et al.* 1988: 6-8). Given that these responses were not further examined for those who were committed Christians, they are not especially illuminating but they do not hint at a smouldering desire to replace ecumenical hymn-singing with *The Old Time Gospel Hour* or *The Jimmy Swaggart Show*.

THE EVANGELIZATION OF THE WORLD IN THIS GENERATION

In 1886, the executive of the British Student Volunteer Missionary Union adopted as its 'watchword' the slogan 'The Evangelization of the World in this Generation' and with the raw enthusiasm common to students, set about trying to persuade the British churches to adopt the same goal (Bruce 1980: 126-31). In an accompanying 'Memorial', the student leaders answered the criticism that they were advocating hurried preaching of the Word without necessary pastoral care:

> We do not understand evangelization to mean, on the one hand, conversion which is the work of the Holy Spirit or, on the other hand, a mere hurried proclamation of the truth of Christ. We understand it to mean that the Gospel should be preached intelligently to every soul in such a manner that the

229

responsibility for its acceptance shall no longer rest upon the Christian Church, but upon each man for himself.

(Quoted in Bruce 1980: 127-8)

By a generation, they meant something like thirty years and they believed that the resources to evangelize the whole world were available, if the Christian churches of western Europe and America could just be galvanized. Two world wars, the destruction of the European empires, and the discovery that there were vastly more languages in the world than had been anticipated put paid to such confidence but now, a hundred years later, evangelization of the world plans are back in fashion.

However, the modern schemes differ from the ones of the last century in that, instead of being promoted by church-based missionary organizations, they are being hatched by religious broadcasters and the organizations that run powerful radio transmitters. The preferred medium for world evangelization is no longer the personal missionary (aided perhaps by some tracts and a translation of the New Testament) but the radio and television programme. In 1988, Far East Broadcasting (FEBA), World Radio Missionary Fellowship (HCJB), TransWorld Radio (TWR), and SIM International (Radio ELWA) pooled resources to sponsor jointly a radio research centre in California. The centre will consider what needs to be done to achieve the evangelization of the world by the year 2000.

Earlier I suggested that a persistent characteristic of televangelism was its mistaking input for output measures. Often by ambiguous or careless use of language, the amount of effort put into evangelism is used to represent the success of that activity; the spending of more money to buy more air-time is taken to be an index of the greater popularity and appeal of the message. It is as if a publisher were to print twice as many copies of a book and imply that this was the same as doubling sales. Clearly evangelists could not turn down the opportunities which radio and television offer but the input/output measure confusion does draw our attention to a significant change in the persuasiveness of missionary work. In direct contact, the missionary might meet relatively few people and might have to suffer a heavy burden of disappointment as many of those contacted remained unimpressed by the new religion on offer. In terms of both financial and psychological resources mass media evangelism is much cheaper. To cover a small language group by radio, one needs only two or three converted speakers of that language. To evangelize in the pre-electronic fashion would require hundreds of Christians trained to speak that language. The use of imper- sonal media is also easier on morale. In pumping the message out into the air, one is leaving it up to potential converts to initiate contact. Only if they are interested, will they make themselves known; if they are obdurate sinners, they will stay where they are, remote, at a distance and unthreatening.

The theology of mission is itself ambivalent on input and output measures. The responsibility of the Christian is to evangelize, not to convert, which after all, is the work of the Holy Spirit and the hearer (in different proportions depending on where one stands on the Calvinism/Arminianism debate). To return to the analogy of the publisher, the evangelical's duty is to publish the book and distribute it in such a way as to make sure that every person has access to a copy. If people choose not to read it, that is their business. Most missionaries would add that the message should be presented in an attractive and intelligent manner, at its most persuasive. Impersonal means of communication are attractive to the producers because they are cheap and give the appearance that a lot is being done but they are also relatively unpersuasive.

The revival of plans to evangelize the world might be seen in some quarters as a sign of evangelical confidence, as the mark of a religion which has come out of its post-imperialism period of self-doubt and is now ready again to Christianize the heathen. It seems more appropriate to see recent schemes for world salvation as representing only the arrival of a technology which so frees pro-selytizers from contact with the heathen that they can suppose that they are doing something persuasive, that they are fulfilling the Great Commission, when from everything we know about mass media effects, we must suppose that they are having very little effect. Such impact as they are having comes, not directly from evangelistic broadcasts, but from social change alienating people from their previously satisfactory world-views, from some local people taking up radio and television messages and incorporating them in persuasive personal communications, and from syncretic re-interpretations of the messages so that they serve local needs.

To turn to the question of the effectiveness of the great prime-time evangelists, I see no reason (other than the claims they themselves make when fund-raising) to suppose that the spread of pentecostalism, or Protestantism more generally, in the Third World would have been markedly different had Roberts, Humbard, Swaggart, Robertson, and others never broadcast beyond the borders of the United States.

Chapter Twelve

CONCLUSION

Most conservative Protestants see televangelism as a powerful new addition to their evangelistic armoury; Armstrong (1979), as executive director of the National Religious Broadcasters Association makes that case. Most mainstream Protestants deride its shallowness and are concerned that the conservative near-monopoly presents, not only a false gospel, but also a false picture of American religious life. Much of the argument between detractors and advocates is made with competing claims about the effects of televangelism. Those who applaud it believe that it takes the gospel to people who would not otherwise be reached. Those who abhor it believe that, by substituting passive watching for active worshiping, it undermines the local church. These and related claims are empirical and their resolution must lie in the world of evidence. We might have expected social scientists to provide such evidence and many have. Unfortunately, some commentators have sought to increase their own importance by inflating that of their subject matter; there seems no other explanation for the wildly exaggerated claims about the importance of televangelism.

One of the main aims of this study has been to deflate the hype of mass media religion. Televangelism is an interesting and important cultural and social institution. Like good furniture, it becomes not less, but more so, for being appreciated in its proper proportion and context.

TELEVANGELISM AND RELIGION

The first and most important point about televangelism was that made at the end of Chapter Five. For all that the audience for religious television is quite large (perhaps 8 per cent of the total viewing population), watching religious television programmes is still an infrequent activity of a small part of the American people. It only appears to be anything else because people who should know better take the most generous estimates of likely audiences for *all* religious television, add them up, and then compare the total with the audience for a *single* popular secular programme. To put it bluntly, not much televangelism is consumed by not many people. Even fewer actually give financial support. And for all the experimentation with new formats and new methods of making the product available, the audience is largely found among less well-educated older women who are already conservative Protestants.

If analysts had started with what is known about why people believe the things they believe or with what is known about the persuasiveness of the mass media, they would have been less likely to exaggerate the influence of televangelism on the ungodly. To return to the theme of Chapter Six, one study involved questioning a sample of people who had phoned religious station WCFC-Channel 38 in Chicago during the previous two and a half years in response to an invitation to accept Christ. Note that this is not a sample of the televangelism audience at large but of those responding to an invitation to accept Christ by calling the station; that is, of those apparently converted through the medium. Of the sample, 30 per cent said they had already been Christians for at least 3 years (that is, their conversion pre-dated their phone claim to have just experienced conversion); 61 per cent identified their conversion with 'a church, a friend, or other situation' (Horsfield 1984: 135). Only 20 per cent associated their acceptance of Christ with either watching television or praying with a television counsellor.

Televangelism exists because there is a large conservative Protestant milieu; not the other way round. Once we get the direction of causality right we can explain the rise of televangelism. Although there were particular reasons related to the financial structure of American broadcasting which exaggerated the tendency, the conservative rise to domination of the air-waves is part of the wider cultural pattern of the relative decline of the mainstream churches. As evangelicals, fundamentalists, and pentecostals have become a larger proportion of American

234

Protestants, so their cultural products have come to be an increasing part of religious broadcasting. I have made the point a number of times but it is worth repeating: presence in the American mass media is largely (although not exclusively) a supply phenomenon. It represents the willingness of conservative Protestants to spend their money on funding this sort of activity. Only secondarily is it an index of demand and it is at best a very rough one.

This does not mean that televangelism does not have some important consequences. It just means that we have to look a little more closely to find them. In Chapter Seven's discussion of fund-raising, I stressed the importance of bricks and mortar projects. Diagnosed as terminally ill by liberal critics at the turn of the century, conservative Protestantism has not only survived but will reach the end of the century in better shape than the mainstream churches (Roof and McKinney 1988). Elsewhere I have argued at length that much of this resilience comes from the way in which its adherents built a supporting sub-society and sub-culture, an enclave in which the faith could be maintained and every subsequent generation raised in the 'old paths in perilous times' (Bruce 1989). The creation of independent conservative Protestant institutions as alternatives to those of the mainstream culture, is expensive. One of the enduring consequences of televangelism will result from its channelling of funds into institution-building. Much of the money raised by faith partnerships, blessing pacts, love offerings, and the like is consumed internally in paying for televangelism (and I will return to that) but much of it has gone into building new conservative churches and training young evangelicals, fundamentalists, and pentecostals in conservative academies. Most prominent is Oral Roberts, University but there is also Falwell's Liberty University, Robertson's CBN University, Herbert W. Armstrong's Ambassador Colleges, and before his scandal Jimmy Swaggart was planning to add a seminary to his Bible college. This extensive plant produces conservative Protestant pastors but it also produces graduates in a variety of disciplines and skills – law, medicine, accountancy, television production, and journalism are just the most obvious. This all strengthens the conservative milieu because it allows that world to acquire expertise and resources which are common in the mainstream without also taking on board the secular world's intellectual and cultural baggage. The conservative milieu possessed colleges – but not a christian 'theme park'! – before televangelism but the extended reach of the electronic mass media has allowed money to be raised from a wide audience on a new scale.

The money which is spent on buying more air-time to show more old time gospel to people who already get quite a lot of that sort of thing might seem wasted but we should not overlook the morale-raising consequence of televangelism. One does not want to exaggerate their sense of inferiority but, as many of Hoover's insightful interviews suggest, born again Christians are troubled by their apparent lack of standing in the world. Pointless as evangelistic exercises, Robertson's *700 Club* or Bakker's *PTL Club* are significant because they have raised the profile of conservative Protestantism and made its adherents feel better about themselves and their place in modern America. Few born again Christians wanted Pat Robertson to be their President – more preferred George Bush – but many were pleased that their man could actually run without looking like a hick.

Increasing respectability is not acquired without cost and this study has stressed the extent to which the gospel now preached by televangelists departs from the conservative Protestantism of the post-war years. The social ethics have changed. Asceticism is dead. More than that, hard work is dead. Jerry Falwell, one of the more conservative religious broadcasters, can say 'material wealth is God's way of blessing people who put him first' (in Horsfield 1984: 49). The Calvinist puritans would have said the same (although less often and not in the context of soliciting). What they would never have suggested is that 'giving money to your pastor' is a sufficient translation of 'putting God first' or that God is as easily pleased as televangelism suggests.

The theology, in so far as it is discernible, has moved a long way from the conservative Protestantism of the inter-war years. There is still a lot of talk about the authority of the Bible but distinctive teaching has been attenuated and its place taken by benign banalities. As Hunter's work (1986) shows, this is a reflection of changes in conservative Protestantism generally but the 'mass' nature of televangelism exaggerates the tendency. A pastor can challenge his congregation because he has an enduring relationship with it. People will not leave him because they dislike one or two sermons. When the relationship between television preacher and viewer (with remote channel changer) is exactly that precarious, blandness becomes an attractive option. Furthermore, evangelists measure their success in the numbers who hear their preaching. Ever-increasing audiences become a 'good thing' in their own right. The more particular one's message, the more one will be confined in recruitment. This is not necessarily a problem. As Swaggart's career pre-scandal showed, it is possible to build a very large following for an orthodox, narrow, anti-Catholic gospel but there is only so much space in the market place for that. Oral Roberts, the Bakkers, and Pat Robertson preferred to reduce the distinctive theological content and go for the broadest possible appeal.

The broad road is the pursuit of self-fulfillment, self-satisfaction, and self-esteem. The 'power of positive thinking', roundly criticized by conservative Protestants for its 'this-worldly' orientation when it was presented by Norman Vincent Peale in the 1950s, now informs most religious television. This is less of a change for Robert Schuller (like Peale a Reformed Church minister and a man who has never claimed to be a fundamentalist) than it is for Oral Roberts, Jim Bakker, or Kenneth Copeland but the ghastly punning title of Schuller's *The Be Happy Attitudes* will stand as a sign of the orientation of most televangelism.

TELEVANGELISM AND POLITICS

Most recent interest in televangelism has centred on the political power of religious broadcasters. In the last chapter of their *Televangelism: Power and Politics on God's Frontier*, Hadden and Shupe predict that:

> In time, the conservative Christian movement has the potential to become solidified enough to 'take over the country'. If the Robertson campaign does not succeed in pulling them together, it will at least demonstrate to conservative Christians the real potential of their movement.
>
> (1988: 286)

Robertson's campaign certainly demonstrated the real potential of their movement: not a lot! As I tried to demonstrate and explain in Chapters Eight and Nine, conservative Christianity is not a particularly fertile soil for political mobilization. Taking just the conservative Protestants who form the core of the televangelism audience and the base for the new Christian right, these people are divided by region, occupation, education, and ethnic background. Not even their religion unites them. As the example of the hostile reception given by pentecostal PTL supporters to fundamentalist Falwell's rescue plans shows, if believers take the details of their religious beliefs seriously, they disagree. Only if they sublimate the particulars and see themselves as defending their shared 'Judeo-Christian' heritage can there be consensus. But commitment to the particulars, the theological and ecclesiological fine print, goes hand in hand with *strength* of motivation. As the distinctive is attenuated enough for various sorts of conservative Protestants (and then conservative Christians) to work together, so the drive to promote a 'conservative Christian' world weakens. One might suppose the problem can be solved by *compartmentalization*. The cadres of Hadden and Shupe's 'solidified' conservative Christian movement might alternate between one set of categories for Sunday (only separatist Baptist fundamentalists are saved) and another for the rest of the week (we welcome the help of our Catholic, Jewish, and Black Baptist brothers). It seems unlikely that many will be able to so easily abandon their anti-Catholic, anti-semitic, and racist attitudes. But more important, to accept that the world can be divided into 'Sunday' and 'the rest of the week', two spheres governed by different criteria of evaluation, is to concede to the modern world precisely the privatization of religion which fundamentalists have historically opposed. Religion is now something for the weekend, for the family, for the home.

With little comparative reference to Europe, Hadden and Shupe miss an obviously instructive case. Holland was initially divided into three 'pillars', each of which encapsulated and provided a wide range of institutions for its people. There were Catholic unions, Protestant unions, and secular trade unions. The triplication was repeated for schools, mass media, sporting associations, and for politial parties. After the Second World War, the Catholic party and the Calvinist Protestant party found they had to make common cause against the secular parties. By the late 1960s, they had formed an alliance. In the early 1980s, they merged to form a conservative Christian party which in turn had to work in alliance with secular conservatives. There is now nothing especially 'Christian' about the party. As I argued at length in *The Rise and*

Fall of the New Christian Right (Bruce 1988), the price conservative Protestants have to pay to achieve political leverage in a pluralistic democracy is the abandonment of almost all of the distinctive platform that initially motivated them to get involved in politics. Any movement which remains seriously 'conservative Christian' will fail; any movement which succeeds will have abandoned its distinctively conservative Christian issues.

But this is to discuss the possibility at its strongest, assuming that most conservative Protestants *want* to Christianize America. In Chapter Nine, I questioned this assumption. It seems very clear to me that most conservative Protestants are not terribly unhappy with America. They might want prayer in schools, a ban on abortion, and the teaching of the oxymoronic 'creation science' but there is no evidence that they want these things badly enough to place them on their agendas above more traditional concerns of politics such as the management of the economy and the pursuit of foreign policy.

For a 'solidified' conservative Christian movement to be created would require a considerable amount of 'consciousness raising'. This is where, in the Hadden and Shupe scenario, televangelism becomes important. Religious broadcasters have lots of money to buy lots of air-time to persuade viewers to coalesce as a conservative Christian movement. This is a vision intended more to sell books than to illuminate the phenomenon. We return to the lack of persuasiveness of television. All the research shows that television is not particularly good at influencing people. We return also to the size and composition of the audience. All the research shows that televangelism is not particularly good at attracting unbelievers. And what difference can televangelism make to the political attitudes of its core audience? The people presently watching Robertson and Swaggart and the like are already likely to be political conservatives.

American religious broadcasting is an interesting phenomenon which tells us a lot about changes in relative strength of different traditions within American Protestantism and about changes in fundamentalist and pentecostal thinking. Whatever it tells Hadden and Shupe, it does not tell me that a popular conservative Christianity will take over the country after the fashion of Iran's Shi'ite Islam. It does not tell me that a cadre of conservative Christians will seize power after the fashion of the Bolsheviks. It tells me only that a minority with a distinctive culture has found a new medium in which to express its beliefs and values and to strive for increasing acceptance and respectability.

NOTES

CHAPTER ONE

1   Although there are some well-known black evangelists, televangelism
    is dominated by whites and attracts a largely white audience. Because
    blacks are a small proportion of many of the samples on which
    quantitative research is based, and because most analysts are
    interested in exploring links with the new Christian right (itself a
    white and sometimes racist movement, despite its leaders' desires to
    enlist black support), most research concentrates on white
    conservative Protestantism. This study is no exception, which is why
    this introductory chapter is a history of white Protestantism. It is based
    on such sources as Weisberger (1958), McLoughlin (1959; 1978),
    Billington (1964), Berthoff (1971), Ahlstrom (1972), Strout (1974),
    and Carroll *et al.* (1979). For excellent studies of black Christianity in
    America, see Frazier (1964) and Fauset (1974).
2   It is not of great importance for my interests but until recently many
    American historians – Ahlstrom, for example – took New England
    puritanism as paradigmatic for the evolution of American Protest-
    antism and rather neglected other influences. For an account which
    stresses regional variation, see Brauer (1985).
3   There is an excellent history of the civilizing process in the many
    works of Norbert Elias. Leftist histories of America describe a similar
    process but see it as a step backward in human development. See, for
    example, Carroll and Noble (1982: 148-50) on the new disciplines and
    the spread of the clock or Ewen and Ewen (1982) on social control
    and advertising.
4   Fundamentalism is often defined in terms of the supposed socio-
    psychological qualities of the belief-system or the supposedly
    pathological personality traits of believers. For reasons elaborated
    elsewhere (Bruce 1983a), I prefer a substantive definition. Although I
    doubt it, it may well be that people who subscribe to fundamentalist
    varieties of Protestantism share some personality traits which are not
    equally often found elsewhere. But this is something which needs to
    be established empirically and not tautologously elided with a

definition. For interesting discussions of the definitional problems, see Warner (1979) and Hunter (1982).

5 For examples of Bundy's work, see his *Apostles of Deceit* (1966) and *How Liberals and Radicals are Manipulating Evangelicals* (1982), both published by his Church League of America in Wheaton, Illinois. An interesting connection between old and new Christian right is evidenced by the fate of Bundy's vast collection of indexed files on ecumenical and liberal churchmen. When he retired, the documents were lodged in the library of Jerry Falwell's Liberty University (*Group Research Reports* May 1985, 24: 18).

6 These statistics were derived from Greeley (1972); Carroll *et al.* (1979: 8-17); Gallup (1985), and *Time* (22 May 1989: 44). For a good recent review and explanation of trends in church membership and attendance see Roof and McKinney (1988).

CHAPTER TWO

1 A further reason for the disappearance of many religious radio stations were the decisions of the FRC to assign religious and educational stations to frequencies to be shared with other stations. 'Within a few years, most noncommercial stations were squeezed off the air along with dozens of other broadcasters with poor equipment and inadequate funding (Schultze 1988b: 293). The FRC favoured stations that would offer a 'well-rounded program to best serve the public. In such a scheme there is no room for the operation of broadcasting stations exclusively by or in the private interests of individuals or groups' (1988b: 294). Schultze believes that the 'FRC regulations were a blessing in disguise for evangelical broadcasters. Instead of remaining on their own low-power, time-shared frequencies, most evangelicals took the FRC's advice, looking to the commercial stations to air their 'propaganda' (Schultze 1988b: 295). Those who sharpened up their acts attracted much bigger audiences than they would have done on their own stations.

2 Not all mainstream churchmen were as triumphalist as Fosdick and periodically attempts were made to reconcile Council and NAE broadcasters. D.G. Barnhouse, a major conservative broadcaster and founding member of NRB, aired his popular *Bible Study Hour* on independent radio for many years but in 1954 he agreed to made a TV programme for the National Council series *Man to Man* (Saunders 1968: 140-4).

3 'Putting out the fleece' is a common evangelical device for ascertaining God's will and is based on the Old Testament story of Gideon asking God:

> Behold, I will put a fleece of wool in the floor; and if the dew be on the fleece only, and it be dry upon all the earth beside, then shall I know that thou wilt save Israel by mine hand, as thou hast said.

> And it was so: for he rose up early on the morrow, and thrust the
> fleece together, and wringed the dew out of the fleece, a bowl
> full of water.
>
> (Judges 6, v. 37-8)

These days it is generally a euphemism for asking people for money.
4 With the exceptions of Kathleen Kuhlman (on whom, see Harrell
1975: 190-1), Alma White, and Aimee Semple McPherson (Clark
1978/9), they have all been men.
5 In 1988 the British government tabled a white paper, the purpose of
which is to further commercialize broadcasting and make it 'customer
driven' on the lines of the American model. For the reasons given in
Chapter Eleven, I do not expect this to make much difference to
religious broadcasting except in so far as one or two minority
language 'ethnic' stations might promote Islam, Sikhism, and so on.

CHAPTER THREE

1 Despite the heated denials of Christian educators, the burgeoning
independent Christian schools movement derives a good part of its
appeal from the fact that most schools are almost entirely white. At a
public meeting in 1967, Falwell expressly said that Lynchburg
Christian Academy would not admit blacks. By 1971 the tune had
changed only so far as to observe the law. Sam Pate, Falwell's father-in-
law, said that they would admit blacks, they just didn't have any
applying (Goodman and Price 1981: 117).
2 There is a similar milieu constructed around the campus of Bob Jones
University in Greenville, South Carolina, but its more rigorously
separatist fundamentalism means that it is expanding less rapidly than
the Liberty organization.
3 With what I suspect is his usual talent for statistical inflation, Falwell
claimed in 1983 that his Liberty Baptist Fellowship for Church
Planting (founded in 1980) had resulted in over 300 new churches
being planted and 400 others being pastored by his graduates (*Group
Research Reports* 24: 11)
4 After he resigned from CBN, Jim Bakker went to work for Paul Crouch
where he was both president of Trinity Broadcasting Systems and
co-host with Tammy Faye of *Praise the Lord*. In November 1973, Crouch
decided to make TBS a uni- rather than inter-denominational network and Bakker left to start his own rival PTL. Although he took his
show with him, he could not take the title which is why the initials PTL
were later to stand for *People That Love* rather than the original *Praise
the Lord*.
5 In a slightly smaller league (producing four hours an evening, seven
days a week) but none the less popular, Eternal Word Television
features Mother Angelica's own lecturing, repeats of Bishop Fulton
Sheen's *Life is Worth Living*, Father John Bertolucci's *Glory to God*, and
repeats of the Bill Cosby show (Elvy 1986: 104-5)

6   In the 1980s, both the Catholic church and the Southern Baptist
    Convention have entered the network business. The Catholic Tele-
    communications Network of America has ambitious plans to link from
    satellite to local broadcast stations and cable systems through
    receivers funded by and located at parish churches. In addition to
    providing religious and wholesome television programmes, the system
    is intended to provide a range of electronic media services such as
    data-processing and e-mail for local churches. Neither it nor SBC's
    American Christian Television (or ACTS!) network has yet achieved
    financial security and there may be a moral in that. With the costs so
    high, it may be that networks can only succeed when they carry, and
    are identified with one highly popular televangelism show.

CHAPTER FOUR

1   There are a wide variety of versions of the argument that television
    presents a systematically biased view of the world. As an example of
    the more radical types, see the studies of British television news
    produced by the Glasgow University Media Group (1976; 1980). A
    more moderate version has been argued for many years by George
    Gerbner, Dean of the Annenberg School of Communication, in his
    work on television violence (Gerbner and Gross 1976; Gerbner et al.
    1980).
2   Between 1977 and 1979 CBN Boston received 36,225 telephone calls
    at its counselling centre. Of the 2,724 that 'asked for salvation', only
    1,118 were referred to local churches or clergymen and many of these
    were for counselling on matters unrelated to their recent conversion
    experiences (Horsfield 1984: 145).
3   But such self-denial needs considerable work and it seems to be only
    communitarian and semi-communitarian introversionist sects with
    distinctive ethnic identities – the Doukhobors, Amish, and Hutterites
    – which prevent increasing affluence undermining commitment. The
    Hutterites prevent wealth becoming an issue by having very large
    families and regularly using profits to buy land to sub-divide
    communities (Wilson 1970: 120-32).
4   Graham is now so much the moderate and father figure that it is
    important to remember that he was a vocal cold warrior until the early
    1970s. He once wrote to Richard Nixon to suggest that the Vietnam
    war could be speedily concluded if the dykes of North Vietnam were
    bombed and millions forced into starvation (The Nation 7 May 1989;
    Wilson 1989).

CHAPTER FIVE

1   The Arbitron data gave data for TV households. For assessing the
    audience for normal evening programmes each household is

reckoned to contain 2.4 viewers. However, most religious television is shown in 'fringe' times (such as Sunday mornings) and even 'deep fringe' times. For these time slots the multiplier used to convert households into individuals is only 1.4.

2   But even if this operated to any significant extent, it would still be an interesting finding that many Americans feel that claiming to watch religious television is a good thing.

3   Another minor source of inaccuracy is the habit of local stations of changing their schedules at short notice. The meters record the setting of the channel switch, not what is actually being shown. It is precisely such low audience programmes as religious television that are liable to be moved.

4   CBN provided Nielsen with an accurate line-up of which stations were showing the *700 Club* at what times. Schedules were not available for the others and so details had to be taken from Nielsen's own central *Report on Devotional Programs* schedule, which omitted some showings. Using the RODP schedule gave an estimated audience 5 per cent lower than using CBN's own details. This suggests that all the following estimates of audience size could reasonably be increased by 5 per cent.

5   Herbert W. Armstrong founded the Worldwide Church of God in 1933. In 1941 he started *The World Tomorrow* on a Hollywood radio station. Three years later the show expanded to broadcasting in early prime time six nights a week coast to coast, and in 1953 it began European broadcasts on Radio Luxemburg. The television show of the same name was added in 1967 and became a daily programme in 1972. European readers can infer the nature of Armstrong's programmes from his free news and opinion magazine *Plain Truth*; they offer slightly right-of-centre social and political commentary on topical concerns. Armstrong's small church has a curious combination of conservative Protestant and adventist beliefs but his mass media output eschews theology, overt proselytizing, and fund-raising and is designed as a 'hook'. Only those people who initiate and maintain contact with the Worldwide Church of God for some time are inducted into church's religious beliefs (Hopkins 1974). Because the Worldwide Church of God is very small and marginal and its programmes deliberately avoid most of the features we think of as characterizing televangelism, I have not dwelt on it in this study.

6   Even more recently, some analysts have claimed a decline (Fore 1987: 84). This may very well be an artefact of the spread of cable. As more and more people get cable fitted, because the reception is much better they switch to it even for network programmes. Because most rating measures neglect cable, audience for syndicated religion programmes will appear to fall when, far from ceasing to watch the programme, many viewers are seeing it more clearly. In favour of the Fore position is the general point, explored later, that the religious television audience differs significantly from the population at large. Overly impressed by the expansion of the audience in the last two

decades, many commentators have missed the point that there is no reason to suppose such growth will continue. The particular identity of the audience suggests that saturation point will soon be reached, if it has not been reached already.

7 The survey was based on a sample constructed by Professor Hollingshead of the Yale Sociology Department so there are no great doubts there, but there is the problem that the measure of viewing was based on self-report and hence has all the obvious problems of poor memory, people wishing to appear more 'religious' than they really are, and so on.

8 Hadden assumes that this is a product of biological age rather than of the experiences and culture of a particular generation. If he is right, this may have considerable implications for the issue of televangelism's potential for political influence discussed in Chapter Nine. But other research – see for example Wingrove and Alston (1974) on church attendance – suggests that age differences are actually cohort effects.

9 Some polarization was however visible in the radio audience. Lazarsfeld and Kendall (1948) note that hillbilly music and religion drew unrepresentatively on the lower classes.

10 That most members of the audience are 'born again' does not mean that most evangelicals and fundamentalists are listeners or viewers. Some object because it is too conservative but others dislike its lack of orthodoxy. In a footnote to her excellent study of a fundamentalist congregation, Ammerman (1987) misses an important implication of her own observation about televangelism viewing, which was not common among her sample:

> available Christian viewing is so scarce. It does not seem to meet the needs of most church families. Some watch Oral Roberts and Jerry Falwell and Billy Graham on independent stations, but other acceptable programming is minimal. The Christian stations' signal, finances and scheduling are spotty at best. The most faithful members also recall that many 'Christian entertainers' (including those who appear on popular Christian television shows such as the '700 Club' or the 'PTL Club' have been condemned by Pastor Thompson as not good examples of the separated life. As a result, Christian television is not nearly so strong an influence as we might expect. This church, unfortunately, cannot serve as a test of the apparently growing influence of televangelists.
>
> (Ammerman 1987: 219)

On the contrary, I would suggest that Ammerman's report is a useful corrective to the usual hysteria about the power of televangelism.

CHAPTER SIX

1 As Barwise and Ehrenburg put it:

> In real life studies (as opposed to laboratory experiments), the results show either no correlation at all or correlations that are statistically significant but very small. The causality is even harder to establish. ... Although sustained television viewing involves seeing a great deal of fictional violence over time, no *dramatic* long-term effects have ever been claimed by serious researchers.
>
> (1988: 141-2)

2 My position is not one of naive empiricism. Even such a 'social constructionist' as Herbert Blumer recognized that some things have the character of 'obdurate reality'. I am not suggesting an absolute division between the material and the ideal but a matter of degree. Different areas of experience clearly vary in testability, even if this is just a matter of inter-subjective consensus rather than objective reality.

3 Butterfield (1986) offers a highly self-perceptive study of being socialized into a belief system which allowed him to turn the frequent rejection of his proselytizing activity into a 'positive' experience. Interestingly, what he was promoting was not a religious belief system but involvement in the direct selling organization Amway (on which see pp. 155–61).

4 The theoretical perspective which informs this discussion (and the whole book) is derived from Gehlen, Weber, and to a lesser extent Durkheim and it is essentially the synthesis of symbolic interactionism, Durkheim, and Weber presented by Berger and Luckmann (1973).

5 On the role of predispositions in conversion, see Greil (1977). For further general models of conversion and references to case studies, see Straus (1979); Bromley and Shupe (1979); Long and Hadden (1983); Stark and Bainbridge (1985); Richardson (1985).

6 One of the most general consequences of television has been the undermining of our 'sense of place' in the social order and the shortening of social distance. 'Many of the traditional distinctions among groups, among people at various stages of socialization, and among superiors and subordinates were based on the patterns of information flow that existed in a print society' (Meyrowitz 1985: 309). Television and radio create the impression of closeness. All Americans have seen and heard Ronald Reagan telling jokes. Very few Americans heard Abraham Lincoln say anything.

7 In a well-documented paper, Wright (forthcoming) persuasively argues that the main impact of televangelism is the welding together of isolated individual believers into a 'moral community'.

8 A further minor function of televangelism, which I have not stressed because it is not much of an improvement over the same thing in print, is that of passing on information which allows mobilization. To

give an example, at a Falwell 'I Love America' rally to celebrate the Fourth of July in Cincinatti, Ohio, in the normal course of conversations I asked a large number of people how they had heard of the rally. Probably two-thirds had been told of the meeting by their pastors; the rest had heard about it from Falwell's *Old Time Gospel Hour*. For similar data on a Carl McIntire march, see Lin (1969).

CHAPTER SEVEN

1 Although I am happy to accept the broad outlines of Frankl's break-down of different sorts of fund-raising appeal, I do not accept her argument that these are in some sense *caused* by the demands of television. To say, for example, that the discrete 'commercial spot' appeal is a television demand is an unhelpful gloss on the more obvious and commonsense view that when a new medium provides preachers with new opportunities they seize them.

2 Perhaps with better information *Newsweek* (6 April 1987) says that $6 million was raised and only $300,000 sent to an organization which helped Vietnamese refugees.

3 Charles Ponzi claimed that, because of the major differences in rates offered for them in different countries after the First World War, he could make large profits by buying and selling international postal orders. He sold notes payable to investors promising the return of their original deposit and 50 per cent profit in 90 days. He made the payments but with money from later investors rather from profits; no international postal orders were bought. Between December 1919 and August 1920, Ponzi took in $9 million (Biggart 1989: 46).

4 In some formulations, this promise is held to be a 'natural law' which holds for non-believers and non-Christians. It is no longer a matter of belief but simply one of ritual action: a reversal of absolutely everything the Reformation stood for!

5 This is not to say that there has been any great equalization of income, only that it has increased absolutely for most people. I am persuaded by Parker (1972) that the post-war period saw no decline in relative inequality.

6 There are a large number of resonances between a DSO like Amway and conservative Protestantism. Although highly entrepreneurial and individualistic, it is *co-operative* rather than competitive individualism which is promoted; a mixture very much like the conservative Protestant view of the church as a fellowship of saved individuals. A Tupperware distributor said:

> 'Everybody wants everybody else to succeed. It's not like the competition you get in some jobs where I don't want you to know what I know because if you do, then you can take my job. I want to share with you what made me successful, so that you can be success too.
>
> (Biggart 1989: 90)

Because of the pyramid nature of the operation: 'In this business you don't get to the top unless you take a lot of people with you' (Biggart 1989: 191). The entrepreneurial emphasis blends readily with the jingoism common among conservative Protestants. Amway is short for 'The American Way' and the front cover of one of Richard De Vos's books (De Vos and Conn 1976) promises that the reader will discover how to attain success and personal fulfillment through belief in 'FREE ENTERPRISE ... HUMAN DIGNITY ... GOD AND HIS CHURCH ... THE AMERICAN WAY'; the final phrase is deliberately ambiguous in its reference both to the company and to the virtues of American capitalism. And it is not just in ethos but in style that Amway is similar to a conservative Protestant church. As Butterfield (1986) shows, it would be very easy to mistake an Amway meeting for an evangelistic revival.

7   What follows is, of course, Max Weber's famous *The Protestant Ethic and the Spirit of Capitalism* (1976) argument.

CHAPTER EIGHT

1   This reminds us of a vital point overlooked by many of the more excited estimates of the power of televangelists: the possibility of a well-organized counter-attack. Many of the early victories of the right – getting 'equal time for Creation Science' bills passed by the state legislatures of Louisiana and Arkansas, for example – were reversed once those who had previously taken for granted their pre-eminence realized they had to work to promote their positions. A good example of the well-organized and imaginative liberal response was seen with Robertson's Constitution Hall rally. He arranged to have it beamed free to a large number of local stations and cable networks. People For the American Way ruined what was to have been good free publicity by presenting the same stations with free anti-Robertson material. Most stations either dropped the Robertson story or balanced his feed with the People For the American Way material.

2   Dispensationalism was popularized by C.I. Scofield and his very popular annotated Bible. The idea is that God treats man differently in different eras. 'Each period of testing [dispensationalists] call a dispensation. They normally claim that there are seven such dispensations – innocence, conscience, human government, promise, law, grace, and the Kingdom' (Cairns 1982: 38). Each period ends with a 'judgement'. The important point about dispensationalism (which is very popular in fundamentalist circles) is that it goes hand-in-hand with the assumption that we are getting very near the 'end times'.

3   In late 1987 Tim La Haye, head of American Coalition for Traditional Values and a leading religious broadcaster, defected from Robertson's campaign to support Jack Kemp who, in order to strengthen his ties to the NCR, made him national co-chairman. La Haye and his wife Beverley, head of Concerned Women for America campaigned hard

for Kemp in Iowa. A week later Kemp sacked La Haye after the *Baltimore Sun* reported La Haye's anti-Catholicism (*Group Research Reports* 26: 40).

CHAPTER NINE

1   There are, of course, many problems with the sort of content analysis which simply sorts words into categories, counts them, and uses the totals as an index of what the programme is saying to its audience. None the less it remains a useful rough guide.
2   It should be noted that the construction of a sample is not without its own problems. For us to generalize with confidence from any sample to a larger population, we need to believe that the sample is representative. It is pretty easy to make a sample represent the grossest demographic characteristics of the population – age, gender, race, and the like – but often we suspect that it is only a part of the population we should really be concerned with. For example, if one is trying to predict an election outcome, it is not the population as a whole but that part of the electorate that will vote which the sample needs to represent. Constructing that sort of sample requires that we know a lot about who does and who does not vote. Thus the construction of the sample will often require assumptions about some of the very things we are trying to discover from the survey which uses the sample!
3   Quite how justices come to their apprehensions of the public good is a mystery but some insight is given in the revealing account of Richard Neely (1981) who was an elected politician before he became Chief Justice of the Supreme Court of West Virginia.
4   *Habits of the Heart* is actually a far better book than Hadden and Shupe's use of it would suggest. It examines in great detail the various images of self and other held by various sorts of Americans and it is essential reading for anyone who wishes to understand the culture of contemporary America.
5   There is a very small but intellectually interesting school of thought associated with R.J. Rushdoony's Chalcedon Foundation and its *Journal of Christian Reconstruction* which is anti-pluralism and anti-democratic, right-wing on most social issues, in favour of 'hard money' but, unusually for the American context, post-millennial in eschatalogy. For a good brief introduction see Clapp (1987).

CHAPTER TEN

1   Were the basics of the case contested by the principals, Hahn's motives would need to be examined and Barnhart has a thoughtful consideration of both her initial reticence and subsequent willingness to tell all and pose nude for *Playboy*. The cosmopolitan reader might wonder how any woman could allow herself to be led into such an

obvious seduction – and hence suppose that Hahn was a willing participant – but one has to allow for the sheltered life led by many pentecostalists and the extent of her admiration for Bakker. Fortunately the basic facts of what occurred are not contested. This account was put together from reports in *Time, Newsweek,* and *Christianity Today* (Frame 1988a and 1988b) in addition to newspaper reports. Barnhart's version is as reliable as any.

2   Although these figures sound large, Hahn was cheated. PTL paid out $115,000 immediately but $94,700 was kept by Roper and an associate as business expenses! A $150,000 trust was established from which interest was to be paid monthly to Hahn. If she kept silent for twenty years she would get the capital. In total she seems to have received only $10,046 (about £7,000) which may well explain her willingness to earn a large sum by posing for *Playboy* and telling her story.

3   There was also a recent argument which instanciated their theological differences. Bakker had dropped Swaggart's shows from his network schedules apparently because he did not think that Swaggart's open anti-Catholicism was in keeping with the ethos of PTL.

4   These figures come from a 'wire' report in *Christian Newsworld* (April 1989: 11). As Chapter Five made clear, there are enormous difficulties in measuring audience size. There is no doubt that there has been a drop in the televangelism audience but it seems implausible, given that the major producers have not reduced the amount of air-time they buy, that it has halved. However, as I argued, air-time is a supply phenomenon and not an index of demand. As the giving from the loyal core has increased, it could be that the audience has fallen dramatically. We will have to wait for better data.

CHAPTER ELEVEN

1   Much of the material in this section comes from a draft of a forthcoming book by David Martin called *Aspiring Flames: The Explosion of Protestantism in Latin America* to be published by Basil Blackwell in 1990. As I have only read a draft I am unable to give detailed page citations but the whole work can be heartily commended.

2   This might seem like a tautology but the detailed evidence which Martin presents supports its claim to be an empirical proposition.

3   As an aside, one might note the pointlessness of the response of some anthropologists to the conversion of indigenous peoples. In mourning the destruction of Indian societies and cultures, and in blaming North American missionaries for taking advantage of social dislocation to promote their alternatives, anthropologists are being unrealistically preservationist. Some missionary organizations – the New Tribes Mission for example (Lewis 1989) – have been active in disrupting Indian villages but many have responded in a humanitarian fashion to changes which were occurring anyway. I have no brief for Protestant imperialism but it is at least arguable that

missionaries, by equipping people with values which might allow them to adapt to the modern urban world, are doing more good than anthropologists who, out of a desire for the unattainable return to the pristine and undisturbed, have nothing at all to offer the displaced of the Third World.

4   Wilson's interesting comments were made in a discussion of Martin's work at the 1989 annual conference of the British Sociological Association's sociology of religion study group, St Mary's College, Twickenham.

5   Harvestime is one of the largest of the post-1970s charismatic 'house church' movements (Walker 1985). Given the miniscule audience for such satellite broadcasts, we may suppose that the activity is undertaken more for the secondary consequences of internal fund-raising and morale-boosting than for the primary purpose of spreading the Word among Europe's heathen.

6   These data were compiled from the various studies organised by Peter Brierley (Bible Society 1980; Brierley 1984 and 1988).

REFERENCES

ABC Television (1968) *Vision and Belief: Religious Broadcasting 1957-1968*, Birmingham: ABC Television.

Abelman, R. (1987) 'Why do people watch religious TV?: a uses and gratifications approach', *Review of Religious Research* 29: 199-209.

Abelman, R. and Neuendorf, K. (1985) 'How religious is religious television broadcasting?', *Journal of Communication* 35: 98-110.

Abelman, R. and Neuendorf, K. (1987) 'Themes and topics in religious television programming', *Review of Religious Research* 29: 152-69.

Abercrombie, N., Hill, S., and Turner, B.S. (1980) *The Dominant Ideology Thesis*, London: George Allen & Unwin.

Ahlstrom, S.E. (1972) *A Religious History of the American People*, New Haven, CT.: Yale University Press.

Aikman, D. (1988) 'Washington scoreboard: evangelical wins and losses during the Reagan years', *Christianity Today* 21 October: 22-3.

Allcock, J.B. (1968) 'Voluntary associations and the structure of power', *Sociological Review* 16: 59-82.

Altheide, D. and Johnson, J. (1977) 'Counting souls', *Pacific Sociological Review* 20: 323-48.

Ammerman, N.T. (1987) *Bible Believers: Fundamentalists in the Modern World*, New Brunswick, NJ: Rutgers University Press.

Apel, W.D. (1979) 'The lost world of Billy Graham', *Review of Religious Research* 20: 138-49.

Armstrong, B. (1979) *The Electric Church*, Nashville: Thomas Nelson Publishing.

Ashman, C. (1977) *The Gospel According to Billy Graham*, Secaucus NJ: Lyle Stuart Inc.

Atkin, C. and Heald, G. (1976) 'Effects of political advertising', *Public Opinion Quarterly* 40: 216-28.

Bachman, J.W. (1960) *The Church in the World of Radio-Television*, New York: Association Press.

Ball, S. (1976) 'Methodological problems in assessing the impact of television programs', *Journal of Social Issues* 32: 8-17.

Barnhart, J.E. (1988) *Jim and Tammy: Charismatic Intrigue Inside PTL*, Buffalo, NY: Prometheus Books.

Barnouw, E. (1968) *The Golden Web: A History of Broadcasting in the United States*, New York: Oxford University Press.

Barnouw, E. (1975) *The Tube of Plenty: The Evolution of American Television*, New York: Oxford University Press.

Barrett, D. (1982) *World Christian Encyclopaedia*, Nairobi: Oxford University Press.

Barrett, D. (1984) 'Five statistical eras in global mission: a thesis and discussion', *International Bulletin of Missionary Research* October: 160-7.

Barrett, D. (1985) 'Annual statistical table on global mission: 1985', *International Bulletin of Missionary Research* January: 30-1.

Barrett, D. (1989) 'Annual statistical table on global mission: 1989', *International Bulletin of Missionary Research* January: 20-1.

Barrett, L. (1988) 'The electability test', *Time* 29 February: 13.

Barron, B. (1987) *The Health and Wealth Gospel*, Downers Grove, IL: Inter-Varsity Press.

Barwise, P. and Ehrenburg, A. (1988) *Television and its Audience*, London: Sage.

Bellah, R., Madsen, R., Sullivan, W.M., Swidler, A., and Tipton S.M. (1985) *Habits of the Heart: Middle America Observed*, London: Hutchinson Education.

Berger, P.L. (1983) 'From the crisis of religion to the crisis of secularity', in M. Douglas and S. Tipton (eds) *Religion and America*, Boston: Beacon Press, pp. 14–24.

Berger, P.L., Berger, B., and Kellner, H. (1973) *The Homeless Mind*, Harmondsworth, Mddx: Penguin.

Berger, P.L. and Luckmann, T. (1973) *The Social Construction of Reality*, Harmondsworth, Mddx: Penguin.

Berthoff, R. (1971) *An Unsettled People: Social Order and Disorder in American History*, New York: Harper & Row.

Bestic, A. (1971) *Praise the Lord and Pass the Contribution*, London: Cassell.

Bettinghaus, E.P. (1968) *Persuasive Communication*, New York: Holt Rinehart & Winston.

Bibby, R.W. and Brinkerhoff, M.B. (1973) 'The circulation of the saints: a study of people who join conservative churches', *Journal for the Scientific Study of Religion* 12: 273-83.

Bible Society (1980) *Prospect for the Eighties: From a Census of the Churches in 1979*, London: Bible Society.

Biggart, N.W. (1989) *Charismatic Capitalism: Direct Selling Organizations in America*, Chicago: University of Chicago Press.

Billington, R. (1964) *The Protestant Crusade, 1800-1860*, Chicago: Quadrangle Books.

Bluem, A.W. (1969) *Religious Television Programs: A Study of Relevance*, New York: Hastings House.

Blumer, H. (1954) 'Public opinion and public opinion polling', in D. Katz, D. Cartwright, S. Eldersveld, and A.M. Lee (eds) *Public Opinion and Propaganda: A Book of Readings*, New York: Holt Rinehart & Winston, pp. 70–8.

Bolton, S.C. (1982) *Southern Anglicanism*, Westport, CT: Greenwood Press.

Bourgault, L.M. (1985) 'The "PTL Club" and Protestant viewers: an ethnographic study', *Journal of Communication* 35: 132-48.

Brauer, J.G. (1985) 'Regionalism and religion in America', *Church History* 54: 366-78.

Brierley, P.W. (1984) *UK Christian Handbook 1985/86 Edition*, London: Bible Society/Evangelical Alliance/MARC Europe.

Brierley, P.W. (1988) *UK Christian Handbook 1989/90 Edition*, London: MARC Europe.

Bright, B. (1965) *Have You Heard of the Four Spiritual Laws?* San Bernadino, CA: Campus Crusade for Christ.

Broadcasting Commission of the General Synod of the Church of England (1973) *Broadcasting, Society and the Church*, London: Church Information Office.

Bromley, D. and Shupe, A. (1979) 'Just a few years seem like a lifetime: a role theory approach to participation in religious movements', in L. Kreisberg (ed.) *Research in Social Movements, Conflict and Change*, Greenwich, CT: JAI Press, pp. 159–86.

Brookeman, C. (1984) *American Culture and Society Since the 1930s*, London: Macmillan.

Brown, J.A. (1980) 'Selling airtime for controversy: NAB self-regulation and Father Coughlin', *Journal of Broadcasting* 24: 199-224.

Browning, D. (1987) 'The Protestant Church in the People's Republic of China', *Christian Century* 4 March: 218-21.

Bruce, S. (1980) 'The Student Christian Movement and the Inter-Varsity Fellowship: a sociological study of two student movements', unpublished PhD thesis, University of Stirling.

Bruce, S. (1983a) 'Identifying conservative Protestantism', *Sociological Analysis* 44: 65-70.

Bruce, S. (1983b) 'The persistence of religion: conservative Protestantism in the United Kingdom', *Sociological Review* 31: 453-70.

Bruce, S. (1984a) 'A sociological account of liberal Protestantism', *Religious Studies* 20: 401-15.

Bruce, S. (1984b) *Firm in the Faith: The Survival and Revival of Conservative Protestantism*, Aldershot: Gower.

Bruce, S. (1985) 'Puritan perverts: notes on accusation', *Sociological Review* 33: 47-63.

Bruce, S. (1988) *The Rise and Fall of the New Christian Right: Conservative Protestant Politics in America 1978-1988*, Oxford: Clarendon Press.

Bruce, S. (1989) *A House Divided: Protestantism, Schism, and Secularization*, London: Routledge.

Bryant, A. (1977) *The Anita Bryant Story*, Old Tappen, NJ: Revell.

Bryant, A. (1978) 'The Playboy interview: Anita Bryant', *Playboy* May: 73-96; 232-50.

Buddenbaum, J.M. (1981) 'Characteristics and media-related needs of the audience for religious TV', *Journalism Quarterly* 58: 266-72.

Butterfield, S. (1986) *Amway: The Cult of Free Enterprise*, Montreal: Black Rose Press.

Cairns, A. (1982) *Dictionary of Theological Terms*, Banbridge, Northern Ireland: Whitefield College of the Bible.

Carpenter, J. (1980) 'A shelter in the time of storm: fundamentalist institutions and the rise of evangelical Protestantism 1929-1942', *Church History* 49: 62-75.

Carroll, J.W., Johnson, D.W., and Marty, M.E. (1979) *Religion in America: 1950 to the Present*, San Francisco: Harper and Row.

Carroll, P.N. and Noble, D.W. (1982) *The Free and the Unfree: A New History of the United States*, Harmondsworth, Mddx: Penguin.

Clabaugh, G.K. (1974) *Thunder on the Right: The Protestant Fundamentalists*, Chicago: Nelson-Hall.

Clapp, R. (1987) 'Democracy as heresy', *Christianity Today* 20 February: 17-23.

Clark, D.L. (1978/9) 'Miracles for a dime: from Chautauqua tent to radio station with Sister Aimee', *California History* 57: 354-63.

Clark, D.W. and Virts, P.H. (1985) 'Religious television audiences: a new development in measuring audience size', paper given at annual meeting of the Society for the Scientific Study of Religion, Savannah, GA, October.

Clelland, D., Hood, T., Lipsey, C.M., and Wimberley, R. (1974) 'In the company of the converted: characteristics of a Billy Graham crusade audience', *Sociological Analysis* 35: 45-56.

Cohen, S. and Taylor, L. (1976) *Escape Attempts: The Theory and Practice of Resistance to Everyday Life*, London: Allen Lane.

Cook, G. (1984) 'The Protestant predicament: from base ecclesial community to established church – a Brazilian case study', *International Bulletin of Missionary Research* July: 98-101.

Davis, L.J. and Volkman, E. (1982a) 'If a business man is to be judged by the company he keeps, then Jerry Falwell may have a lot of explaining to do', *Penthouse* February: 63-70, 84, 186-90.

Davis, L.J. and Volkman, E. (1982b) 'Jerry Falwell, Part II, the prophet motive', *Penthouse* March: 65-72, 182-4.

Dennis, J.L. (1962) 'An analysis of the audience of religious radio and television programs in the Detroit metropolitan area,' unpublished PhD thesis, University of Michigan.

De Vos, R. and Conn, C.P. (1976) *Believe!* Old Tappan, NJ: Revell.

Dinwiddie, M. (1968) *Religion by Radio: Its Place in British Broadcasting,* London: George Allen & Unwin.

Dobson, E. and Hindson, E. (1986) 'Apocalypse Now? What fundamentalists believe about the end of the world', *Policy Review* Fall: 16-22.

Dollar, G.W. (1973) *A History of Fundamentalism in America,* Greenville, SC: Bob Jones University Press.

Douglas, M. and Tipton, S.M. (1983) *Religion and America: Spirituality in a Secular Age,* New York: Beacon.

Duin, J. (1988) 'Why the Assemblies of God dismissed Swaggart', *Christianity Today* 13 May: 36-9.

Durkheim, E. (1970) *Suicide: A Study in Sociology,* London: Routledge & Kegan Paul.

Ellens, J.H. (1974) *Models of Religious Broadcasting,* Grand Rapids, MI: W.B. Eerdmans.

Elvy, P. (1986) *Buying Time: The Foundations of the Electronic Church,* Great Wakering, Essex: McCrimmons.

Elwood, D.J. (1968) *Churches and Sects in the Philippines: A Description of Contemporary Religious Group Movements,* Dumaguele City, Philippines: Silliman University Press.

Emery, W.B. (1969) 'The American system of broadcasting: a rationale', in his *National and International Systems of Broadcasting,* East Lansing, MI: Michigan State University Press, pp. 5–16.

Ewen, S. and Ewen, E. (1982) *Channels of Desire: Mass Images and the Shaping of American Consciousness,* New York: McGraw-Hill.

Falconer, R. (1977) *Message, Media, Mission: The Baird Lectures 1975,* Edinburgh: Saint Andrew Press.

Falwell, J. and Towns, E. (1971) *Church Aflame,* Nashville: Impact Books.

Falwell Ministries (1981) *We've Come This Far By Faith: Jerry Falwell Ministries 1956-1981,* Lynchburg, VA: Thomas Road Baptist Church.

Fauset, A.H. (1974) *Black Gods of the Metropolis: Negro Religious Cults of the Urban North,* New York: Octagon.

Ferguson T. and Rogers, J. (1986) 'The myth of America's turn to the right', *Atlantic Monthly* May: 43-53.

Firebaugh, G. (1981) 'How effective are citywide crusades?', *Christianity Today* 25: 412-17.

Fitzgerald, F. (1981) 'A disciplined, charging army', *New Yorker* 18 May: 53–110.

Fore, W.F. (1969) 'A short history of religious broadcasting', in A.W.

Bluem (ed.) *Religious Television Programs: A Study of Relevance*, New York: Hastings House, pp. 203-11.

Fore, W.F. (1984) 'Religion and television: report on the research', *The Christian Century* 18-24 July: 710-12.

Fore, W.F. (1987), *Television and Religion: The Shaping of Faith, Values and Culture*, Minneapolis, MN: Augsburg Publishing House.

Forster, A. and Epstein, B.R. (1964) *Danger on the Right: The Attitudes, Personnel and Influence of the Radical Right and Extreme Conservatives*, New York: Random House.

Frady, M. (1979) *Billy Graham: A Parable of American Righteousness*, Boston: Little Brown & Co.

Frame, R. (1988a) 'PTL: a year after the fall', *Christianity Today* 18 March: 44-9.

Frame, R. (1988b) '$8 million worth of unanswered questions', *Christianity Today* 15 July: 36-7.

Frankl, R. (1984) 'Television and popular religion: changes in church offerings', in D.G. Bromley and A.D. Shupe (eds) *New Christian Politics*, Macon, GA: Mercer University Press.

Frankl, R. (1987) *Televangelism: The Marketing of Popular Religion*, Carbondale, Ill.: Southern Illinois University Press.

Frazier, E.F. (1964) *The Negro Church in America*, Liverpool: Liverpool University Press.

Freed, P.E. (1979) *Towers to Eternity: Reaching the Unreached*, Chatham NJ: Transworld Radio.

Gaddy, G.D. (1984) 'The power of the religious media: religious broadcast use and the role of religious organizations in public affairs', *Review of Religious Research* 25: 310-63.

Gaddy, G.D. and Pritchard, D. (1985) 'When watching religious TV is like attending church', *Journal of Communication* 35: 123-31.

Gallup, G. Jnr (1985) *Religion in America. 50 Years: 1935-85*, Princeton, NJ: Princeton Religion Research Center.

Gasper, L. (1963) *The Fundamentalist Movement*, The Hague: Mouton and Co.

Gaustad, E.S. (1962) *A Historical Atlas of Religion in America*, New York: Harper and Row.

Gerbner, G. and Gross, L.P. (1976) 'Living with television: the violence profile', *Journal of Communication* 26: 173-99.

Gerbner, G., Gross, L.P., Morgan, M., and Signorielli, N. (1980) 'The mainstreaming of America: violence profile 11', *Journal of Communication* 30: 10-29.

Gerbner, G., Gross, L.P., Hoover, S., Morgan, M., Signorielli, N., Cotugno, H., and Wuthnow, R. (1984) *Religion and Television: A Research Report by the Annenberg School of Communication*, Philadelphia: University of Pennsylvania and the Gallup Organization.

Gerlach, L.P. and Hine, V. (1968) 'Five factors crucial to the growth and spread of a modern religious movement', *Journal for the Scientific Study of Religion* 7: 23-40.

Gerlach, L.P. and Hine, V. (1970) *People, Power and Change: Movements of Social Transformation*, New York: Bobbs-Merrill.

Glasgow University Media Group (1976) *Bad News*, London: Routledge & Kegan Paul.

Glasgow University Media Group (1980) *More Bad News*, London: Routledge & Kegan Paul.

Goethals, G. (1985) 'Religious communication and popular piety', *Journal of Communication* 35: 149-57.

Goldstein, C. (1985) 'What Ronald Reagan needs to know about Armageddon', *Liberty* 80: 2-6.

Goodman, W.R. Jnr and Price, J.J.H. (1981) *Jerry Falwell: An Unauthorized Profile*, Lynchburg, VA: Paris & Associates.

Goodman, W.R. Jnr and Price, J.J.H. (1983) 'Falwell', *Penthouse* April: 79-82, 168-70.

Greeley, A.M. (1972) *The Denominational Society: A Sociological Approach to Religion in America*, Glenview, IL: Scott, Foresman & Co.

Greil, A.L. (1977) 'Previous dispositions and conversion to perspectives of social and religious movements', *Sociological Analysis* 38: 115-25.

Grupp, F.W. and Newman W. (1973) 'Political ideology and religious preference: The John Birch Society and Americans for Democratic Action', *Journal for the Scientific Study of Religion* 12: 401-13.

Gusfield, J. (1963) *Symbolic Crusade: Status Politics and the American Temperance Movement*, Urbana, IL: University of Illinois Press.

Hadden, J.K. (1980) 'Soul saving via video', *Christian Century* May, pp. 609-13.

Hadden, J.K. (1985) 'Religious broadcasting and the mobilization of the New Christian right', address at the Society for the Scientific Study of Religion, Savannah, GA, October.

Hadden, J.K. (1986a) 'Taking stock of the New Christian right', *Christianity Today* 13 June: 38-9.

Hadden, J.K. (1986b) 'The great audience size controversy', *Religious Broadcasting* January: 20-2.

Hadden, J.K. (1986c) 'Getting to the bottom of the audience size controversy', *Religious Broadcasting* February: 88, 116, 122-8.

Hadden, J.K. and Frankl, R. (1987a) 'Star wars of a different kind: reflections on the politics of a religion and television research project', *Review of Religious Research* 29: 101-10.

Hadden, J.K. and Frankl, R. (1987b) 'A critical review of the *Religion and Television* research report', *Review of Religious Research* 29: 111-24.

Hadden, J.K. and Shupe, A. (1988) *Televangelism: Power and Politics on God's Frontier*, New York: Henry Holt.

259

Hadden, J.K. and Swann, C.E. (1981) *Primetime Preachers: The Rising Power of Televangelism*, Reading, MA: Addison-Wesley.

Halevy, E. (1937) *A History of the English People*, London: Pelican Books.

Harrell, D.E. (1975) *All Things Are Possible: The Healing and Charismatic Revivals in Modern America*, Bloomington, IN: Indiana University Press.

Harrell, D.E. (1985) *Oral Roberts: An American Life*, Bloomington, IN: Indiana University Press.

Haught, R. (1980) 'The God bizz', *Penthouse* December: 102-6, 250-7.

Herberg, W. (1960) *Protestant, Catholic, Jew: An Essay in American Religious Sociology*, Garden City: Doubleday.

Hill, D. (1986) 'Preacher for President? Don't say Pat Robertson doesn't have a prayer', *TV Guide* 15 March.

Hill, S.S. (1977) *Religion in the Old South*, Chicago: University of Chicago Press.

Hoge, D. and Roozen, D. (1979) *Understanding Church Growth and Decline 1950-78*, New York: Pilgrim Press.

Hollinger, D. (1989) 'Enjoying God forever: an historical/sociological profile of the health and wealth gospel', paper given at the British Sociological Association Study Group of Religion conference, St Mary's College, Twickenham, April.

Hoover, S.M. (1987) 'The religious television audience: a matter of significance or size', *Review of Religious Research* 29: 135-51.

Hoover, S.M. (1988) *Mass Media Religion: The Social Sources of the Electronic Church*, Berkeley: Sage.

Hopkins, J. (1974) *The Armstrong Empire: A Look at the Worldwide Church of God*, Grand Rapids, MI: W.B. Eerdmans.

Horsfield, P.G. (1984) *Religious Television: The American Experience*, New York: Longman.

Horsfield, P.G. (1985) 'Evangelism by mail: letters from broadcasters', *Journal of Communication* 35: 89-97.

Horton, D. and Wohl, R.R. (1956) 'Mass communication and para-social interaction', *Psychiatry* 19: 215-29.

Howe, D.W. (1972) 'The decline of Calvinism: an approach to its study', *Comparative Studies in Society and History* 14: 306-27.

Humbard, R. (1971) *Miracles in My Life*, New York: New American Library/Signet.

Hunter, J.D. (1982) 'Operationalizing evangelicalism: a review, critique and proposal', *Sociological Analysis* 42: 363-72.

Hunter, J.D. (1983) *American Evangelicalism: Conservative Religion and the Quandary of Modernity*, New Brunswick, NJ: Rutgers University Press.

Hunter, J.D. (1987) *Evangelicalism: The Coming Generation*, Chicago, University of Chicago Press.

Janowitz, M. (1978) *The Last Half-Century: Societal Change and Politics in*

America, Chicago: University of Chicago Press.

Jenkins, J.W. (1981) 'Toward the anti-humanist new Christian nation', *The Humanist* 41: 20-2.

Johnson, C.A. (1955) *The Frontier Camp Meeting: Religion's Harvest Time,* Dallas: Southern Methodist University Press.

Johnson, D.L. (1980) 'Electronic fundamentalism: supply and demand', *The Christian Century* 28 May: 606-7.

Johnson, N.R. (1973) 'Television and politicization: a test of competing models', *Journalism Quarterly* 50: 447-55.

Johnson, S.D. and Tamney, J.B. (1982) 'The Christian right and the 1980 presidential election', *Journal for the Scientific Study of Religion* 21: 123-31.

Johnson, S.D. and Tamney, J.B. (1985) 'Mobilizing support for the Moral Majority', *Psychological Reports* 56: 987-94.

Johnstone, R.L. (1971-72) 'Who listens to religious radio broadcasts anymore?', *Journal of Broadcasting* 16: 91-102.

Jones, C.E. (1974) *Perfectionist Persuasion: The Holiness Movement and American Methodism 1867-1936,* Metuchen, NJ: Scarecrow Press.

Jones, M.A.J. (1960) *American Immigration,* Chicago: University of Chicago Press.

Jorstad, E. (1970) *The Politics of Doomsday: Fundamentalists of the Far Right,* Nashville: Abingdon.

Jorstad, E. (1981) *Evangelicals in the White House: The Cultural Maturation of Born Again Christianity 1960-1981,* New York: Edwin Mellen Press.

Katz, E. (1957) 'The two-step flow of communication: an up-to-date report on an hypothesis', *Public Opinion Quarterly* 21: 61-78.

Katz, E. (1960) 'Communication research and the image of society: convergence of two traditions', *American Journal of Sociology* 65: 435-40.

Katz, E. (1971) 'Platforms and windows: broadcasting's role in election campaigns', *Journalism Quarterly* 48: 304-14.

Katz, E. (1980) 'On conceptualizing media effects', *Studies in Communications* 1: 119-41.

Katz, E., Gurevitch, M., and Haas, H. (1973) 'On the use of mass media for important things', *American Sociological Review* 38: 164-81.

Katz, E., Gurevitch, M., Danet, B., and Peted, T. (1969) 'Petitions and prayers: a method for the content analysis of persuasive appeals', *Social Forces* 47: 447-63.

Katz, E. and Lazarsfeld, P.F. (1955) *Personal Influence: The Part Played by People in the Flow of Mass Communication,* Glencoe, IL: Free Press.

Korpi, M.F. and Kim, K.L. (1986) 'The uses and effects of televangelism: a factorial model of support and contribution', *Journal for the Scientific Study of Religion* 25: 410-23.

Krohn, F.B. (1981) 'The language of television preachers', *Et cetera*

Spring: 51-63.

Lacey, L.J., (1978) 'The electric church: an FCC established institution', *Federal Communications Law Journal* 31: 235-75.

Lane, R.E. and Sears, D.O. (1964) *Public Opinion*, Englewood Cliffs, NJ: Prentice-Hall.

Lang, K. and Lang, G. (1960) 'Decisions for Christ', pp. 415-27 in M.R. Stein, A.R. Vidich, and D. White (eds) *Identity and Anxiety*, Glencoe, IL: Free Press.

Lawton, K.A. (1988) 'CT poll: what do Christians want from the candidates?' *Christianity Today* 17 June: 50-1.

Lazarsfeld, P.F., Berelson, B., and Gaudet, H. (1948) *The People's Choice*, New York: Columbia University Press.

Lazarsfeld, P.F. and Kendall, P.L. (1948) *Radio Listening in America: The People Look at Radio – Again*, New York: Prentice-Hall.

Lears, T.J.J. (1983) 'From salvation to self-realization: advertising and therapeutic roots of the consumer culture, 1880-1930', in R.W. Fox and T.J.J. Lears (eds) *The Culture of Consumption*, New York: Pantheon Books, pp. 1-37.

Leiss, W., Kline, S., and Jhally, S. (1986) *Social Communication in Advertising*, Toronto: Methuen.

Lernoux, P. (1988) 'The fundamentalist surge in Latin America', *The Christian Century* 20 January: 51-4.

Lessnoff, M. (1981) 'Protestant ethic and profit motive in the Weber thesis', *International Journal of Sociology and Social Policy* 1: 1-18.

Lewis, L.S. and Blisset, D.D. (1986) 'Sex as God's work', *Society* 23: 67-75.

Lewis, N. (1989) 'A harvest of souls', *Independent Magazine* 1 April: 20-8.

Liebman, R.C. (1983) 'Mobilizing the Moral Majority', in R.C. Liebman and R. Wuthnow (eds) *The New Christian Right*, Chicago: Aldine, pp. 50-73.

Lin, N. (1969) 'The McIntire march: a study of recruitment and commitment', *Public Opinion Quarterly* 38: 562-73.

Lipset, S.M. and Raab, E. (1978) *The Politics of Unreason: Right-wing Extremism in America, 1790-1977*, Chicago: University of Chicago Press.

Lipset, S.M. and Raab, E. (1981) 'Evangelicals and the elections', *Commentary* 71: 25-31.

Lofland, J. (1966) *Doomsday Cult: A Study of Conversion, Proselytization and Maintenance of Faith*, Englewood Cliffs, NJ: Prentice-Hall.

Lofland, J. and Stark, R. (1965) 'Becoming a worldsaver: a theory of conversion to a deviant perspective', *American Sociological Review* 30: 862-75.

Long, T.E. and Hadden, J.K. (1983) 'Religious conversion and the concept of socialization: integrating the brainwashing and drift models', *Journal for the Scientific Study of Religion* 22: 1-14.

Lowenthal, L. (1944) 'Biographies in popular magazines', in P.F. Lazarsfeld and F. Stanton (eds), *Radio Research: 1942-43*, New York: Duell, Sloan & Pearce.

McConnell, D.L. (1988) *A Different Gospel: A Historical and Biblical Analysis of the Modern Faith Movement*, Peabody, Mass: Hendrickson Publishing.

McLoughlin, W.G. (1955) *Billy Sunday Was His Real Name*, Chicago: University of Chicago Press.

McLoughlin, W.G. (1959) *Modern Revivalism*, New York: Ranald Press.

McLoughlin, W.G. (1978) *Revivals, Awakenings and Reform*, Chicago: University of Chicago Press.

McLuhan, M. (1964) *Understanding Media: The Extensions of Man*, London: Routledge & Kegan Paul.

McNamara, P.H. (1985) 'Conservative Christian families and their moral world: some reflections for sociologists', *Sociological Analysis* 46: 93-9.

McQuail, D. (1983) *Mass Communication Theory: An Introduction*, London: Sage.

MacRobert, I. (1988) *The Black Roots and White Racism of Early Pentecostalism in the USA*, London: Macmillan.

Mariani, J. (1979) 'Television evangelism milking the flock', *Saturday Review* 3 February: 22-5.

Marsden, G. (1980) *Fundamentalism and American Culture*, New York: Oxford University Press.

Martin, D. (forthcoming) *Aspiring Flames: The Explosion of Protestantism in Latin America*, Oxford: Basil Blackwell.

Martin, M. and Gelber, L. (1981) *Dictionary of American History*, Totowa, NJ: Rowman & Littlefield.

Martin, W.C. (1970) 'The God-hucksters of radio', *Atlantic Monthly* June.

Martin, W.C. (1974) 'This man says he's the divine sweetheart of the universe', *Esquire*, June.

Martin, W.C. (1981) 'Television: the birth of a media myth', *The New Yorker* June.

Martin, W.C. (1982) 'Waiting for the end: the growing interest in apocalyptic prophecy', *Atlantic Monthly* June: 317.

Marty, M. (1976) *A Nation of Behavers*, Chicago: University of Chicago Press.

Matthews, D.G. (1977) *Religion in the Old South*, Chicago: University of Chicago Press.

Merton, R.K. (1957) *Social Theory and Social Structure*, Glencoe, IL: Free Press.

Meyer, M. (1958) *Madison Avenue USA*, London, Penguin.

Meyrowitz, J. (1985) *No Sense of Place: The Impact of Electronic Media on*

Social Behavior, New York: Oxford University Press.

Miller, S. (1985) 'Radio and religion', *Annals of the American Academy of Political and Social Science* 1117: 135-40.

Mills, C.W. (1956) *White Collar*, New York: Oxford University Press.

Mobley, G.M. (1984) 'The political influence of television ministers', *Review of Religious Research* 25: 314-33.

Moody, W.R. (1937) *The Life of Dwight L. Moody*, Kilmarnock: John Ritchie.

Morris, J. (1973) *The Preachers*, New York: St Martin's Press.

Mueller, C. (1983) 'In search of a constituency for the "New Religious Right"', *Public Opinion Quarterly* 47: 213-29.

Mumper, S.E. (1986a) 'The missionary that needs no visa: how gospel radio is reaching behind closed borders', *Christianity Today* 21 February: 24-6.

Mumper, S.E. (1986b), 'Where in the world is the church growing?', *Christianity Today* 11 July: 17-21.

Murdoch, G. and Golding, P. (1978) 'Theories of communication and theories of society', *Communications Research* 5: 339-56.

Neely, R. (1981) *How Courts Govern America*, New Haven, CT: Yale University Press.

Neill, S. (1975) *A History of Christian Missions*, Harmondsworth, Middx: Penguin.

Neuendorf, K. and Abelman, R. (1987) 'An interaction analysis of religious television programming', *Review of Religious Research* 29: 175-98.

Neuhaus, R.J. (1984) *The Naked Public Square*, Grand Rapids, MI: W.B. Eerdmans.

Norman, E.R. (1981) *Christianity in the Southern Hemisphere: The Churches in Latin America and South Africa*, Oxford: Clarendon Press.

Orbison, C. (1977) '"Fighting Bob" Schuller: a radio crusader', *Journal of Broadcasting* 21: 459-72.

Ostling, R. (1988) 'Now it's Jimmy's turn', *Time* 7 March: 28-30.

Packard, V. (1960) *The Hidden Persuaders*, Harmondsworth, Middx: Penguin.

Parker, E.C. (1957) *Religious Radio*, New York: Harper.

Parker, E.C. (1961) *Religious Television*, New York: Harper & Brothers.

Parker, E.C., Barry, D.W., and Smythe, D.W. (1955) *The Television-Radio Audience and Religion*, New York: Harper & Row.

Parker, R. (1972) *The Myth of the Middle Class*, New York: Harper.

Pierard, R. (1970) *The Unequal Yoke: Evangelical Christianity and Conservatism*, New York: J.B. Lippincott.

Pollock, J. (1966) *Billy Graham: The Authorised Biography*, London: Hodder & Stoughton.

Pusateri, C.J. (1977) 'FDR, Huey Long and the politics of radio regulation', *Journal of Broadcasting* 21: 85-95.

Richardson, J.T. (1985) 'The active vs passive convert: paradigm conflict in conversion/recruitment research', *Journal for the Scientific Study of Religion* 24: 119-236.

Roberts, O. (1970) *The Miracles of Seed-Faith*, Tulsa: Oral Roberts.

Roberts, O. (1972) *The Call: An Autobiography*, Garden City, NY: Doubleday.

Roberts, O. (1974a) *Twelve Great Miracles of My Ministry*, Tulsa: Pinoak Publications.

Roberts, O. (1974b) *How to Live Above Your Problems*, Tulsa: Pinoak Publications.

Robinson, H.W. (1964) 'A study of the audience for religious radio and television broadcasts in seven cities throughout the US', unpublished PhD. thesis, Ohio State University.

Rogers, E.M. (1962) *Diffusion of Innovation*, Glencoe, IL: Free Press.

Roof, W.C. and McKinney, W. (1988) *American Mainline Religion: Its Changing Shape and Future*, New Brunswick, NJ: Rutgers University Press.

Rosenberg, T. (1983) 'Diminishing returns: the false promise of direct mail', *The Washington Monthly* June: 33-8.

Roy, R. (1953) *Apostles of Discord: A Study of Organized Bigotry and Disruption on the Fringes of Protestantism*, Boston: Beacon.

Sandeen, E. (1970) *The Roots of Fundamentalism*, Chicago: University of Chicago Press.

Saunders, L.S. (1968) 'The National Religious Broadcasters and the availability of commerical radio time', unpublished PhD. thesis, University of Illinois.

Schuller, R. (1969) *Self-love*, Old Tappan, NJ: Revell.

Schuller, R. (1983) *Self-esteem: The New Reformation*, Waco, TX: Word Books.

Schuller, R. (1985) *The Be Happy Attitudes*, Waco, TX: Word Books.

Schultze, Q.J. (1988a) 'The wireless gospel: the story of evangelical radio puts televangelism into perspective', *Christianity Today* 15 January: 18-23.

Schultze, Q.J. (1988b) 'Evangelical radio and the rise of the electronic church, 1921-1948', *Journal of Broadcasting and Electronic Media* 32: 289-306.

Seymour-Ure, C. (1974) *The Political Impact of Mass Media*, London: Constable.

Sholes, J. (1979) *Give Me that Prime-time Religion*, New York: Hawthorn Books.

Shupe, A. and Stacey, W. (1982) *Born Again Politics and the Moral Majority: What Social Surveys Really Show*, New York: Edwin Mellen Press.

265

Shupe, A. and Stacey, W. (1983) 'The Moral Majority constituency', in R. Liebman and R. Wuthnow (eds) *The New Christian Right*, Hawthorne: Aldine, pp. 104-17.

Sigelman L. and Presser, S. (1988) 'Measuring public support for the new Christian right: the perils of point estimation', *Public Opinion Quarterly* 52: 325-37.

Simpson, J.H. (1983) 'Moral issues and status politics', in R. Liebman and R. Wuthnow (eds) *The New Christian Right*, Chicago: Aldine, pp. 187-205.

Smith, T.L. (1965) *Revivalism and Social Reform: American Protestantism on the Eve of the Civil War*, New York: Harper Torchbooks.

Solt, D.C. (1971) 'A study of the audience profile for religious broadcasts in Onondaga County', unpublished PhD thesis, Syracuse University.

Stacey, W. and Shupe, A. (1982) 'Correlates of support for "The Electronic Church", *Journal for the Scientific Study of Religion* 21: 291-303.

Stark, R. and Bainbridge W.S. (1980) 'Networks of faith: interpersonal bonds and recruitment to cults and sects', *American Journal of Sociology* 85: 1376-95.

Stark, R. and Bainbridge, W.S. (1985) *The Future of Religion: Secularization, Revival and Cult Formation*, Berkeley: University of California Press.

Straus, R. (1979) 'Religious conversion as a personal and collective accomplishment', *Sociological Analysis* 40: 158-65.

Strober, G. and Tomczak, R. (1979) *Jerry Falwell: Aflame for God*, Nashville: Thomas Nelson.

Strout, C. (1974) *The New Heavens and New Earth*, New York: Harper & Row.

Svennevig, M., Haldane, I., Spiers, S., and Gunter, B. (1988) *Godwatching: Viewers, Religion and Television*, London: John Libbey and Co./IBA.

Tamney, J.B. and Johnson, S. (1984) 'Religious television in Middletown', *Review of Religious Research* 25: 303-13.

Target, G.W. (1968) *Evangelism Inc.*, London: Allen Lane.

Taylor, P. (1987) 'Robertson campaign persists amid setbacks', *Washington Post* 31 March: A8.

Thomas, N.E. (1987) 'Evangelization and church growth: the case of Africa', *International Bulletin of Missionary Research* October: 165-70.

Towns, E. (1973) *Jerry Falwell: Capturing a Town for Christ*, Old Tappan, NJ: Revell.

Tran, M. (1986) 'TV preacher hits trouble on road to White House', *Guardian*, 23 October.

Wacker, G. (1985) 'The holy spirit and the spirit of the age in American Protestantism 1880-1910', *Journal of American History* 72: 45-62.

Walker, A. (1985) *Restoring the Kingdom: The Radical Christianity of the House Church Movement*, London: Hodder & Stoughton.

Wallis, R. (ed.) (1982) *Millennialism and Charisma*, Belfast: The Queen's University of Belfast.

Wallis, R. and Bruce, S. (1983) 'Accounting for action: defending the common-sense heresy', *Sociology* 17: 102-11.

Wallis, R. and Bruce, S. (1986) *Sociological Theory, Religion and Collective Action*, Belfast: The Queen's University of Belfast.

Ward, D.A. (1980) 'Toward a normative explanation of "Old Fashioned Revivals"', *Qualitative Sociology* 3: 3-22.

Warner, R.S. (1979) 'Theoretical barriers to understanding evangelical Christianity', *Sociological Analysis* 40:1-9.

Weber, M. (1964) *The Theory of Social and Economic Organization*, London: Free Press.

Weber, M. (1976) *The Protestant Ethic and the Spirit of Capitalism*, London: George Allen & Unwin.

Weber, T. P. (1979) *Living in the Shadow of the Second Coming: American Pre-millennialism: 1875-1925*, Oxford: Oxford University Press.

Weisberger, B. (1958) *They Gathered at the River: The Great Revivalists and their Impact upon Religion in America*, New York: Quadrangle Books.

Whitam, F.L. (1968) 'Revivalism as institutionalized behavior: an analysis of the social base of a Billy Graham crusade', *Southwestern Social Science Quarterly* 48: 115-27.

Whyte, W.H. (1960) *The Organization Man*, Harmondsworth, Mddx: Penguin.

Wilcox, C.D. (1988) 'Seeing the connection: religion and politics in the Ohio Moral Majority', *Review of Religious Research* 30: 47-58.

Wilson, A.N. (1989) 'God's leading man', *Independent Magazine* 27 May: 42-7.

Wilson, B.R. (1968) 'Religion and the churches in contemporary America', in W.G. McLoughlin and R. Bellah (eds) *Religion in America*, New York: Basic Books, pp. 73-110.

Wilson, B.R. (1970) *Religious Sects*, London: World University Press.

Wilson, E.A. (1988) 'The Central American evangelicals: from protest to pragmatism', *International Review of Missions* 77: 94-106.

Wingrove, R.C. and Alston, J.P. (1974) 'Cohort analysis of church attendance', *Social Forces* 53: 324-31.

Wolff, K.M. (1984) *The Churches and the British Broadcasting Corporation 1922-1956: The Politics of Broadcast Religion*. London: SCM Press.

Wright, C. (forthcoming) 'Preaching to the converted: conversion language and the constitution of the TV evangelical community',

Sociological Review.

Wuthnow, R. (1983) 'The political rebirth of American evangelicalism', in R. Liebman and R. Wuthnow (eds) *The New Christian Right,* Hawthorne: Aldine, pp. 167-85.

Wuthnow, R. (1987) 'The social significance of religious television', *Review of Religious Research* 29: 124-34.

INDEX

269